DEVELOPMENT ACCORDING TO PARENTS

The Nature, Sources, and Consequences of Parents' Ideas

Development According to Parents
The Nature, Sources, and Consequences of Parents' Ideas

Jacqueline J. Goodnow
Macquarie University

and

W. Andrew Collins
University of Minnesota

LAWRENCE ERLBAUM ASSOCIATES, PUBLISHERS
Hove and London (UK)   Hillsdale (USA)

Lawrence Erlbaum Associates Ltd., Publishers
27 Palmeira Mansions
Church Road
Hove
East Sussex, BN3 2FA
U.K.

British Library Cataloguing in Publication Data

Goodnow, Jacqueline *1924*
Development according to parents : the nature, sources and consequences of parents'
ideas
1. Children. Development. Role of interpersonal relationships with parents
I. Title   II. Series
155.418

ISBN 0-86377-160-2 (HBK)
ISBN 0-86377-161-0 (PBK)
ISSN 0959-3977 (Essays in Developmental Psychology)

Printed and bound in the United Kingdom by BPCC Wheatons, Exeter

CONTENTS

ACKNOWLEDGEMENTS

Financial support for this project has come primarily from the Australian Research Committee, in the form of a research grant to the first author, and from Macquarie University, in the form of a Visiting Scholar Program that made it possible for Andy Collins to spend time at Macquarie. The project has derived major benefit from the many scholars who generously sent us material not yet in print, from discussions about parents' ideas with the "Monday group" (Jenny Bowes, Judy Cashmore, Jackie Crisp, Laurel Bornholt, Lesley Dawes, Rosemary Leonard, Pamela Warton), and from constructive comments on earlier drafts by several readers: Bob Goodnow and Joan Grusec in particular.

CHAPTER 1

INTRODUCTION

We have been asked to review the current state of research in a particular area and to point forward by noting gaps, trends, and possibilities. This short opening chapter will provide an indication of what the reader may expect to find.

In essence the book is about the ideas that parents bring to the work of parenting: the nature of these ideas, their sources, and their consequences. The ideas are not only about children (the conventional focus) but also about parents, and about the relationship of "family". We are concerned, for instance, not only with ideas about the needs of children, the contributions of heredity, and the way children change over time, but also with ideas about the joys and difficulties of parenting, the value of advice, the obligations of family members to one another, and the way family members are linked to various parts of the community.

To introduce the material, we provide in this chapter the briefest of histories for research in the area, a summary of the distinctive features of our account, an outline of the chapters, and an explanation of why we use the term "ideas" rather than some other term to refer to the content of parents' developmental psychology.

A LITTLE HISTORY

Parents' ideas are of interest to a wide range of social scientists, with developmental psychologists representing only one group among them. We shall, for instance, draw from material written by clinicians, family therapists, parent educators, and a range of psychologists, anthropologists and sociologists. Scholars in all these groups have developed an interest in parents' ideas in the course of seeking to understand the social context of development, to learn about problem-solving in everyday life, to explore the way one family or one cultural group differs from another, or to determine the way one generation passes its ideas on to another. No one group has a monopoly of knowledge about parents' ideas, and each may learn from the other. As an opening device, however, we shall base this brief history on research by developmental psychologists, noting as we proceed the ways in which they have turned to other sources as the research area has progressed.

Starting Points.   A first wave of interest focussed on parents' expectations and attitudes as an expression of "naive psychology" (e.g. Baldwin, 1965) or as determinants of parental action and parental satisfaction (e.g. Emmerich, 1969; Ewart & Green, 1957; Hess & Handel, 1959; Stolz, 1967). This wave opened up several issues that still remain inadequately explored. To take one example, there has been only limited testing of Baldwin's (1965) proposal that children acquire first the ideas on which there is most agreement among adults. To take another, there has been little follow-up of Hess and Handel's (1959) analysis of "family themes", an analysis emphasising ideas about the "good family" rather than about the "good child".

This first wave lost momentum during an era of insistence on the value of attending only to overt behaviour. It reappeared in the course of critical comments on psychologists' exclusive attention to actions and to the details of contingencies between the actions of parents and children: Bell's (1979) comment, for instance, that this emphasis ignores the fact that parents are thinking beings and Parke's (1978) even sharper observation that psychologists often credit mothers with about as much cognitive complexity as they do babies.

The reawakening of interest was not an isolated event. On the one hand, it was an extension of cognitive approaches to child development. Increasingly, analyses of children's development had moved towards arguing that the effects of instruction or of exposure to any social event (television, abuse, time in hospitals) depended on the child's interpretations and the child's capacity to assimilate what was happening. The same viewpoint was now being advocated for parents. The reawakening also fitted well with approaches towards interpreting the effects of early experience on later personality in terms of the "internal models" that people develop about the nature of relationships: models based on their own childhood experiences, carried forward, and acting as filters through which the behaviours of one's own children are viewed (e.g. Belsky, 1984; Crowell & Feldman, 1988; Main, 1985).

The stirring of interest in parents' ideas was also part of change outside the developmental area. It was, for instance, very much in line with moves towards asking about the nature of "everyday" psychology, and its connections to formal psychology, moves marked by an increasing respect for the everyday variety and a shift in labels, from "naive" (e.g. Baldwin, 1965) to "common sense" or "informal" psychology (e.g. Moscovici & Hewtstone, 1983; Wegner & Vallacher, 1977). It was also in good agreement with an increased interest in "social" and "everyday" cognition: that is, in the categories, scripts, images, or schemas that people bring to understanding the world around them or acquire in the course of everyday practices and interactions (e.g. Rogoff & Lave, 1984; Rogoff & Wertsch, 1984). As in social psychology, this cognitive emphasis left to one side the more affective components of attitudes, but it nonetheless made it easier for part of the earlier interest in parents' attitudes to be resurrected, and it continues to provide a link between research on parents' ideas and research on the general nature of cognition.

A Marked Increase in the Empirical Data, and the Emergence of Ways to Order it.   The comments of Bell (1979) and of Parke (1978) coincided with the emergence of reports demonstrating empirical ways to proceed. Ninio's (1979) study is a prominent early example, reporting differences in the age at which mothers in several ethnic groups in Israel expected infants to display various skills. An independent study in Japan and the U.S.A. adopted a similar approach (Hess et al., 1980). So also did a further study in Australia, begun separately but revised to use the same measures as those used by Hess et al. (1980) (Goodnow, Cashmore, Cotton, & Knight, 1984). Since the early studies, the number of empirical studies has increased dramatically, along with extensions to applied topics such as the impact of depression on parents' views of children (e.g. Kochanska & Radke-Yarrow, in press), the links between parents' expectations and child abuse (e.g. Bugental, Blue, & Cruzcosa, in press ; Trickett & Susman, 1988), or the reasons for parents' bringing to clinics children who appear to be functioning well (e.g. Rickard et al., 1981). With the increase has come the need to find ways of ordering the data. The approach most often used has been to organise material in terms of some recurring questions: questions dealing with ways of describing and eliciting ideas, and with the nature and bases of multidirectional links among ideas, actions, affect, and outcomes for both children and parents (e.g. Goodnow, 1984; 1988a; Holden & Edwards, in press; Miller, 1988). This approach (organisation around central questions) is the one we shall follow in this book.

Beginnings of Concern About the Empirical Data and its Gaps.   This concern takes several forms. The field displays a bias towards ideas about young children and early parenting, as if later phases were of less interest. It lacks developmental and longitudinal data. It concentrates on ideas about individuals and interactions within dyads at a time when the goal increasingly set in developmental psychology is one of finding ways to consider interactions and consequences for triads or family units. And it concentrates on information gained from direct experience with parenting to the neglect of information from other people, from books, and from the images conveyed by books, television, or the extent to which public space makes any provisions for parents or children (Clarke-Stewart, 1978; Goodnow, 1990a; Quinn & Holland, 1987).

The concern with these gaps is not simply with holes in the data bank. On the contrary: These particular holes are of interest because they represent a sensed need for research directed from a conceptual base and a recognition that the wheel need not be completely re-invented. There are, in fact, concepts and methods available in other areas of research that can serve as a borrowable base (Goodnow, 1988a). Two broad solutions are emerging. One is to stay within developmental psychology, turning to theoretical analyses of cognitive development among children. It should be possible, for instance, to extend Piagetian analyses from child development to adult development (e.g. Sameroff & Feil, 1985), or to extend Vygotskian analyses of instruction and guided participation to the analysis of parents' teaching actions and parents' definitions of learning situations (e.g. Lloyd, 1987; Palacios, 1986; Wertsch, Minick, & Arns,1984).

A second broad solution is to look beyond developmental psychology. For some analysts of parents' ideas, the major turn has been towards concepts contained in general analyses of cognition and learning. The turn may be, for instance, towards information processing, regarding parents as engaging in problem-solving or decision-making, as proceeding from noting an event to comparing it with knowledge or schemas already available, and then moving from the discrepancy to action (e.g. Holden, 1988; Mancuso & Lehrer, 1986; Rubin, Mills, & Krasnor, in press; Vedeler, 1987). The turn may also be towards attribution theory, placing parents' ideas about the causes of behaviour (their own or their children's) within the framework provided by general analyses of attribution patterns and their bases or consequences (e.g. Dix & Grusec, 1983; 1985; Dix, Ruble, Grusec, & Nixon, 1986; Hess & McDevitt, 1986; Holloway, Hess, Azuma, & Kashiwagi, in press).

For others, the major turn has been towards concepts drawn from positions that are, in Reiss, Oliveri, and Kurd's (1983) phrase, more "down-from-society" than "up-from-the-individual". These positions share the argument that the self-construction of ideas could never account for their acquisition, or would at best be a laborious way to proceed. Attention is drawn instead to the way that every society contains a number of available ideas or forms of knowledge, often not completely consistent with one another or respectful of each other. Formal theories of education, for instance, exist side-by-side with parents' common sense theories and with the views known as "alternative" approaches to education. Attention is drawn also to the way these available ideas are passed on or conveyed to people in a variety of ways. Ideas about children and families, for instance, are embedded in language, in folk-lore, in the way schools are structured, in the way teachers are trained, in the legal approval given to some kinds of families rather than others.

In effect, each society contains "social representations" or "cultural models" of the ideas that individuals come to hold. The critical questions then have to do with the extent to which ideas are shared among people in a society, the way in which ideas spread from one social group or one generation to another, the way individuals absorb, accept, doubt or resist the ideas of others, and the way in which people reconcile conflicting social representations (reconcile, for instance, differences between formal and informal developmental theories). Starting from this orientation, for example, Reid and Valsiner (1986) have asked which ideas about the punishment of children are shared by U.S. parents in various income groups, while Goodnow, Cashmore, Cotton, and Knight (1984) have asked about the relative influence of cultural group and personal experience on mothers' implicit developmental timetables. Harkness, Super, and Keefer (1986) have asked about the meaning that parents give to terms such as "stage". Mugny and Carugati (1985) and Emiliani and Molinari (1988; in press) have asked how parents reconcile or choose among conflicting social representations about the way children learn. Triana and Rodrigo (1989) have asked whether literature presenting environment-centred vs. child-centred explanations of children's behaviour is read differently by parents who know both traditions but prefer one to the other.

These several starting points and theoretical turnings, the reader should note, do more than display the way that social scientists are beginning to borrow from one another. They also shape the questions asked. We can best illustrate such effects—and put some of our own interests and values on the table—by offering a brief account of the way we ourselves have come to be interested in parents' ideas, to choose particular research topics within that area, and to lean towards some particular theoretical orientations.

One of us (WAC), for instance, has a background of interest in the way people interpret events, presented either in real action or by way of television, and in the way interpretations vary as a function of the experience and competence of the observer and of the signals or cues that the events provide (e.g. Collins, 1983). The topic first chosen as a way of exploring these questions had to do with the way television is understood by children. This topic turns out to allow a number of questions about interpretations, but it is not the optimal base for exploring several others. It does not, for instance, bring out the way that individuals operate within a context or network of relationships. Nor does it do justice to the importance of "mutual cognitions" (each party interpreting the behaviour of the other) or lead readily to the analysis of interactions. In a sense, the topic is likely to leave the individual acting in solo fashion.

The study of parents with adolescent children (Collins, in press) offers a contrasting case. When parents observe adolescents, they are interpreting a changing event, and they bring to any current interpretation both ideas about children in general and a history of past observations. We may readily ask: How far do ideas about "typical" or "ideal" children coincide with ideas about one's own child? What changes in their own child do parents observe? How do they come to notice change? What signals are being given and noted? Which ideas show easy or slow change? Moreover, parents with adolescents are themselves being observed and interpreted, by observers—their adolescent children whose position may also be expected to change over time. We may ask the same questions about adolescents that we asked about parents and see how far there is congruence between interpretations or expectancies. We may also ask whether a lack of congruence or a shift in either party's viewpoint leads to a change in the interactions between them or to the presence of conflict. At a research level, then, a topic emerges that allows a multiple set of questions to be asked. At a conceptual level, the shift in topic and in questions is accompanied by special attention to analyses of relationships and their functions in the development of individuals (e.g. Grotevant & Cooper, 1986; Hinde & Stevenson-Hinde, 1988; Kelley et al., 1983).

In contrast, the other of us (JJG) has a background of interest in the way people think or solve problems, and in the influence of both direct experience and social or cultural conditions on the ideas that children or adults come to hold. That background prompts an interest in finding ways to define that often-used term "social context", and an interest in a particular definition: namely, context as the set of ideas or assumptions that people encounter, either in stated form or embedded in everyday practices and routines. These everyday ideas need not be held only by parents, or deal only with parenting. In fact, the first set of ideas chosen for analysis had to do with "cognitive values": ideas about intelligent vs. not-so-bright behaviours, trivial vs. significant problems, stodgy vs. elegant solutions, "proper" vs. inappropriate approaches to learning (Goodnow, 1976, 1990b). The ideas that parents hold, however, have some special advantages as a research topic. They allow one to ask how adults come to hold the ideas they do, and how changes occur in adults' thinking. Moreover, since parents' ideas are also likely to be the ideas most closely encountered by children, one may use the same research topic to study the nature and the acquisition of ideas for both generations.

The first substantive topic chosen—namely, parents' developmental timetables or the ages at which they expected various skills or qualities to appear—again allowed some questions to be explored but was an incomplete base for exploring others. The alternative now being pursued has to do with the ideas held by parents and children about household work patterns and the values these express. Here is a topic that is salient to both generations, loaded with affect, marked by differences in viewpoint among family members and cultural groups and by an unexpected slowness of change in actions. It is also theoretically difficult to account for by conventional accounts of labour, of families, or of ideas as constructed solely from one's own direct experience. The topic, and its background, are again accompanied by a particular theoretical turn. In this case, the turn is towards giving a larger conceptual space than usual to material that is often termed "social": that is, material from social psychology, anthropology and sociology which deals with the way ideas are shared by people and are passed with varying degrees of acceptance and resistance from one social group, one generation, or one family member to another.

SOME FEATURES OF OUR APPROACH

Four features will mark our approach:

1. *A variety of sources.* The reader can expect to find an emphasis on material from developmental psychology, supplemented by material from "social" sources and from general studies of cognition. The references to "social" material reflect our shared view that we cannot understand parents' ideas unless we consider parents in the context of particular responsibilities, particular social conditions, particular relationships, and a cultural history of ideas about childhood, parenting, and the course of development. The references to studies of cognition reflect our view that parental cognition is not some strange new form of

thought, for which we need to invent totally new principles, or which tells us only about parents. Parental cognition is part of cognition. It is illuminated by general studies of cognition and in turn helps to extend our general understanding of the nature of knowledge and thought.

2. *The use of research from several countries.* The research itself is international and we have tried to depart from exclusive attention to material that comes from North America or is written in English. These citations, however, are within the limits of our knowledge and reading skills, and we are aware that there is still material we have neglected.

3. *A restricted number of references.* To our regret, the constraints of space in these essays have placed limits on our ability to cite all the research that we would like to cite. We have had to select examples rather than cover all studies and, in some cases, to cite only a recent reference for a particular topic, with the hope that the interested reader will be able to track the earlier research from that source.

4. *A research agenda.* There are now available some reviews of research on parents' ideas (Goodnow, 1984; 1988a; Holden & Edwards, 1989; Miller, 1988) as well as three edited books that cover a variety of research material (Ashmore & Brodzinsky, 1986; Duveen & Lloyd, in press a; Sigel, 1985b). The field would be poorly served if we were simply to summarise these sources.

The field would also be poorly served if research now proliferated in shopping list fashion. It could easily do so. Interest has now been sparked, for instance, in the issue of similarity between formal and informal or parental developmental psychology. Why not work our way through all the parts of developmental psychology—all the ideas that formal psychologists hold—and see which of these ideas are held by parents? Interest has also risen in differences among cultural groups in some concepts of children, e.g. in the developmental timetables that are expected. Why not now ask if cultural groups differ on a variety of other ideas about children or families? Why not simply keep adding to the list of cultures? Such extensions may be readily resisted as "too broad". Take, however, the beginnings of evidence that parents vary in the cues they use to assess a child's developmental level or the state of a move into adolescence. Why not work through one cue after another to determine their impact or their relative weights?

We see it as more useful, and more in keeping with the intent of these Essays in Developmental Psychology, if we draw material together in a way that points to gaps and that asks: What questions need to be answered? What are the possible methods and models that one might draw from? What directions, out of the many possible, seem especially worthwhile and feasible?

Each chapter is accordingly oriented to both completed and missing pieces. Each chapter also ends with a section labelled "Items for a Research Agenda": a section in which we have chosen one or two particular research problems as the ones we see as most in need of attention. This does not mean, however, that only the research agenda section is oriented towards research gaps. Nor does it mean that we set our sights only at the identification of research topics. Throughout all the chapters, we shall be emphasising the need to become aware of theoretical approaches that can inform research on parents' ideas, to attend to the processes that underlie links among actions, feelings, and outcomes, and to locate ways of aligning parenting with other activities or other forms of work, bringing out its special features but not leaving it in some esoteric theoretical limbo.

THE ORGANISATION OF CHAPTERS

Chapters 2 and 3 are concerned with the nature of parents' ideas. These chapters provide the baseline material needed before plunging into the more detailed accounts of possible sources and consequences. They are also relevant to basic early research decisions because, without a specification of the ways in which parents' ideas vary, there is no base to which we may link variations in sources or consequences. Readers already versed in research on parents' ideas may wish to skim Chapters 2 and 3, read only the research agenda sections at the end of the chapters, or move directly to the later chapters that best fit their interests. Readers who are relatively new to the area should find that Chapters 2 and 3 are a useful introduction to both completed research and research possibilities.

The division between Chapters 2 and 3 is between descriptions of the content and of the quality of ideas. Content refers to differences in the substance of ideas (parent X, for instance, considers that boys are more vulnerable than girls or that homosexuality has a completely biological base, while parent Y does not). Quality refers to characteristics that may cut across content: characteristics such as the degree of certainty and openness to change, the degree of accuracy or elaboration, the degree of interweaving with other ideas, or the degree of consistency between verbal statements and other actions.

Chapters 2 and 3 differ also in the research agenda items discussed at the end of each chapter. The starred item for Chapter 2 has to do with the need for expanded research on ideas about families and family relationships, supplementing the more widespread attention to date on ideas about children or parents as separate units. The starred item for

Chapter 3 has to do with the need for research on connections among parents' ideas: research that explores, for instance, the extent to which ideas about goals and methods are inter-related and the extent to which a collection of ideas shows any hierarchical structure, with some ideas occupying a superordinate role and implying others. In both chapters, we have aimed not only at pointing out a need but also at suggesting some possible leads.

Chapter 4 looks specifically at the sources of parents' ideas. It presents first a summary of parental research, noting the initial emphasis on direct experience with children as the major source and the rise of interest in other sources. The chapter then outlines some of the larger traditions from which parental research might draw and to which it can contribute: the traditions of information processing, cultural models, and social representations. These traditions vary in some respects (e.g. in the extent to which they see the information encountered as containing one vs. several accounts of development) but are similar in others (e.g. all three pay some attention to ideas being acquired or kept not on the basis of "rational" processes but because they serve some protective function or vested interest). The chapter ends with two items starred for the research agenda. One has to do with the need for data over time, concentrating on changes and lags in parents' ideas as children change. The other derives more from a cultural or social view of sources and has to do with parents' trust or confidence in their own ideas and those of others, encountered either in a search for information or by way of unsought advice.

Chapters 5 and 6 turn towards the analysis of consequences. We start with an emphasis on consequences for parents (Chapter 5) and then consider children (Chapter 6). That order may be disturbing for some readers. It might be justified by the argument that parents' ideas, actions and feelings are earlier steps in a chain that ends with child outcomes. We have as well a different rationale in mind. For us, an exclusively child-centered view is limited. Child development is not the whole of developmental psychology. Moreover, parents are interesting in their own right. Their experiences, satisfactions, and development are topics to be explored without any necessity to justify the exploration on the grounds of effects upon children. Consequences for children are certainly important to consider, but they are not the necessary or the only basis for interest in parents' ideas.

The chapter on consequences for parents deals first with affect and then with actions and interactions. We place affect first partly because it is both a source and a consequence of ideas (mood, for instance, influences the ideas we hold and is influenced by them), partly because of proposals to the effect that feeling may be the critical mediating step in moving from ideas to actions (e.g. Weiner, 1986), and partly because we ourselves are challenged by the relative lack of attention to what is one of the major features to the parenting experience: namely, the highs and lows of feeling that often accompany parenting. We shall note especially two general ways of accounting for why affect is such a feature of parenting. One is that the experience often involves expectations both met and "violated" (e.g. Belsky, 1985; Ruble, Hackel, Fleming, & Stagnor, 1988). The other is that the work of parenting is a particular kind of job, often marked by frequent evaluation, ambiguous criteria, and what Engstrom (1988) has called—in the analysis of some other occupations—"impossible demands".

Chapter 5 also covers parental actions, noting both that a number of difficulties and possibilities remain in the analysis of congruence between ideas and actions, and that the theoretical turn is toward recognising that effects are bidirectional (from actions to ideas as well as from ideas to actions). Present also in this chapter is a basic concern with the wisdom of separating ideas from actions, when many of our definitions of objects or people are in fact descriptions of actions or procedures. Chairs, for example, are to sit on, X is a person you can trust, good parents are people who protect their children.

Chapter 5 ends with two starred items for the research agenda. One has to do with affect: namely the need to dissect the occasions when parental affect runs high, locating the ideas that contribute to this level. The other has to do with interactions. Rather than stop at a concentration on the links between parent's ideas and parents' actions, we propose, we would do well to explore interactions and their links to "mutual cognitions" (Maccoby & Martin, 1983): to the ideas, for example, that each party to the interaction has of the other or of what the relationship between them should be like.

Chapter 6 concentrates on outcomes for children. In the research literature, outcomes have been primarily considered in terms of a child's intellectual growth and level of adjustment. We shall also give attention to the degree to which children's ideas (e.g. ideas about important values, causes of success, the proper organisation of family life and the definition of family) match those of parents, and the bases of varying degrees of agreement or disagreement. Two items are starred for the research agenda. One has to do with developing ways of considering two sets of influences on children's ideas: the ideas of parents and the ideas encountered outside the family. The other has to do with comparability. To what extent are the same processes involved in parents' and in children's acquisitions of ideas about children, parenting or families? Considering the two together may well illuminate both. It is also a return to the questions about sources asked in Chapter 4, allowing us to ask whether the same accounts of sources for parents' ideas can also be used for children (and vice versa).

The final chapter retains the theme of research possibilities. We do not intend to summarise the variety of research possibilities noted in the several chapters. That could become a seemingly endless list. We shall instead emphasise some issues that cut across topics. One of these has to do with selecting measures. A second has to do with sampling within and among families. The third has to do with aiming for some general orientations or "perspectives" that cut across a variety of topics. There seems little point at this stage in arguing for any single grand theory of parents' ideas. There are, however, as in developmental psychology in general, some useful general orientations or "perspectives". From life-span psychology we have borrowed the terms "socio-historical", "contextualist", and "transactional", but we argue for amendments to each of these.

A LAST COMMENT BEFORE PROCEEDING

The reader may have noted that we have used the term "ideas" rather than some available alternatives such as "internal cognitive states", "representations", "beliefs" or "belief systems".

We find "internal cognitive states" a rather clumsy phrase, although we like the breadth of the definition: "The internal state may involve an attitude, a belief, an attribution, or an inference about one's own physiological state, such as pain or hunger" (Quattrone, 1985, p.4). "Representations" has a variety of meanings depending especially on the social psychological or anthropological theory it comes from (e.g. Durkheim, 1895; Farr & Moscovici, 1984). "Systems" suggests that ideas are linked to one another, and this is a quality that may or may not be present. "Belief" is less easy to set aside. It is now in fairly wide usage (e.g. Sigel, 1985b). It captures the sense of parents' ideas as constructions, as "statements of truth" from the parents' viewpoint (Sigel, 1985a). It avoids the unhappy connotation of ideas as consisting of some "inert mental state" (Bogdan, 1986, p.8). It has also the appeal of suggesting some of the features we wish to see acknowledged in research on parents' ideas: namely, the recognition that parents' ideas are often marked by a touch of myth, are linked to action, have a possible "executive" function, are suffused with affect, and are often accompanied by a sense of attachment and ownership on the part of the believer.

Nonetheless, "belief" remains for us an awkward term. It has a wide variety of meanings (see Bogdan, 1986, and Stich, 1983, for reviews). It has at the one time both the connotation of certainty (e.g. "I will die for my beliefs") and a suggestion of doubt or "cognitive hesitation" (Bogdan,

1986, p.2) (e.g. "I believe so" or "imagine so" rather than "know so"). The term "belief" also leads one quickly into an extensive philosophical literature about relationships between belief and knowledge, with positions ranging from the assertion that statements such as "I believe so" represent linguistic habits (e.g. Austin, 1979) or an attitude to mental content rather than mental content in itself, to the view that beliefs or propositions about the world are the essential part of mental content (e.g. Fodor, 1983).

To us, the losses outweigh the gains. We shall resist the appeal of "beliefs" and retain the term ideas, with occasional use of the term "cognitions" and the term "expectancy" (used especially when the issue is one of linking ideas to actions). We shall, however, assert from the start that ideas are neither "inert" nor "cold". They are, instead, always linked to actions and suffused with some degree of feeling. In effect, we can explore these aspects of thought without adopting the term "belief" and entering the philosophical maze.

THE NATURE OF PARENTS' IDEAS: DESCRIPTIONS BY CONTENT

In Chapters 4 to 6, we shall concentrate on some specific issues in research on parents' ideas: issues related to particular sources and particular consequences. To provide a background of general knowledge, we begin with two chapters that serve a double purpose. They provide a broad picture of the field and they concentrate on some early decisions in research: What ideas, or what aspects of ideas, should we choose to work with? How can we describe the difference between one parental idea and another?

We shall start by dividing material into descriptions by *content* as against descriptions by *quality*. Chapter 2 will deal with variations in content: the difference, for example, between person X's view that infants are extremely vulnerable and person Y's view that infants are extremely resilient. Chapter 3 will deal with variations in quality: differences, for example, in such aspects as the degree of accuracy, certainty, differentiation, openness to change, centrality for other ideas, consensus or congruence with the ideas of others. In the course of both chapters, the reader will be introduced to a number of hypotheses about the sources and consequences of of parents' ideas. Broadly speaking, our discussion of the content of parents' ideas will contain material on both sources and consequences but will emphasise sources, while—as a contrast—the chapter on quality will place more emphasis on consequences.

Throughout the chapter, we shall point to research gaps and possibilities. The research agenda section at the end of the chapter selects one research topic and explores it in more detail than others noted as we proceed. The item for this chapter has to do with the need for content on parents' ideas about relationships and families: that is, ideas not simply about children, or about parents, but about the way family members combine, interact, and form some kind of unit.

Throughout the chapter, we shall draw material from research that deals directly with parents' ideas and research that deals with the nature of ideas in general. The latter areas—e.g. the study of cognition or of cognitive anthropology—offer concepts and frameworks that may be drawn upon or applied to research dealing specifically with parents. They offer also a way of placing research with parents into the larger picture of how people come to think in some ways rather than others about the nature of the world in which they live.

The content considered for parents' ideas covers much of the ground that is also covered by formal developmental psychology. We have divided the material into two major categories: research concerned with ideas about the directions of development, and research concerned with ideas about the conditions of development. Research on *directions* covers: parents' goals; ideas about starting points (expectations, for instance, about infants or what life with a first child will be like); and ideas about the course of the journey (the timetable of change and the stages or phases along the way). Research on *conditions* covers ideas about: the relative contributions of internal and external conditions (heredity and environment, or effort and luck); the influence and responsibility of parents; and the methods that parents may use to achieve various goals.

In each main section, we shall introduce some of the reasons for interest in particular aspects, describe some completed research, and indicate some remaining questions. The overall goal, however, is to reduce the almost infinite variety of differences in content that could be considered. Our aim is a limited set that allows us to give a sense of links both to sources and to consequences, together with a sense of what has been considered and where the major gaps exist.

GOALS

Why do people wish to have children? What do they want children to be like? How important is it that children be obedient, loyal, independent, happy, healthy, able to support themselves, observant of the family religion, not too different from most other boys or most other girls? Such questions are of interest in research on the sources of parents' ideas, since the goals parents emphasise provide clues to the relative importance of various sources. Some goals, for instance, may reflect ongoing environmental factors, while others reflect traditions that no longer have a clear anchor in today's pressures. Goals are of interest also for the study of consequences, not only because the goals parents have are expected to influence their actions (whether they have children or not, whether they prefer sons or daughters, how they bring up children), but also because unrealistic goals may set the scene for disappointment, poor relationships, and possibly abuse. In the words of an abusive mother quoted by Helfer and Kempe (1986, p. 14): "I waited so long to have my baby and when she came she never did anything for me."

Parents' goals may seem infinite in their variety. They can, however, be reduced to a manageable number. We shall start with a useful distinction between goals related to what parents want *from* their children as against *for* their children (LeVine, 1974; 1988). This distinction is allied to two contrasting research traditions: one related mainly to population research (e.g. research on fertility or the use of contraception), the other related more to research on socialisation. The distinction is not the only one possible. LeVine (1974; 1988), for instance, adds a distinction between short-term and long-term goals, and we would add a distinction between goals related to individuals and goals related to the family as a unit. In addition, goals for parents and goals for children are not always completely distinct. Goals for children, for instance, are often explored by way of the question: What qualities do parents wish to see their children develop? These qualities may well be influenced by what parents need or want for themselves. To take an example from Poffenberger and Poffenberger (1973), when parents need children to support them economically, and when daughters are expected, upon marriage, to contribute to the support of the husband's parents, sons will be preferred to daughters and parents will value highly the development of a sense of filial obligation in their sons. Nonetheless, the distinction between "from" and "for" children is a useful entry point into research on goals.

What Parents Want from Their Children

In broad terms, societies may be divided into those where resources are mainly expected to flow from children to parents and those where resources are expected to flow from parents to children. There has been some debate as to whether the usual expectation in modern Western countries—a flow from parents to children—may be reversed as parents live longer and run more risk of exhausting their own resources (Hagestad, 1984). Most of the research to date, however, indicates that throughout the life-span the flow from parents in Western countries continues to be larger than the flow to them (e.g. Kendig, 1986).

A more detailed breakdown of parents' hopes comes from a large cross-national study of the value of children to parents (Hoffman, 1988, provides a summary). In each of the nine countries, parents were asked to describe "the good things about having children compared with not having children at all" (Hoffman, 1988, p.109). The good things most often mentioned were parents' needs for economic help, primary ties and affection, stimulation and fun, expression of self, and adult status or social identity. The frequencies with which various needs were mentioned, however, varied considerably from country to country.

What gives rise to variations in such goals? Overall, the utilitarian value of children is mentioned more often in countries and regions with predominantly rural as compared with industrialised economies. At base, the critical quality is probably not rural vs. urban *per se* (Singapore, for instance, has little rural quality left to it but 47% of mothers mentioned the economic utility of children) so much as the level of income and the availability of other forms of support for parents. The availability of alternate ways to meet one's needs seems likely also to affect the perception of other advantages to having children, from the sense of achievement or social identity to the provision of entertainment (Hoffman, 1988). Heath's (1983) analysis of rural black families in the United States certainly supports such a proposal. In the face of few other sources of entertainment, children are praised for their ability to joke, tell a good story, sing, or act as a pleasant distraction from an adult's dull or difficult day. In effect, children in these circumstances have amusement value.

The Qualities Parents Want to See Their Children Develop

Here again the possibilities might seem endless. We shall reduce them by selecting two aspects that have been linked to some particular proposals as to why parents value some goals more than others.

Level in a Hierarchy. The most detailed attention to parents' perceptions of current and future needs, allied to an explicit way of distinguishing among goals, comes from LeVine (1974; 1988). As a way of comparing goals across diverse cultures, he has proposed a hierarchy that starts from physical health and survival, and progresses through the acquisition of economic capacities ("good job", "self-supporting" etc.), to the "attainment of whatever other cultural values are locally prevalent" (LeVine, 1988, p.4). The latter group includes being sociable, honest, happy, attractive, conforming, curious, loyal, clearly masculine or clearly feminine.

In essence, LeVine suggests several working hypotheses: (1) that parents move up the hierarchy as each lower-level goal is satisfied, (2) that the level of major concern will show a strong influence from the hazards (and perhaps the opportunities) in a particular environment, (3) that in times of rapid social transition all levels may be found operating relatively simultaneously, and (4) that in times of social change parents may also show a lag in the modification of ideas that were previously adaptive. The most extensive data so far come from the analysis of hazards. To take one example, in societies where children are an economic asset and infant mortality is high, the mother's attention is expected to be concentrated on ensuring infant survival, with relatively little attention or value given to social or mental stimulation, and with a ready transfer of the same concentrated concern to the survival of the next infant. This is certainly the pattern of values and actions observed in groups such as the Gusii of Africa (LeVine & LeVine, 1988).

LeVine's proposals have offered an excellent base for a series of studies in several cultural groups. These studies have led to some qualifications and reservations related to the original position. Briefly, these are that:

● Mothers in some modern societies where infant mortality is low—Sweden, for instance—often show extreme concern about an infant's survival, with most planning to breast feed for health reasons and with many reluctant to buy things for the baby before it is born "in case things go wrong" (Welles-Nystrom, 1988). The incidence of infant mortality or morbidity may be low, but the salience of risk seems to be high.

● Parents in societies where high-level goals might seem unlikely because of subsistence demands may nonetheless display a great interest in the emotional development of children and in social play and communication with their infants. In similar fashion, people with equivalent subsistence demands may nonetheless vary in their interest in emotional development (Richman, Miller, & Solomon, 1988).

● The important qualities may be determined by expectations as to who will be the child's caregivers. The Gusii, for instance, appear to aim at quiet, docile infants who will give minimal trouble to their sibling minders (LeVine & LeVine, 1988). The Fijians, in contrast, appear to aim at sociable children who will respond positively to a variety of adults and children, whether or not the mother is present (West, 1988, p.23).

● The values covered at the top level require some subdividing, especially when they represent all the goals mentioned by parents. A case in point is provided by Richman et al. (1988, p.68) in a study of 20 Boston families. In that sample, 19 of the 20 mothers "mentioned the importance of independence: Children should make their own decisions and establish separate existences . . . . Seventeen out of twenty mentioned the importance of inner psychological qualities: Children should be happy regardless of the material conditions of their lives . . . The third goal involved relationships with others: Children should be generous, honest, and respectful of the rights of others." These goals are clearly not all alike, but LeVine's (1974) system—developed for a diversity of cultures—places them all in the one group. Some further divisions among top level goals are clearly needed, together with further proposals as to why some of these are more highly valued than others.

A Contrasted Pair of High-level Qualities: Conformity/Independence.
Interest in conformity vs. independence has been sparked especially by Kohn's (1977) proposal that a higher value placed on conformity vs. self-direction, by either mothers or fathers, reflects the degree of self-direction in the father's occupation. The proposal has generated replication of the original research in several countries (e.g. Hoffman, 1988; Burns, Homel, & Goodnow, 1984; Luster, Rhoades, & Haas, 1989), along with critical comment on the need to consider more fully the basis for a spread of values from fathers to mothers, the place of the mother's occupation, and the extent to which occupation alone is the critical source (e.g. Gecas, 1979). It has also been supplemented by proposals that concentrate on a particular aspect of conformity: namely conformity to gender stereotypes. The value placed on this particular goal may reflect parents' views of their own gender roles, together with their views of what the future may demand. It may also vary with the gender of the parent and of the child. Fathers are more concerned than are mothers with conformity to gender stereotypes for both sons and daughters, and especially so for sons (e.g. Antill, 1987; Brooks-Gunn, 1985; Siegal, 1987).

A different view of conformity/independence comes from the cross-national study reported by Hoffman (1988). This arises from a thought-provoking correlation in several countries between valuing children for the way they strengthen a marriage and hoping that children will be independent. "The data suggest that when children are wanted to enhance the marriage, it is expected that they not intrude too much on the marriage; they should be independent" (Hoffman, 1988, p.119). Independence apparently is seen in these cases as serving to ensure that a relationship seen as critical in its own right—the relationship between spouses—is not swamped by that with children.

An apparently reverse expectation emerges in the Italian town studied by New (1988). Here husbands and wives live essentially separate lives but children mingle freely in both men's activities and women's activities. The children are physically as well as emotionally "go-betweens" or "the tie that binds" and are valued for that intrusive, interlinking role. Both reports are an interesting change from the more frequent emphasis on the occupational advantages of independence. Both also suggest ways of linking research on a quality valued in children to an emerging definition of families as consisting of sets of relationships (e.g. parent/parent, parent/child) that may be seen as supplementing, competing, or intruding upon one another (Belsky, Rovine, & Fish, 1989).

IDEAS ABOUT STARTING POINTS

Like research on goals, research on parents' ideas about starting points takes a variety of forms, covering ideas about (1) the initial nature of children; (2) the nature of life with a young child; and (3) the nature of new parents. All three aspects attract attention because of some suspected links to actions. Historically, for instance, the image of children as possessing an original innocence, easily lost in a corrupt world, appears to underlie moves to isolate children from the world of adult activities and adult concerns (Ariès, 1962; Hoffman, 1970). The same link may also hold for contemporary parents. Images of children are also at the heart of a debate over the sources of ideas about children. These images might represent the state of current objective knowledge about children, becoming more accurate with each generation or with experience. On the other hand, they also seem to vary with social or economic conditions, and to be driven by adults' vested interests. Children may be seen, for instance, as able to benefit from time in day care when mothers are needed in the paid work force, but as requiring her constant presence when the labour force is managing nicely without the presence of mothers. In effect, some of our images of the intrinsic nature of children may be "social constructions" (Gergen, 1985) or cultural "inventions" (Kessen, 1979).

The Initial Nature of Children

Are infants "imps of darkness", marked by "original sin", or angels trailing clouds of glory? Are they resilient or vulnerable? Do they need soothing or stimulating? Are they "blank slates" or do they have some directional tendencies of their own? Are they "small adults" or have they quite different natures from those of adults? Such questions have been pursued with an eye to describing cultural differences and, within a culture, differences from one historical period to another.

From a variety of material on contemporary and past ideas, we shall first draw out two proposals that have to do with the extent to which children need adult control. One has to do with the child's moral nature (imp or angel, original sin or original innocence). Depending on the image, the consequence may be protection for the innocent child, or pressure designed to bend a wilful, self-centred soul into a more pliant or altruistic state.

The second proposal has less of a moral overtone. It has to do with ideas about the extent to which children are externally controlled or self-directive. In Kojima's (1986; 1987) view, this dimension of children's basic qualities accounts, both in the past and the present, for the emphasis in Japanese child rearing on setting the child on a proper course. Since the concept of a child as self regulatory is not a completely familiar one in Western views (it is not an exact opposite to "blank slates"), it may be best to quote directly. Reviewing Japanese writings from the mid 17th to mid 19th century, Kojima (1986, p. 323) comments that "the early Japanese emphasis on environmental factors as the explanation for differences among children does not mean that they conceived of children as passive beings in relation to experience . . . . Japanese writers thought educational intervention to be necessary to keep the autonomously developing child on the morally right course from the standpoint of adult society." A continuing view of self-regulatory power, Kojima (1987, p. 10) argues, accounts for the perceived need "to make the learner understand the whole procedure" as a way "to regulate their own behavior by themselves towards goals set by adults". Needed then are parental practices that guide the child in the right direction (especially in the direction of faithfully executing one's assigned task), and encourage self-regulation in the maintenance of that direction (activities, for example, that encourage and give practice in concentration, patience, and a step-by-step mastery of procedures).

Are there original qualities that have attracted attention but that do not deal with the need for adult control? One that is quite different in quality has to do with whether infants are seen as "all alike" or as "different from the start": a distinction seen as having particular flow-on effects to other ideas about infants and parents. The notion of babies as "all alike", for instance, has been seen as related to the view that "infants just need to eat and sleep" (Emiliani & Molinari, 1988). The notion that they are all uniquely different has been seen as linked to the view that parents have a special responsibility to "divine" their infant's individual temperament and capacities, starting even during the first 24 hours of a child's life (e.g. Fischer & Fischer, 1963). The sources of emphasis on "all alike" or "all different" are so far not clear, but both these and the potential links to actions are certainly of interest.

The Start of Life with Children

Will children change one's life? Will they "settle a man down", alter the relationship between the parents, be a source of delight or irritation to the other children? How well will one cope as a parent? Especially if we are interested in families, we need to know not only what parents think children will be like, but also what they think life with a child will be like. Such expectations have been neglected as research topics, even though they are widespread and seem to have effects both on people's actions and on their sense of satisfaction or discontent. We do know, however, that people who are about to have their first child see infants as causing less of an upheaval (and as more competent) than do people who describe themselves as not yet ready to have children (Pharis & Manosewitz, 1980). Both expectations may be regarded as serving a protective function, reassuring the first group and supporting the second group's decision to delay. We also know that mothers in the U.S. often expect that the increased work of running the house and looking after the child will be shared, to a greater extent than often turns out to be the case, with the effect of a drop later on in satisfaction with their partners (Ruble, Hackel, Fleming, & Stangor, 1988).

Parents also seem to expect a mixture of feeling competent and incompetent. On the one hand, they are told that "maternal instinct" will be helpful (after the child is born, mothers believe in "maternal instinct" less than fathers do [Russell, 1983]). On the other, there is the view that looking after infants will require a great deal of "learning on the job", buttressed by the arguments that "it's different for everybody", "you'll learn by trial and error", and "you'll work it out together" (Backett, 1982). The uncertainty about what will be needed must both heighten concern about one's competence and about the vulnerability of infants, and serve to increase the sense of achievement and of togetherness as novel situations are coped with and learning does take place. Uncertainty and the necessity of one's own learning also seem likely to contribute to the appeal of some particular views about infants. If one must learn by trial and error, for instance, it would clearly be reassuring to believe that infants respond to good intentions rather than once-off actions, that their early needs are minimal ("they just need to eat and sleep"), and that parents have many "second chances" to recover from a poor start.

A great deal remains to be learned with regard to expectations about life with children and the impact of these on actions and on satisfaction.

One general point to note in any future study is the difference between expectations that are essentially additive (the child will add to, or strengthen, the existing relationships), and those that are essentially subtractive (e.g. the wife-mother or husband-father has only so much love or attention to give and it will now be divided among more people). This general division provides some integration of possibilities, and should make it easier to identify correlates in future research.

STEPS ALONG THE ROAD: THE COURSE OF DEVELOPMENT

We shall group the diverse material and the possibilities it suggests into three sets, starting with broad expectations about divisions or sections of the life-span, then moving to ideas about the significance of early behaviours and early experiences for later behaviours, and finally to more specific expectations about when various skills or qualities will appear. These ideas about the course or timing of development have attracted attention both because they seem to influence the timing of parents' actions, and because they seem to provide the basis for assessment, for noting whether a child's progress or one's own progress as a parent is "on time" or "off time". As long as children are "at an age when they don't know any better", for instance, a variety of misbehaviours may be excused, and a parent's anger seen as unjustified. Once they "should know better", however, parents may well feel more disturbed, perceiving the child's actions now as more likely to spring from the child's disposition and as less likely to change (e.g. Dix & Grusec, 1983; Dix, Ruble, Grusec, & Nixon, 1986; Mancuso & Lehrer, 1986; Rubin, Mills, & Krasnor, in press).

Divisions and Stages

Parents and formal psychologists tend regularly to divide the life-course of childhood and parenting into sections. Children move from being infants or toddlers to being "terrible twos", preschoolers, "in middle childhood", sub-teens, teenagers, youths, or young adults. Parents make a "transition to parenthood", followed by a variable period of parenting and moving to stages with a variety of labels: "revolving door", "empty nest", "post-parenting", or "child-free adulthood".

At issue now are ways to test the nature, sources and consequences of such time divisions. One might start by asking where divisions into stages, periods, or phases are made and how they are described. Are children in all social groups, for instance, described as becoming "terrible twos" or is the occurrence and the expectation of this phase, like the expectation of *Sturm und Drang* in adolescence, linked to particular combinations of parental control and children's interests? We know at least that some very general differences seem to be expected by adults in many cultures. In almost all of the cultures in the Human Relations Area Files, adults expected several major transition points in cognitive and social competence during the second year of life, around the ages of 6 or 7 years, and at the time of puberty (Rogoff et al., 1975).

More subtly, social scientists are now beginning to ask when parents use a term such as "stage", or "being ready", and what features of behaviours prompt the use of such terms. Belsky et al. (1989) have argued especially for analysis of what parents have in mind when they describe a child as "being ready", but unfortunately no such analysis seems available. There is available, however, a close analysis of the use of two terms ("stage" and "independence") in the ongoing descriptions of a child by parents in Boston (Harkness et al., 1986). The analysis starts by noting that the term "stage" serves to integrate several behaviours. The child's "wanting to help with everything", for instance, and "wanting to do everything himself", are seen as two parts of a new stage of wanting independence. This integrative function, however, cannot be the sole basis for using the term. The two-year-old who objects violently to having his diapers changed (and is seen by his parents as "getting to the point where it's insulting") does not object to being buckled into a car seat. In contrast, another child who fights against the car seat does not object to being diapered. Why, the observers ask, do parents use such general-level terms as "stage" to describe behaviour that seems so situational? The hypothesis proposed is that terms such as "stage" are used to cover some particular occasions:

● The behaviour is seen as having a temporal dimension ("it began a couple of months ago").

● The behaviour is seen as initiated spontaneously by the child, rather than growing out of some particular environmental conditions or interaction patterns between parent and child.

● The behaviour "requires a new set of responses from the parent, new responses which require effort and may challenge the parents' perceived ability to cope successfully" (Harkness et al., 1986, p.12).

● The term allows parents to redefine the child's behaviour in a positive light. The struggle to "do everything myself", for instance, becomes a sign of growth in the direction of a valued quality, "independence".

These proposals about parents' use of "stage" with reference to two-year-olds might well be checked against uses of the term when children are older: when children are, for instance, going through the "stage" of adolescence (Grusec, personal communication). The later check would allow one to determine if all of the features noted for the term "stage" at age two appear again with its use in reference to adolescence, or whether the main common property is the connotation that parents are justified in taking no action other than waiting for the behaviour to run its course.

Links Between One Phase and Another

Links over time may refer to a relatively short time-span. Parents have been asked, for instance, to observe videotaped sequences of behaviour and to mark the beginnings and ends of episodes (Hayes, Gunn, & Price, 1982; Vedeler, 1987). What is seen, for example, as the beginning of an infant's reach for an object or the start of a burst into tears? The technique has been useful in distinguishing between parents and non-parents. (Parents see earlier beginnings to an episode than do non-parents). The same technique of marking episodes could well be adapted to longer periods of time. What do parents see, for instance, as the beginnings of a new "stage" of open conflict, the start to a breakdown in communication between themselves and an adolescent, or the first signs of a new base for interacting with an adult child?

In practice, research approaches to ideas about time usually deal with a long developmental span. One approach, for instance, asks about the general view of childhood in relation to adulthood. Is childhood seen as a time to be endured until one reaches the pleasures of adulthood, a view Wolfenstein (1955) saw as prevalent in France? Or is it a time to be enjoyed, a period of relative license before one takes up the inevitable hardships of adulthood? "Let them play while they can", in effect or, in the words of a Lebanese-born mother in Australia, commenting on whether her 10-year-old daughter had any specific household tasks: "Why should she? She'll get lumbered with them soon enough."

A second approach asks whether parents value precocity, seeing it as a sign of distinction. The answer seems to vary with the domain and the cultural group. Against the notion of early maturity as always "a good sign", for instance, may be set some other examples of parental thought: the low value most parents seem to place on "precocious" sexual interest or sexual behaviours even when they are delighted by early achievements in many other areas; the Chinese proverb "early ripe, early rot"; and the observation by Blount (1972) that in some cultural groups the early acquisition of language may attract the suspicion of witchcraft. The last observation may seem remote from parental ideas in modern secular societies but a sense of unease about some forms of early achievement can still be noticed. We have certainly seen "modern" parents who felt there was something "freakish" and a little "alien" about very early reading or mathematical skills in their children, especially when these appear before any exposure to school and do not "run in the family".

The third type of approach asks whether parents see the behaviour displayed at one age as likely to last or to change. There are now several studies where parents have been given a list of skills or qualities and asked: "If a child is like this, say at the age of 6 years, is he or she likely to be the same at age 12, or are things likely to change?" The result is nicely consistent across several cultural groups. Behaviours or qualities regarded as desirable (e.g. is friendly, catches on quickly, talks nicely, is generous to others) are regarded as likely to be stable. Behaviours regarded as undesirable (e.g. is easily upset by mistakes, is rude, cries easily) are expected to change (Becker, in press; Goodnow, Cashmore, Cotton, & Knight, 1984; Knight, 1986). They are also more likely to be attributed by mothers to situational factors while prosocial behaviours are attributed to dispositions (Dix et al., 1986; Gretarsson & Gelfand, 1988).

The final form of interest in connections across time is the one to which we shall give most space. This has to do with the view that early phases have significant effects upon later ones. This view is well represented popularly in phrases such as "give me a child until the age of seven, and he (or she) is mine for life", or "as the twig is bent, the tree will grow". This may not, however, be the only view that parents may hold. They may well believe, as Tizard (1977) encourages us to do, in "second chances" (used in her case with reference to adoption, especially beyond infancy). Of the two concepts, the notion that early experiences are decisive seems to receive the larger endorsement by parents, perhaps because it reduces the sense of ambiguity about what children need, or perhaps because the alternative (second chances) has not been as widely publicised or as widely endorsed by formal theory.

More broadly, there appear to be two general views about the significance of early experience, especially early learning. One proposes that behaviours should be built in as early as possible, the other that behaviours or skills can wait until the individual needs to learn them. One we shall label a *role-theory point of view*. A mother may assume, for instance, that a daughter does not need any early learning of household skills. When she moves into the role of married woman, she will of course acquire the appropriate skills and display the appropriate willingness. The other view we shall label a *trait-theory view*. If, for instance, a child does not acquire at an early age an attitude of willingness and some skill in work around the house, he or she as an adult will never accept the tasks willingly or do them well.

Parents may hold both views, simply differing in the items that they class as needing to be learned early and the items that can "be left until later" without consequences for later development. We do not know which skills or qualities fall into the "role" or the "trait" category for various parents. The topic strikes us, however, as especially worth pursuing, not only as a way to understand parents' views of their own children, but also as a way to understand the kinds of judgments that are made, as formal or informal psychologists, about other people's views of development. As Westerners, for instance, we are often struck by the apparent "discontinuity" in the actions and expectations of parents in other cultural groups (e.g. Benedict, 1938). How, we ask, can children go from an indulged childhood into schools that emphasise control and discipline and may even be downright authoritarian? How can Lebanese-born mothers who strike Anglo-Australians as "indulgent" worry that Australian teachers are "too soft" with kindergartners and first graders? The "discontinuity" seems to stem from our expectations that a number of behaviours require early practice or slow transitions rather than the expectation that, when people move into a role, they will act as the role requires and as they have been told ahead of time that this is what the role requires.

Developmental Timetables

The term is used to refer to parents' ideas about the ages at which a particular skill or quality would be expected to appear (Goodnow et al., 1984). Parents may be given alternatives (e.g. before the age of 5, around the ages of 5 or 6, or later than that) or asked to estimate an age in more open-ended fashion. The ideas may refer to motor changes (e.g. can sit up by self), social changes (e.g. can disagree with friends without fighting, can take disappointment without crying) or cognitive shifts (e.g. can count from one to ten, knows the names of colours or shapes, can benefit from being read to). Most of the items studied so far have been relevant to young children, although two studies have now appeared which deal with timetables for adolescents (Feldman & Quatman, 1988; Rosenthal & Bornholt,1988).

In some studies, the intention has been one of asking about the accuracy of parents' judgments, using formal scales as the norm (Miller, 1988, provides a review of these with special attention to parents of children showing either normal progress or developmental delay). In others, the intention has been to compare the expectations of one cultural group with another, or one experiential group with another: parents with non-parents, parents with teachers, parents with children at about the age for which questions are asked as against parents with children several years older.

Overall, the results have brought out the effects of several sources. Culture certainly has an effect. Japanese mothers, for instance, expect earlier emotional control but not earlier scholastic achievement than do American-born mothers (Hess et al., 1980). Lebanese-born mothers in Australia have more relaxed timetables (expect achievements at later ages) than do Australian-born mothers (Goodnow et al., 1984). The same is true for Israeli mothers with "Eastern" as against "European" backgrounds (Ninio, 1979). Experience has also been shown to have an impact (Edwards & Gandini, 1988), but it is complicated by the effects of responsibility. Mothers and workers in day-care centres with young children, for instance, expect competence in self-care at an earlier age than do non-parents or teachers of older children (Hess, Price, Dickson, & Conroy, 1984). The experience of the former group may be the source of their perceptions of competence. So also may the need to perceive and expect competence.

Despite the several studies, gaps still remain in our understanding of developmental timetables. One has to do with *the range of age-expectations*. At what point, for instance, is an age seen as "seriously late" or "too late"? How much of a delay is a strong cause for worry? How far do parents agree on any age-grading? A second has to do with *the sources of variations in age-expectations*. The contributing factors are certainly of several kinds. Mothers appear to expect at an early age, and perhaps press for, qualities and skills that they see as valuable for the child, as not likely to be achieved by the child without help, and as demonstrating to the world that they are "good mothers". The weights of these contributing factors are not yet known. A third concerns *the bases of interest in age-grading and age-norms*. At least in the Western world we are uneasy when dealing with a child whose age we do not know, just as we are uneasy in dealing with an infant whose gender is not known. Not all cultures, however, share the same degree of interest. The concern with age may perhaps reflect the extent to which life in general involves competitive comparisons and evaluations. The fourth and last area where more research is needed has to do with *the consequences of a difference between expectations and reality*. We shall take this up again in Chapter 5, when we consider the issue of affective consequences to discrepancy. At this point, however, it is important to note that for new parents the absolute difference is less important than the direction of difference (Belsky et al., 1989). Pleasant surprises are different from disappointments.

THE CONTRIBUTIONS OF INTERNAL AND EXTERNAL CONDITIONS

We turn at this point from parents' ideas about the course of development to their ideas about the conditions that influence development, starting, in this section, with their ideas about the contributions of internal and external conditions, and progressing, in the following two sections, to ideas about the influence and responsibility of parents and about optimal and feasible methods. In theory, some ideas about conditions should accompany some ideas about the directions of development. A major role for environmental factors, for instance, should accompany a view of children as initially "blank slates". In practice, however, researchers may deal with one concept without considering others that might go with it, and parents may vary considerably in the degree of consistency within the ideas they hold (Palacios, 1986). In this chapter we shall accordingly treat only ideas about the conditions that influence development, deferring until the next chapter the issue of whether ideas about conditions and directions form particular clusters.

The Contributions of Heredity and Environment

We shall draw mainly from two studies. One is by Antill (1987), dealing with parents' views about biological and environmental contributions to the development of sex differences and gender identity. Parents' behaviours were scored for the extent to which they encouraged or discouraged same-sex and cross-sex behaviours. Parents who believed that homosexuality has social rather than biological causes, or that cross-sex behaviour is associated with later homosexuality, encouraged same-sex and discouraged cross-sex activities. The link was stronger for fathers than for mothers and was especially pronounced among fathers of sons.

The second study deals with parents' views about the sources of intelligence (Mugny & Carugati, 1985). It requires longer comment, partly because we wish to draw upon it in Chapter 4 when considering a particular theoretical approach to sources, and partly because of its delayed accessibility to English readers (all quotations are translations from French and are our responsibility. Readers should note, however, that an English-language version is to become available in late 1990). The sample is from two cities (Geneva and Bologna). It is large (506 females, 221 males) and designed to reflect various forms of "socialisation into representations of intelligence" (Mugny & Carugati, 1985, p.58): socialisation that may come from professional training (checked by comparing trainee-teachers or teachers with students in other areas or graduates in other professions), or from parenting (checked by comparing parents with non-parents, and by comparing parents with one child with parents of more than one). The questionnaires asked for degrees of agreement with statements dealing with a number of themes. We shall concentrate on the results from items dealing with general aspects of intelligence and its development (questionnaires 1 and 2), and from the comparisons designed to check the effects of being a parent (Mugny & Carugati, 1985, pp. 67-108).

In essence, parents differed significantly from non-parents in the extent to which they saw intelligence as a gift. They were, for instance, significantly *less* likely than were non-parents to endorse familial factors: to endorse, for example, items such as "like father, like son; this is true also for intelligence"; "intelligent children come only from families which value intelligence"; or "show me the profession of the parents, and I will tell you the intelligence of the child" (Mugny & Carugati, 1985, p.77). Parents were also less likely to endorse the influence of schools (e.g. less likely to agree with items stating that the school accentuates, reveals or creates differences in intelligence).

In contrast, parents were *more* likely to endorse a biological unfolding of intelligence, agreeing with items such as "the development of intelligence unrolls according to a programme fixed at birth"; "intelligence does not develop, it is an hereditary gift"; "the child develops spontaneously an innate intellectual capacity"; or "you can teach good manners to a child, but not intelligence" (Mugny & Carugati, 1985, pp.86-87). What is more, parents with more than one child, compared with parents of one, were more likely to endorse statements about natural inequalities in the gift of intelligence, and more likely to take a non-developmental or biological unfolding view.

How may such differences be accounted for? Socialisation into a view of intelligence is certainly one possible explanation. More broadly, Mugny and Carugati (1985, pp. 180-183) regard parents' views of intelligence as reflecting the way that parents select, from a number of views available in the culture, positions which are both socially acceptable and "personally gratifying" in the sense that they assign less rather than more responsibility to the family milieu and provide a protective buffer against a loss of one's identity as an effective parent.

Attribution Studies

In a broad sense, studies asking about the perceived contributions of heredity and environment are attribution studies. The latter term is usually reserved, however, for studies that consider a particular set of factors: in the case of academic achievement, factors such as effort, ability, the quality of teaching, the difficulty of the task, and luck; in the case of misbehaviours, factors such as the nature of the situation, the child's understanding or knowledge, and the child's disposition. Such studies offer a breakdown of internal and external factors. They have as well the attraction of carrying implications as to whether action is worthwhile and who should take action (who, for instance, should increase the effort they are making), together with the appeal of linking material on parents' ideas to the analysis of parental actions (e.g. discipline and abuse) and to an established body of theory dealing with conditions that influence attribution patterns.

We shall deal with these studies briefly since the format for attribution studies is relatively familiar and since we have already noted one major result: the way that parents generally expect desirable behaviours to be more stable and more dispositional than are undesirable behaviours. Several other results will be considered in the chapters on sources and consequences. For the moment, it will be sufficient to note three points:

• The results with parents show many of the effects found in classical attribution studies. The actor/observer effect, for instance, appears in the way that parents, who are observers of children's school performance, are generally more likely to make attributions to stable internal factors than are the main actors in school: the children themselves. For explanations of failure or of less success than might be possible, the children lean towards attributions of lesser effort or of circumstances (e.g. Bar-Tal & Guttman, 1981; Cashmore & Goodnow, 1986).

• Attributions provide a vantage point for considering changes in parents' ideas with the changing age of the child. The sharpest data come from attributions for the misdemeanours of older vs. younger children. The older the child, the more parents are inclined to make attributions to the child's disposition and, reasonably, to be upset by the child's actions (e.g. Dix & Grusec, 1985; Dix et al., 1986).

• Negative affect and abuse may be related to particular patterns of attributions. In an interesting move beyond the usual set of attributions, Bugental and her colleagues have asked about the consequences of mothers attributing various degrees of power to themselves and to children. In one of these studies, the children are confederates, trained to be assertive or shy, resistant or cooperative towards the adult they are to work with in a teaching/learning situation. Adults with low perceived control respond with greater negative affect to "difficult" children (Bugental & Shennum, 1984). Similar results have been found in a later study that has refined the measure, providing a scale that taps the perceived balance between control by the caregiver and by the child over success and failure, and extended the sample to families where abuse has occurred (Bugental et al., 1989). A mother's sense of control and her past history, however, are not the only factors operating. Adults who were not related to the abused children differed in the way they reacted to children who had received more abuse in a family than they did to those who had received less than others (Bugental et al., 1989). To account for abusive actions, it is argued, we shall need a transactional model that takes account of the caregiver's perception of control (these perceptions act both to sensitise parents and to buffer them against the challenge of a child's behaviours), the characteristics of the child (e.g. those characteristics that provide stress or difficulty for the caregiver), the affect experienced or expressed by the caregiver, and the child's interpretation of and response to the caregiver's actions (Bugental, 1989).

THE PARTICULAR INFLUENCE AND RESPONSIBILITIES OF PARENTS

We shall group examples of research into two main clusters: work related to (a) concepts of influence and (b) concepts of responsibility. We shall use the former term to refer to ideas about what one can influence, and the latter for ideas about what one should attempt to influence, with the recognition that the two sets of ideas seem to be linked and to affect one another.

Ideas About Influence

It is clearly uncomfortable to fail in one's attempts at influence and still be expected to sustain the view that influence is possible. Worth particular note in this connection is a set of results from Emmerich (1969) relating degrees of satisfaction to ideas about influence. Parents felt the most dissatisfaction with their parenting when dealing with a characteristic that they perceived as in principle open to influence, and usually influenced by most parents, but not amenable for some reason to their own attempts at influence. The discrepancy in such a case is not only from their own expectations of themselves but also from the achievements of their peer group, leaving little room for explanations other than the peculiarity of one's child or one's own inadequacy.

Do people always believe that influence is maximal when the child is at a young age? Such a view is certainly not universal. Among Aboriginal Australian groups, for instance, a father may be absent for several years but return when children—boys especially—are around 12. At that age, the father is seen to exert a strong and a much needed influence, more so than in earlier years (Ruth, 1984). Relevant also is the comment that mothers in Singapore see the need to take time out of paid work not when the children are in the preschool years but once they start school and need close supervision of their school work (Michael Lamb, personal communication). Both of these examples contain a mixture of *can* influence and *should* influence, and the two aspects are difficult to separate. Both run counter, however, to the notion that all is lost if influence is not applied at early ages.

Ideas About Parents' Responsibilities

Parents are often described as having responsibility for children and as feeling responsible. What the term covers, however, is far from clear. Popular opinion, for instance, often takes the form of seeing parents as responsible for supplying a child with one or more siblings ("it's not good for children to be an only child") even in the face of formal evidence that first-borns and only children are generally high achievers and well-adjusted rather than "hopelessly spoilt". Popular opinion, and some formal theory, may argue as well for the responsibility to provide two parents. In Lidz's (1963) view of family functioning, for instance, one parent is needed to love and one to use as a model. Single parents might well disagree.

We are, in fact, far from clear as to what parents regard as the essentials or the limits of responsibility, and what the conditions are that give rise to different definitions. The lack of clarity applies to the length of a commitment. How is it, for instance, that some parents can close the door and say "my job is ended", while others see no finish to the obligation and little change in the nature of their responsibility? Even less clear are the areas for which parents see themselves as having primary responsibility and the areas where they see responsibility as shared with people outside the family: from day-care staff to teachers or police officers.

Areas of Parental Responsibility. Suppose we begin with what parents see as needing to be supplied from within themselves. Backett (1982) comments perceptively on the view of Scots parents that they "should try to understand their children": a view that seems likely to be held by parents in many other "modern" groups. The meanings and expected functions of "understanding", however, are yet to be well explained. The responsibility, one suspects, is probably most deeply felt in situations where parents are expected to persuade rather than to command, to enter into some negotiations with children, to supply children with reasons for actions, and perhaps to model an interactive style that children should extend to others. There is at least some formal evidence that adults whose perceptions of each other are in relative agreement are more likely to try working through a problem rather than disengaging from one another (Knudson, Sommers, & Golding, 1980). But we cannot yet tell whether parents operate from an intuitive knowledge of such effects or whether the goal of "working things out" is part of a broader view, e.g. the view that families should be characterised by intimacy rather than by emotional distance and by attempts at consensus rather than authoritarian commands.

Few people in modern societies would quarrel with the view that parents should try to understand their children. More variable are likely to be opinions about responsibilties that begin to involve others and that stretch outside the home. How much responsibility, for instance, do parents have for attempting to influence a child's choice of friends, a child's outside activities, the type of school a child attends, or the particular teacher assigned in a school? And do children agree with these views? We know so far that adolescents in the U.S. and in Canada come with age to regard a number of such areas as more within their personal jurisdiction than as falling within parental responsibility, while their parents see parental responsibility as tending to last longer than adolescents perceive it as doing (Smetana, 1988), but this research could well be taken further.

Shared Responsibility.   A parent is seldom—if ever—the sole holder of responsibility in any situation. Responsibility may also be held (or perceived to be held) by the child, by the other parent, by kin, by schools, by health-care personnel, by the state and its various welfare agencies. We need to ask about parents' perceptions of spheres of influence in relation to each other, to siblings, or members of the larger community. Needed also is a deeper understanding of the way some actions by these several people are perceived as "failing to take responsibility" while others are seen as "interfering".

What avenues of research are there? One relevant line of research has to do with the responsibilities of siblings. We know that cultures vary considerably in the extent to which older children act as caregivers, language teachers, and task models for their younger sibs (e.g. Weisner & Gallimore, 1977). What we now need to understand are the principles that underlie what parents regard as reasonable or unreasonable to expect of an older child and the way these expectations vary with the age or the gender of that child.

A further line of research has to do with the sharing of responsibility among adults. The adult of main concern may be the child's father. One of the outcomes of family therapy, for instance, is that fathers come to perceive that they have some responsibility for a problem and its solution as against responsibility resting entirely with the mother and/or child (e.g. Watson & Russell, 1988). This type of outcome, in the form of fathers taking increased responsibility for playing with a child, has also been noted as an outcome of a parent education programme with a middle-class non-clinic sample (Larsen & Harris, 1989).

A broader form of sharing is involved when one asks about the expectations that a custodial parent has of a non-resident parent or a step-parent, or that parents have of caregivers outside the family: of a day-care mother, for instance, or of the workers in day-care centres (Graeme Russell and Jodie Watson, work in progress). In time, we may begin to learn from such research what it is that parents regard as neglectful or as taking over, why they come to regard some patterns of responsibility or involvement as less or more than what is expected, and what they regard as better vs. poorer ways of organising responsibilites among family members and among the several contributors to a child's development.

OPTIMAL AND REASONABLE METHODS

In this final section on the content of parents' ideas we shall concentrate on ideas about "how" to proceed rather than "when" to proceed. The material is in two parts, dealing with some particular bases for interest, and some parental preferences among methods and their sources.

Some Particular Bases for Interest

Parents use a variety of methods in bringing up children, and social scientists often wish to account for why some are used rather than others. This wish is especially sharp when parents' methods violate one's sense of the norm for reasons that are not obvious. Abuse within the family is such a case. Physical abuse and sexual exploitation violate our general sense that the weak should be protected and our specific sense that families should be safe havens. Given these assumptions, how are abusive and exploitive methods to be understood? The search for causes has spanned the parents' history, the child's qualities, the social isolation of parents, the general acceptance in the community of violence as a way of resolving problems, and—of particular interest to us—parents' ideas about why children act as they do and what the best methods are for treating misbehaviours (e.g. Bugental et al., 1989; Trickett & Susman, 1988; Twentyman & Plotkin, 1982).

The appeal of considering parents' ideas about methods is all the greater because of the hope that parents' actions may be altered by changing their ideas about optimal or possible methods. There is in fact some evidence that ideas about methods may be the area where change most readily occurs. Kohn (1963), for instance, has proposed that the changes in permissiveness noted by Bronfenbrenner (1958) for the U.S. over a 25-year period reflect primarily changes in ideas about methods rather than changes in ideas about goals. Backett (1982) notes that information about methods—"something that works"—is what parents seek.

In effect, if one is looking for historical change or if one wishes to feed information to parents, ideas about "how" are probably the best place to begin. This is, in fact, where a family therapist may also begin. According to Ford (1984, p.178), "A therapist interested in a client's control cognitions might ask, 'What could you do to get what you want?' . . . 'What do you usually do?' 'What else could you do?' 'Are there better ways to get what you want?' 'What do you do when something goes wrong?' 'How do you make yourself feel better?' 'How can you get one thing without giving up the other?' ". One note of caution needs adding, however, before starting enthusiastically with questions about methods. It comes from Trickett and Susman's (1988) comparison of abusive with non-abusive mothers. The two groups they selected did not differ in their degree of approval of physical punishment. Nor did they disagree on the frequency of its use (both groups used it frequently). The difference lay in the quality of its use. The control group, for instance, did not strike with an object, hit in the face, or pull a child's hair. In effect, ideas about methods may have to be pursued with some subtlety if the aim is to differentiate among groups of parents.

Preferences Among Methods

Parents clearly prefer some methods to others. Some, for instance, favour the supply of a small number of toys while others believe in novelty and profusion. Some favour power assertion over reasoning when a child is not meeting parental expectations. Some will hint at their need for help rather than make a direct request. Some will pay children to do work around the house while others regard payment as a last resort.

Why do parents distinguish among methods and prefer some methods to others? Three factors stand out. Two are in the form of other ideas that parents hold: the importance of the underlying goal, and parents' categories of actions. The third has to do with the knowledge of past effects.

The *significance of the goal* emerges most clearly in studies of methods related to discipline. The use of rationales, for instance, needs to be understood in terms of whether a parent's goal is compliance *per se* or the encouragement of particular styles of negotiating. A child's learning that "whatever you do, don't whine", for instance, may be as important or more important to a parent than whether the child complies or not (Leonard, 1988). In related fashion, the nature of the goal influences the extent to which parents prefer rationales over power assertion methods. The strongest evidence for this connection comes from a study in Holland (Nijmegen) (Janssens, Gerris, & Janssens, 1987; Siebenheller, Gerris, & van Leeuwe, 1988). Both parents, in a large sample of families, were given descriptions of hypothetical situations that could involve discipline and were asked: How do you feel in such a situation? What do you do or say? Why do you do or say that? Discipline behaviours were coded as emphasising power assertion or induction, and the analysis was directed towards determining the factors that best predicted preference for one rather than the other. The strongest predictive value came from the parents' emphasis on conformity (determined from a set of questions dealing with the parents' orientation to child rearing values). The greater the emphasis on conformity, the more frequent the reports of using power assertion rather than reasoning.

Parents' categories of actions provide the second cognitive factor influencing a parent's preference for particular methods. From studies of prosocial/antisocial behaviour comes evidence to the effect that parents distinguish between actions that are active transgressions (e.g. hitting another child) and actions that are failures to be prosocial (e.g. failing to help or to share with another child). Parents are more likely to ignore the latter than they are the former, on the grounds that failing to help is less of a transgression and asks more of a child (asks them, for instance, to take another child's perspective or to set aside their own interest) (Grusec & Kuczynski, 1980). From material on household work comes evidence of distinctions between "regular" vs. "extra" jobs (payments in money may be acceptable for the latter but not the former) and between "self-care" and "family-care" jobs. "Self-care" covers tasks such as putting away one's own clothes or toys, "family-care" tasks such as clearing the table or taking out trash. The methods in this case refer to whether a piece of work, if not done, can be asked of another sib, as against being left for the original owner of the task or "taken back" by the mothers. Australian mothers regard family-care tasks as transferable to another child. In contrast, they disapprove of asking another child to pick up another's self care task, on the double grounds that the request would not be well received and that the job "belongs" to the first child (it is "their" job) (Goodnow & Delaney, 1989; Goodnow & Warton, in press).

The *importance of the results of past use* is illustrated particularly in research by Mancuso and Lehrer (1986). They asked adults to indicate the degree of "change power" they would expect various kinds of reprimand to have (using "reprimand" to cover all forms of control or discipline). The main result is that people were reluctant to see much change power in single reprimands, unless they knew something of the outcomes of previous reprimands. A similar point is made by Holden and

Ritchie (1988) in discussing consistency, or its lack, between observed actions (e.g. how a parent responds in a supermarket to a child's pulling items off the shelves) and reports of what one would do or did do in such situations. Such analyses, they argue, need to proceed not only by gaining reports from as close a re-enactment of the actual situation as possible (e.g. setting up a computer simulation of an interaction). They also benefit considerably by noting how far a parent feels that a particular method has worked well in the past or how far a method has, on this supermarket occasion, been tried but turned out to be ineffective. In short, parents' ideas about optimal or reasonable methods may be an area where the need for data over time, as against the single snapshot of opinions, is particularly sharp.

RESEARCH AGENDA: IDEAS ABOUT FAMILIES AND RELATIONSHIPS

The aims of this chapter have been twofold. One is to introduce a number of the ways in which researchers have explored the content of parents' ideas, paying attention sometimes to ideas about the direction of development (e.g. the goals it should reach or the timetable of change) and sometimes to ideas about conditions that influence development (e.g. the role of heredity, the responsibility of parents, or the methods most likely to be effective). These forms of attention to content, we have noted, arise sometimes in the course of attempting intervention (e.g. what ideas *do* these parents hold about their areas of influence or responsibility?) and sometimes in the pursuit of questions about the sources or consequences of parents' ideas.

The second aim of the chapter has been to note a number of gaps and difficulties. We have noted a number of these throughout the chapter. We now wish to move to a practice we shall also follow in later chapters: singling out one or two special items for a major place on the research agenda. For this chapter, we shall take only one item: the need for research on ideas about relationships and about families.

Our concern with that item stems from the way most material on the content of parents' ideas concentrates on individuals, a concentration not yet in keeping with the emerging recognition that we need to think also in terms of people as embedded in relationships and of families as containing people whose goals and paths of development influence and intersect with one another. The emphasis currently falls, for instance, on goals for the child, or for the parent, rather than explicitly for the relationship or for the family. The methods discussed are more often for achieving a child's compliance or achievement than, say, tolerable or warm relationships among siblings. The course of development considered is usually the child's rather than that of several independent family members.

The emphasis on individuals is understandable, but it is also limiting. How could we explore ideas about relationships and families? As a basis for working through some possibilities, we shall take ideas about goals. One could take ideas about the course of family development or about methods for producing the kind of family one hopes to see. Conceptually, however, goals provide a nicely superordinate point from which to start. In addition, ideas about goals have been the main concern in several discussions of what it may mean to be a family. Points of entry for research are suggested by three types of material: (1) analyses of the way parents combine goals for various family members; (2) analyses of families described as placing the interests of family above the interest of individuals; and (3) proposals from family system theory as to what dimensions differentiate one family from another, combined with related proposals from analyses of differences among relationships (relationships within or outside the family).

Combining Goals for Various Family Members

How do parents combine goals for themselves and their children? How do they combine goals for the several children in a family? Where do they set priorities if these goals are incompatible? What do they see as reasonable compromises? Data related to such questions is scarce. We do know that parents, in considering requests for household help from their teenage children, consider both the need for the work to be done and the level of discussion or "hassle" likely to be involved (Goodnow, Bowes, Dawes, & Taylor, 1988). We also know, however, that the compromises are not always on the parents' side. In Western countries, for instance, Super and Harkness (1986) see the conflict between children's demands for attention and parents' wishes for time to themselves as resulting in an expectation that children will sleep for periods that tax their physiological limit.

Families Described as Placing Family Above Individuals.   It is often said that some cultural groups take a "collectivist" rather than an "individualist" orientation towards families or other social units. The general concept is useful for the analysis of parents' ideas when it is accompanied by some more specific description of expectations. Soccio's (1977) description of immigrant families in Australia with Italian backgrounds helps pinpoint some of these. Older children may be expected to leave school early so that the later-borns may be well-educated; parents may encourage delay in the marriage of one daughter until the older daughter is first married; children are expected to contribute time to the family business; children are expected to consult their parents about marriage partners and to respect their advice; and children are seen as responsible—by virtue of their appearance, their grooming and their deportment—for the "figura" and the honour of the family.

Descriptions of such families bring out not only ideas about the way children should behave or develop. They contain also material on preferences for particular methods. New (1988) sees, for instance, the establishment of a sense of concern for "la famiglia" as starting with early interactions with infants. Infants and toddlers may be teased by others; they may be awakened if someone wants to play with them or show them off; their attempts at exploration (likely to result in soiled clothing) are discouraged in favour of "bella figura"; their feeding times are aligned with the family feeding times; and there are "few accommodations made for the infant . . . (who is) hungry ahead of schedule or even . . . sleeping when it was time to eat" (New, 1988, p.59). In these several ways, "the constant reminders of the . . . infant's immature status with respect to the family hierarchy may be seen as . . . discouraging autonomous behavior or independent daily routines" (New, 1988, p.62). Heath's (1983; 1990) description of rural black families in the U.S. has less hierarchical overtones. The goal in this case is seen as one of seeking "to fix and stabilize the identity of individuals as members of their own group and as outsiders to others' cultural groups" (Heath, 1990, p.499). The methods emphasised are collective: the joint reading of newspapers, the telling and retelling of stories, the criss-crossing of narrative and comment in the joint production of a story. The two reports, in effect, point to different ways by which a "family" identity may be established. The need now is to expand the descriptions and to ask when and why some approaches are preferred to others.

Ideally, developmentalists would also hope to know whether an emphasis on "family" changes over time. Margaret Mead, for instance, (cited by Wolfenstein, 1955) suggests that such changes may vary from one cultural group to another. In Anglo-Saxon families, she argues, parents regard the family as a "launching pad", a base preparing children to move into a world of peers who will, in time, become more important than family. In contrast, ties within European families are expected to deepen rather than to diminish. The comment helps clarify some cultural differences. It also emphasises the need to regard parents' goals as changing rather than static, and the value of data that considers more than one age-point or one life-phase.

Proposals From Family System Theories and From
Analyses of Relationships

There is some overlap between proposals about the markers or norms of "family" from family system theory and those from analyses of relationships (e.g. Clark, 1984). We shall first consider proposals that are predominantly from family system theory alone, and then move to some that are shared by the two approaches.

As markers of "the good family", parents may value and use criteria such as the following:

An investment in more than one relationship. The suggestion comes from Belsky et al. (1989). Concerned with the ambiguity of many statements to the effect that families form "systems", they have proposed that a system may be defined as a set of intersecting relationshps: mother/father, mother/child, father/child, sibling/sibling, etc. To be closely involved with one's wife, but uninterested in one's child, or with one's child but not one's partner, are then taken as signs of a family not functioning well as a system. Ideally, one suspects, the parental goal for a family may not be simply an investment in more than one relationship, but some "proper" balance of investments.

A sense of boundaries or of territory, applying not only to space ("my room" etc.) but also to activities and privileges (Minuchin, 1985). Family therapy is often especially concerned with families that contain weak boundaries or reversed territories between generations. Parent plays child, for instance, and/or child moves into the role of parent (e.g. Minuchin, 1985; Sroufe et al., 1985). The concept of boundaries suggests as well the value of research on the way family members define boundaries and base these on generation or gender. Since the concept may not be clear in abstract form, we offer a concrete example from an Australian mother, commenting on a time when her 12-year-old son, who had begun a part-time job and was contributing financially to the family, expected her to make coffee for him at breakfast: "I had to let him know that he might be earning money, but I did that only for his Dad".

A Way of Dealing With the World That is Not Family. The previous point dealt with boundaries within families. Boundaries apply also in distinctions between "family" and "not-family". Family systems theories again offer an example of this dimension as a way of defining a family that is functioning well: namely, that "family relationships should neither prevent outside contact nor force outside contact as an escape" (Walsh, 1981, p.19). Ideally, the attitude toward the outside society should be "open and hopeful". All families may not be responsive to such a view. In some, the outside world may in fact not be a safe or rewarding place, to be approached with trust and optimism. In others, the notion of the outside world as threatening and dangerous may be the cement that holds a family together and creates a sense of unity. It seems likely, however, that all families will have some implicit norms about the nature of the outside world, the proper lines of communication with it (Should a child under 16, for instance, be allowed to seek independent legal or medical advice?), the importance of a united front, and the occasions when a family must appear as a unit or must agree to present the same view. What we now need to understand more fully are the content, the sources, and the consequences of such views.

Of particular attention in this respect are proposals from Reiss and his colleagues (e.g. Oliveri & Reiss, 1982; Reiss, Oliveri, & Kurd, 1983). They have asked families to engage in tasks such as working together on a novel problem in the laboratory (also new to them) and then observed the way various family members approach the task and regard the laboratory staff. This procedure and others have led to some particular distinctions among families. Some are described, for instance, as "distance-sensitive": "the outside world of people, places, events and things is lived in but neither explored or understood" (Reiss et al., 1983, p.81). Other families are "achievement-sensitive"; they " do not see themselves as part of a group but as individuals operating on their own to secure success in a tough but masterable world" (Reiss et al., 1983, p.81). Overall, families vary in their "family paradigms", with paradigm referring to "the set of assumptions, convictions, or beliefs that each family holds about its environment . . . [and that] guide the family to sample some segments of its world and ignore others" (Reiss et al., 1983, pp.79-80). We would wish to add that a concern with "family paradigm" may obscure differences in viewpoints among family members. The critical question may then be one of determining whose view prevails. We would also add attention to the ideas that family members hold about who should be responsible for dealing with various segments of the outside world. Should mothers, for instance, be expected to deal with schools and physicians, while fathers tend to any financial or legal segments? These additions aside, the proposals and the several research studies related to them, both in the U.S. and in Israel (e.g. Shulman & Zohar, in press), provide an especially interesting example of how to take account of the ways in which family members view the outside world.

Expectations about ways to reach agreement or to resolve conflict. From family system theories comes the proposal that all families contain rules or principles about the right or the best ways to approach problems (cf. Walsh, 1981). Clark (1984) makes a similar point in her general analysis of relationships. Communal relationships, in her view, should be marked by the use of consensus to reach a decision rather than the use of authority only or a resort to a majority vote with little concern for the minority. Both suggestions point to a route by which one could differentiate among parents' ideas about what families should be like. Should family members, for instance, be expected to "make allowances" for each other, to avoid assuming the worst of motivations? Should they aim at some agreed-upon level of conflict or drama, or at least be aware of each other's sensitivity to confrontations or explosions? There is the beginning of attention to such questions in research on the use of drama in Greek-Australian and Anglo-Australian families by Rosenthal and Bornholt (work in progress).

Expectations about reciprocity. Ideas about reciprocity offer a promising way of exploring what people regard as proper for a family. That statement applies first of all to time-frames for reciprocity. From family system theory comes the proposal that families hold expectations about when any favour or help should be returned, any debt repaid. In some families, the ledger of benefits and debits may be expected to balance only across generations (Baszormeny-Nagy & Spark, 1973). Parents do well by their children, in this view, and children do well by their children, rather than making a return directly to their parents. The time-frame may be shorter than this but, at least in some models of family therapy, "short-term reciprocity is thought to be characteristic of distressed relationships, while long-term exchanges tend to characterize more functional relationships" (Walsh, 1981, p. 18).

Do families and family members vary in their time-frames for reciprocity? Australian mothers offer some anecdotal evidence of a long-term time frame, in the form of spontaneous references to children having done "their share of housework over the years". There is clearer evidence that it is not until the ninth grade that children begin making spontaneous references to being willing to take over a job for a sib on the grounds that "it will even out in the end" (Warton & Goodnow, in press). We have, however, a great deal yet to learn about parents' views on time-frames for reciprocity: where they set the limits, for instance, or what they regard as warranting a short-term, long-term, or "never" time-frame.

A further aspect of reciprocity is emphasised by Clark (1984) in her distinction between "exchange" and "communal" relationships. This aspect has to do with the content of reciprocity: with what counts as an appropriate return for a favour or a benefit. In Clark's (1984) view, one mark of communal relationships (defined mainly by responsiveness to the needs of others) consists of avoiding returns in direct kind (one bed-making or one dinner for another, for instance) and avoiding repayment in money.

For the avoidance of money, we do have some information that is specific to families. One piece of information has to do with the ambivalence parents often display about paying children to do work around the house (Goodnow & Delaney, 1988; Newson & Newton, 1976). Family members may be paid an allowance or pocket money, but this should not become the primary reason for making a contribution. In the words of one Australian mother, "I'm happy to pay them if they do the jobs, but I wouldn't pay them in order to get them to do it: that would be bribery." Further information comes from an historical analysis of debates, in U.S. journals for parents, about pocket money for children. The prevailing view, at least until the 1930s, was that the "world of commerce" and the "world of family" need to be kept distinct (Zelizer, 1985, p.107). This aspect of ideas about reciprocity is all the more interesting because of indications that children also absorb the distinction. Wittner (1980), for instance, reports that children in foster homes sometimes regarded their foster families as not "real" families, on the grounds that there was too much concern with being paid to look after a child and with how much expenditure a child actually involved.

In sum, there are some challenging and available ways to explore the content of parents' ideas about relationships and about families. To the information we already have on ideas about children or about parents as separate members of a unit, research along these lines would add a better understanding of parents' ideas about the way various family members are, or should be, related to one another.

CHAPTER 3

THE NATURE OF PARENTS' IDEAS: DESCRIPTIONS BY QUALITY

To repeat a comment at the start of Chapter 2, we have adopted a working distinction between attention to content (Chapter 2) and attention to quality. Quality refers to characteristics that could apply to ideas in a variety of content areas. The six we consider are: (1) accuracy; (2) differentiation; (3) agreement or shared meaning; (4) awareness and accessibility; (5) intensity or attachment; and (6) structure or connectedness. The six fall roughly into two groups, in the sense that the first three are often seen as having particular links to consequences for child development, while the second three are often regarded as having particular links to the possibilities of change in parents' ideas.

The chapter begins with a brief statement of why people come to consider the quality of ideas, rather than focus only on their content or in addition to their content. It then proceeds to outline research on the six chosen characteristics, noting for each the reasons for interest, the kinds of measures used, the kinds of results obtained and the questions that remain. The chapter ends, as did Chapter 2, with a major item for the research agenda. In this case, the item has to do with the connectedness of parents' ideas: the extent to which they form clusters or are marked by some central premises, core images, or superordinate concepts. As in Chapter 2 also, the aims throughout are twofold: to introduce a variety of ways in which quality has been explored and related to sources or consequences, and to bring out directions and

47

possibilities for further research. To repeat the advice given in Chapter 1, the knowledgeable reader may wish to read only the research agenda section or move directly to Chapter 4.

As we discuss the specific qualities, we shall pick up a number of particular reasons for research that concentrates on them. As advance advice, however, we shall point out that there are three general bases that cut across several qualities.

One of these has to do with using the *quality of parents' ideas as a marker for the direction of development*. An example is the property known as degree of elaboration or degree of differentiation: the extent, for instance, to which people see differences among children rather than seeing them as "all alike", or the extent to which they see themselves and the task of parenting in terms that allow some shades of grey rather than only stark black-and-white. In some theoretical positions, increasing differentiation attracts research interest as a sign of cognitive development among both children and adults.

A second general base has to do with *links between the qualities of ideas and the possibilities of change*. If, for instance, one wishes to change the ideas that neglectful, abusive, or unhappy parents hold about themselves or their children, then it becomes useful to know how far various ideas are open to change. Which ideas, for instance, does a parent hold most dearly and yield most reluctantly? For the same purposes, it becomes useful to know whether people are aware of the ideas they hold. It is, for instance, difficult to discuss an alternative to a parent's current view of the world if that view is not recognised by them as theirs, or cannot be put into discussable words. For the same purposes of predicting or inducing change, to take one last example, it becomes useful to know how ideas are connected to one another and which ideas are central. There is little value, for instance, in concentrating one's research efforts or intervention efforts on ideas that are so peripheral that change in them brings in its wake change in that idea only and in nothing else.

A third recurring base has to do with *links between the qualities of ideas and consequences for parents and for children*. One widespread position in psychology, for instance, takes the form of proposing that the optimal condition for development consists of a reasonably good match between the capacities or style of one person and the expectations of the other. A good match, for instance, is likely to promote a reasonable climate for learning, with parents presenting to children tasks that are neither too difficult nor too easy. From this point of view, one will clearly wish to explore such qualities as the accuracy of parents' ideas and their openness to change once a mismatch becomes apparent. We shall also be interested in the degree of "shared meaning", regarding its occurrence in the family as an influence on actions and as a way of defining successful parenting, and its occurrence in society as influencing the extent to which parents see some ideas as more "natural" or"factual" than others.

Should a researcher then ignore the content of ideas, or feel forced to choose between working on content or on quality? We propose attention to both features. For examples of benefit to both, we shall reach outside the developmental literature. One example comes from research on teachers by Fry (1984). Fry asked primary, secondary, and tertiary teachers not only for descriptions of an "ideal student" (attention to content), but also for lists of the characteristics they found most difficult to tolerate (an index of the degree of attachment to a particular preference). Both types of question brought out differences among teachers, with the question about intolerability eliciting the sharpest differences (secondary and tertiary teachers, for instance, showed large differences in tolerance for sexual misconduct, drug abuse, and disagreement). The second example comes from Argyle and Henderson (1985). They have analysed "the anatomy of relationships" by asking people to indicate the rules that apply (e.g. rules about being faithful, about not telling another person what was told in confidence, or about sticking up for someone criticised in their absence). The set of rules rated as important for a relationship defines the relationship: in effect, specifies its content. A further rating, however, explores the degree to which a single rule is a critical feature. If this rule were broken, Argyle and Henderson (1985) asked, would that mean the end of the relationship? What people do in practice, it turns out, depends not only on the content of the rules that they see as applying to a relationship but also on the status of any single rule within the set. In effect, the best research strategy will probably combine attention to content and to some particular qualities.

We turn to the six qualities chosen, noting for each how it has been defined or measured, and some proposals about conditions that influence the degree to which parents' ideas display this quality, and the consequences that may follow.

THE ACCURACY OF PARENTS' IDEAS

Can parents predict which problems a child will be able to solve? Are they correct in their assessments of what children understand or what they know about their parents? About the views their children hold on a variety of issues or about what their children are likely to do if a conflict or a difficulty arises at home or at school?

All such questions imply the presence of some standard that is taken to reflect the "true" state of affairs. The standard may need to be the child's own report. Only he or she may know, for instance, the extent of intimacy or the depth of involvement in a current friendship. Alternately, the standard may be some measure that stems from outside the family: a count of problems actually solved, or a school report, an intelligence test, a personality inventory, a teachers' rating, or the opinion of someone regarded as an expert in the area.

By and large, comparisons between a parent's report and a child's report are placed under the label of "inter-generation agreement", while issues of "accuracy" involve comparisons with some "expert" or "objective" standard. The distinction may clearly become arbitrary. We shall, however, follow it by concentrating in this section on the standards represented by expert opinion, deferring inter-generation agreement until Chapter 6. In both cases, the reader should note, questions occur about the sources and the consequences of differences between judges.

Influences on Accuracy

We have already noted in Chapter 2 that parents, like people in general, may lean towards ideas that serve a task-sustaining or ego-protecting function. The same type of function should be expected to occur for issues of accuracy. One should expect to find that parents maintain some degree of "illusory glow" (Lewinsohn, Larson, & Munoz, 1982) about their own performance as a parent and the ability or personality of their children.

What else might be added? From parental research comes evidence that the judgments by parents and by experts may come to diverge because of differences in the bases of judgment: more specifically, in the cues, categories, or images used to form a judgment.

Mugny and Carugati (1985) provide a first example. What counts as intelligence and, by implication, what will be used as the basis for judgments, may be social or "cybernetic" intelligence. Definition in terms of "social" intelligence is indicated by agreement with statements such as "intelligence is the capacity to adapt to the society in which one lives", or "to be intelligent is to know how to benefit from the opportune moment". Definition in terms of "cybernetic" intelligence is indicated by agreement with statements such as "logic and mathematics are the prototype of intelligence", or "the measure of intelligence is the capacity to think abstractly". The greater the experience with children and schools, the higher the agreement with the "cybernetic" view. According to Mugny and Carugati (1985), parents took this view significantly more often than did non-parents (p.207), and teachers took it significantly more often that did student-teachers (p.215). Mugny and Carugati

(1985) see the difference as a sign of socialisation into a world where school-based results or psychometric tests set the standards for all judgments about intelligence.

A contrasting position sees divergence from an expert position as based upon the nature of thinking. The effects may stem, for instance, from the well-documented human tendency to use short-cuts or heuristics. In research on parents, this kind of tendency appears in two interesting forms. One has to do with the influence of gender schemas on judgments. Regardless of actual achievement or effort, for instance, parents may rate mathematics as more natural to boys and as requiring less effort from them (Parsons, Adler, & Kaczala, 1982). The other short-cut takes the form of relying upon some particular images related to age. When parents and teachers are asked to estimate the ages at which children could succeed on a number of items on intelligence tests, the assessments (and the direction of errors in estimation) display a developmental pattern, accounted for by some changing general images or "stereotypes" of children. People underestimate what 2-year-olds can do (they see them as "babies" and are then surprised by competence), while they overestimate what 6-year-olds can do (children are now "growing up" and observers are surprised by the signs of incompetence) (De Grada & Ponzo, 1971; D'Alessio, 1977, 1990). The results and the general concept of stereotyped images now challenge us to ask whether there are similar core images that underlie judgments about children of other ages (adolescents, for instance) and about the competence of parents. Small signs of competence among fathers, for instance, may lead to inflated judgments of their skills with children, while small signs of incompetence in mothers—the parents expected to operate well on the basis of instinct—may have a disproportionate effect upon the judgments made by others or by themselves.

Given these several conditions leading towards parents diverging from expert views, does agreement ever occur? It can, in fact, occur even when the test-makers and the parents do not come from the same social or cultural group. When African or Guatemalan parents, for instance, are asked to nominate which child they would select to deliver a complicated message or how well various children might do on a novel task, their predictions match quite well with the kind of rank order that emerges from Western psychometric measures of verbal and social competence (Nerlove et al., 1974; Serpell, 1974).

The Effects of Accuracy or Error

We need to distinguish two lines of effect: one from lack of agreement, the other from the wish for accuracy in the face of uncertain information.

The Effects of a Lack of Agreement.   Does it really matter if parents misjudge their children's competence, knowledge, or personality? The effects turn out to depend upon the direction of error and upon parents' response to discrepancy (assuming, that is, that they become aware of its existence).

The direction of error is a factor we have noted before (Chapter 2): pleasant surprises after underestimating a child are preferred to disappointments (Belsky et al., 1989). The response to discrepancy is more complex, as illustrated by results reported by Entwisle and Hayduk (1981). The evidence of discrepancy in their study comes from school report cards in the first three years of school, set against the estimates of grades that parents had made before the report cards came in. Some parents scaled down their expectations, others maintained their high expectations by virtually ignoring the report cards, and still others changed not their view of their own child so much as their sense of the norm or the reference group (e.g. by the inference that their child had encountered an unusually bright class).

The results fit some general data in the study of cognition: namely the occurrence of several ways of responding to dis- crepancy—accommodation to the evidence, flat resistance to change, and resisting by way of sub-typing or creating exceptions (e.g. Rothbart, 1981). The addition lies in Entwisle and Hayduk's (1981) evidence that middle income parents (who presumably are following the situation more closely) change their expectations or propose an exception more than low income parents do. These parents are also the more likely to understand the implications of school reports and of results from aptitude or intelligence tests, although even middle-class parents may have only an incomplete understanding of what test results may imply for decisions about their children (Evans et al., 1989).

The Effects of Difficulty in Achieving Accuracy.   Asking about the effects of being inaccurate assumes that parents are able to make an assessment and to locate some standard against which they can set their own judgment. Still relatively unexplored are the ways in which parents cope when such conditions do not apply. When a child is developmentally delayed, for instance, where do parents turn for a comparison? How do they make a judgment as to the length of time a task may take, the level a child may reach, or the degree to which parental effort may make a difference?

Many of the sources to which parents turn (books, discussions with other parents) may now be far from useful. The result may be both an increase in error and in lack of confidence (Miller, 1988). It may also be an increased reliance on expert opinion: a result suggested by Frankel and Roer-Bornstein's (1982) study of immigrant mothers in Israel. Although the children in this sample are not delayed, their mothers do not have the usual access to grandmothers and folk wisdom, and the traditional views may be looked upon with scorn by the establishment health service. These mothers are then particularly likely to hold inaccurate and uncertain ideas about the sources of health problems and to turn to hospitals, clinics, and other modern experts for even the minor health problems that their children develop.

DEGREE OF DIFFERENTIATION

We noted in Chapter 2 one version of an undifferentiated view of infants: namely, that they are "all alike" rather than displaying marked individual differences. To that version we shall now add another based on an extension of Piagetian theory from child development to the development of adults. The material comes from Sameroff and Feil (1985), from Newberger (1980), and from Shulz (1989). They bring to the study of parents' ideas an interest in a particular quality of cognitive structure: namely, the extent to which parents focus on one factor (e.g. "It's all in the genes" or "I've been a terrible father") as against achieving a more differentiated, multidimensional view (e.g. "it was a difficult birth, she was not an easy baby, I didn't know what to do, and I wasn't getting much help").

Influences on Differentiation

From Piagetian theory, Sameroff and Feil (1985) adopt the expectation that the main source of change in parents' ideas will be encounters with viewpoints that differ from one's own. These encounters, it is argued, account for why parents in societies that are relatively traditional and contain less diversity of opinion (Mexico and England are their examples) are more likely to display one-dimensional views than are parents in countries, such as the U.S.A., which are more diverse and give more approval to the discovery of new ways.

A similar view—in the sense that differentiation is regarded as a higher level of development—may be found in Klein's (1965) integration of a large number of studies of child-rearing practices in England. Klein uses the term "cognitive poverty" (p.87) to cover thinking that is marked by little speculation as to why children or events should be the way they are ("life is just like that"), little reflection over one's own ideas, and little differentiation among ideas (children are "all alike", as are men or women, while people outside one's own social group—authorities especially—are grouped as "them"). Klein attributes these qualities of thought to a lack of control over one's circumstances and to a pattern of socialisation that emphasises a distrust of introspection, reflectiveness and "words", and a preference for action. The same pattern, in Klein's (1965, p.162) view, accounts also for results indicating that "working-class men show a greater cognitive poverty and unimaginativenss than the women". In agreement with Sameroff and Feil (1985), Klein sees experience with the views of others, often occurring in the course of moving to a new area, as potentially leading to more differentiated ideas. Klein (1965) also proposes, however, that some parents may react to such encounters by clinging more steadfastly than ever to their old beliefs and by restricting their circle so that few encounters occur that might demand reflection or change.

Are there other ways of viewing the bases of differentiation? As a start, one might be alert for the presence of value judgments: "Cognitive poverty" is itself a loaded term. In addition, one might turn to an interesting alternative present in social psychology and extendable to work on parents' ideas. The relevant research deals with a phenomenon labelled the "outgroup homogeneity effect" (e.g. Linville & Jones, 1980): the hypothesis that the degree of differentiation in ideas about oneself and others is a function, not of the level of mind, but of the relationship. The members of my own group, for instance, are seen as possessing a variety of characteristics and as holding a variety of views, all subtly different despite a common core. The viewpoints of people outside one's own group, however, are likely to be seen as fairly homogeneous ("they all act that way, they all believe that . . ."). Moreover, the degree of perceived homogeneity is considered to reflect the degree of social distance. (The closer you perceive a social group to be in relation to your own, the more you are inclined to take a view of them that allows for individual differences.)

Extended to parents' ideas, the concept of "outgroup homogeneity" could provide one way to understand and explore the perception of children as "all alike" vs. "all individuals". To the extent that children are seen as quite different from adults, and adults are seen as individuals, then children should be perceived as "pretty much like one another". Parents might also see other people's children as more alike than they do their own. They are certainly known to use more complex bases when judging their own children than when judging other people's. Faced with children of equal activity level, for instance, they respond to the unfamiliar child in terms of immediate cues but to their own child in terms of his or her typical level of activity (Halvorson & Waldrup, 1970). Finally, the differentiation of parents' ideas might be expected to show some particular patterns of change over time. After considering infants as "all alike", for example, parents might perceive individual differences as beginning to emerge at the same time as adult-like qualities. In effect, some testable predictions might be made that do not require the assumption that degrees of differentiation reflect higher vs. lower levels of thought.

Effects from Varying Degrees of Differentiation

We shall single out two effects that suggest interesting research possibilities. One has to do with an effect on communication patterns, the other with an impact on parents' feelings about themselves or their children.

The issue of communication patterns is raised most explicity by Klein (1965). Her general argument is that when differentiated terms are lacking, "discussion of family problems is fraught with danger . . . and a fear of 'argument' " (p.173). Within the family, the heavy reliance on clichés will mean that the nature of a problem or a decision will seldom be adequately described, and that the means by which people seek to get what they want from others will be limited, relying heavily on an authoritarian stance or on devious manoeuvres. With people outside the family, perhaps with middle class interviewers especially, the result can again be little exchange. Drawing from research by Bott (1957), Klein (1965, p.173) notes that asking about ideals or obligations for husbands, wives, or children often yielded very little: "the usual reaction was either a prolonged uncomfortable silence or an immediate reply to the effect that there was so much variation that one could not generalize" . The basic difficulty is likely to lie not in total "cognitive poverty", but in the content areas for which each social group considers it important to develop differentiated ideas or a wide range of terms. The results are nonetheless a reminder that a verbal exchange of viewpoints is not likely to be full or sparkling if one or both parties sees the issue in black and white terms.

An impact on feelings is suggested by two lines of research. One provides data to the effect that the "complexity" with which mothers think about the decision to have a first child is correlated with the degree of dissatisfaction felt during the first year of child-rearing: a correlation not found among fathers (Shulz, 1989). Still to be determined is the degree to which complexity and dissatisfaction are correlated with education and degree of responsibility for care of the child.

The other line of research is represented in studies by Snyder and Fromkin (1979) that may well be extended to the understanding of parents. To be told that one is similar to others is not always palatable. It can, in fact, lead to a drop in self-esteem, a lowered opinion of those who have failed to perceive one's uniqueness, and moves to conform less and so reduce the appearance of similarity. We would now be tempted to ask when parents are pleased to see that their child is like others and when not. Pleasure from perceived similarity, we suspect, comes from concern with unwanted behaviour and the realisation that the tantrums, moodiness, or messiness of one's child are not the sign of some deviant disposition or some failure in upbringing. "Ah, I now see that they all do that." In contrast, pride in uniqueness and the perception of differences among children should occur more often with judgments about pleasing behaviours or desired achievements.

THE EXTENT OF SHARED MEANING

The extent to which an idea is shared with others is a feature that first surfaced in the preceding chapter when we considered the proposal that parents' ideas often reflect "social representations" rather than opinions carefully constructed on the basis of individual experience. We may now take a broader look at sharing as a property of ideas, asking—as with the earlier properties—both about ways of defining the term and at the expected consequences when ideas are marked by various degrees of sharing. The treatment will be brief as the issue appears again in the chapter given specifically to the sources of parents' ideas (Chapter 4) and, in the form of agreement between parents and children, in Chapter 6.

We start by noting some definitions of shared meaning. Sharing may refer to the degree of agreement between two parents, between parents and children, between members of a social group, between parent and teacher or physician, between the ideas of an individual and ideas that represent the mainstream or the dominant culture. The concern in all cases is the degree to which two or more parties share the same meanings, the same definitions of a situation. As a rule, the reference is to actual sharing rather than to perceived sharing (that is, to whether two people do hold the same views rather than whether one or both misguidedly assumes that this is the case).

Closer definitions are possible when shared meaning is assigned a particular term: namely, intersubjectivity. Intersubjectivity is of interest both to psychologists and to cognitive anthropologists. Among the former, it is often seen as the essential basis for face-to-face communication between parent and young child (e.g. Kaye, 1982). Among the latter, the presence of shared meaning is the main criterion for designating a viewpoint as a "cultural model" (e.g. Quinn & Holland, 1987). As a definition, we shall take a statement from a cognitive anthropologist (D'Andrade, 1987, p.113), in part for the sake of novelty and in part because it contains a proposal about consequences for communication: "A schema is intersubjectively shared when everybody in the group knows the schema, and everybody knows that everyone else knows the schema, and everyone knows that everyone knows that everyone knows." Under these conditions, a minimal sign conveys the message. When these conditions apply to money under teapots, for instance, "then anyone's glance toward the teapot is understood by all, including the one giving the glance, as a potential reference to the money" (p.113). In effect, "a great deal of information need not be made explicit" (p.113).

Effects from the Extent of Shared Meaning

There is little material available on the sources that give rise to varying degrees of shared meaning for parental ideas. We shall accordingly concentrate on effects, where there are some specific proposals.

The lines just quoted from D'Andrade (1987) proposes a first effect: namely, the absence of a need to spell things out. D'Andrade makes the same point even more explicit in the course of analysing the way two people knowledgeable about the game of baseball discuss a particular play. To people who know the rules of the game, it will be obvious that a particular pitch is a "ball" ("one would have to be blind to miss it"), and the narrator "can reasonably assume that what obviously must happen . . . does not need to be stated" (p.113).

A further consequence has to do with the likelihood of considering alternate views: "One result of intersubjective sharing is that interpretations . . . are treated as if they were obvious facts of the world" (D'Andrade, 1987, p.113). A similar point is made by psychologists who have explored the nature of discussion in groups that vary in their emphasis on consensus or challenge (e.g. Berkowitz, 1985; Leadbeater, 1988). In groups where "empathic or affirming . . . non-competitive transacts predominate, points of conflict and logical inconsistencies may go unexplored" (Leadbeater, 1988, p.313). The way is now open to use such insights as bases for analysing the influence of shared meaning, and of the value placed on consensus, upon dialogue and communication between adults and children.

One beginning in such research takes the form of asking whether shared meanings between some members of a family may have consequences for others. Where a mother and father share the same definitions of a situation, for instance, children seem more likely to become at least aware of parents' views, even if they then reject them (Cashmore & Goodnow, 1985). More broadly, shared meanings are likely to affect the sense of being a unit, and the sense of satisfaction with a relationship. For these outcomes, however, the critical factor may be less the degree of shared meaning than the feeling that others will respect a difference in viewpoint. As Smetana (1988) notes, parents and adolescents may disagree as to who should have the final authority on an issue, but there will be less sense of conflict if the two generations at least reason in the same way and approve of each other's reasoning style, even if they come to different conclusions.

DEGREES OF AWARENESS AND ACCESSIBILITY

Some ideas come more readily to mind than do others. In the language of cognitive social psychologists, they are more "accessible" than others, and the degree of accessibility can be measured by the likelihood that, with little or no priming, people will notice some events rather than others and interpret events in some ways rather than others (e.g. Higgins & King, 1981).

Some ideas are also more readily expressed in words than are others: a feature that makes them both more retrievable in discourse and more amenable to reflection. The degree of reflection given, however, may still vary considerably from one idea to another. This is the feature noted by the sociologist Schütz (1953), writing about the way some ideas are marked by "reflexivity" while others are not, and about the extent to which one's sense of being comfortable in a culture depended upon having the non-reflexive "recipe knowledge" of the culture (the kind possessed by cooks who no longer need to rely on books). Psychologists make something of the same distinction when they speak of some ideas or responses to a situation as being "automatic" while others are more intentional, more controlled, more fully processed or subject to deliberation (e.g. Bargh, 1982; Higgins & King, 1981).

Cognitive anthropologists sound a similar theme. Shweder (1982), for instance, distinguishes among cultural rules or messages in terms of the extent to which they are expressed in stated rules or are, with little explicit statement of the rule, embedded in practices that contain the rule. To manufacture an example, parents may say explicitly that "You should clean your teeth at night, not tell lies, pay attention when I speak to you", etc. They are, however, less likely to state explicitly that time is a valuable commodity. Instead, the importance of time is conveyed by anxiety about "being late", "not having enough time", "running out of time", by frequent questions about "what time it is", and by the use of time as a justification for actions ("We don't have time now"; "it's too late for lunch"). Even when words are used, the ease and nature of retrieval may vary. According to Quinn and Holland (1987, p.8):

It is no doubt true that some knowledge is more habitually, hence more readily, put into words than other knowledge; that some . . . is tidily "packaged" in memory, hence easily retrieved for the telling; and that some knowledge is under conscious and voluntary control whereas other pieces are less available for introspection and articulation.... At another extreme, some linguistic outputs, but by no means most, have the "canned" quality of well-worked and well-rehearsed rationalizations or idealizations.

Influences on Awareness

What gives rise to varying degrees of reflexivity or awareness? Again there is little material that comes directly from research with parents. From some anthropological material, however, we shall draw some proposals that could well be extended. The proposals fall basically into two sets: those emphasising the nature of the idea, and those emphasising the demands experienced, either for careful statement or for disguise.

The Nature of the Idea.   From the anthropologist Caws (1974) comes the proposal—so far untested—that "operational" ideas are less likely to be put into words than are "representational" ideas. The former have to do with the way people should act, the latter with the way the world is. We note the proposal especially because of an overlap with the distinction psychologists draw between "global beliefs" and "praxis beliefs" (Sigel, 1985a) and between "declarative" and "procedural" knowledge (e.g. Rumelhart & Norman, 1981).

The Nature of Demands.   Demands for reflection and for explicit statement may arise either from the task of being interviewed or having to account for oneself (Quinn & Holland, 1987) or from being in the position of the transmitter rather than the recipient for a message, especially when shared meanings cannot be assumed. Demands for disguise seem to be less often commented upon, but strike us as more common in anthropology/sociology than in psychology. We shall take as an example Bourdieu's (1977) comments on the description of their society offered by the Kabyles in Algeria. In accounts of who marries whom, the verbalised principles have to do with kinship. The realities struck Bourdieu as having more to do with control over property (non-kin, for instance, might be adopted or declared as relatives if that move provided labour that was needed or enabled two adjoining properties to be merged). In Bourdieu's view, naked self-interest threatens the sense of a social group, and reality may come to be disguised both from others and from oneself. Parents who disguise the presence of disagreement and insist that "we all agree" (Elias & Ubriaco's, 1986, "agree" families) seem to display a similar pattern.

Effects

Does the degree of awareness or verbalisability matter, especially for parents or for family interactions? One type of consequence is for the receiver of any message. Without verbal statements from parents, for instance, children may need to rely more upon catching the emotional quality and the implications of parents' actions. The disadvantage to that situation is that there may be no explicit statement which can be reflected upon or argued against. The advantage perhaps is that the child's awareness of the parental message can be legitimately denied ("How was I to know that you felt that way?").

The consequences proposed for the original idea-holder (in our case, the parent) have more to do with the possibilities of change. One such proposal comes from Ford (1984), in a discussion of cognitive-behavioural therapy. In smooth everyday life, he considers, awareness of one's ideas may not be needed. When things cease to function well, however, a rise in the level of awareness may facilitate a change in the assumptions or definitions that are creating difficulty. A further proposal comes from Bugental (1989) in an interesting extension to abuse within families. One of the challenging phenomena within abusive families, she points out, is the high likelihood of parents repeating abusive actions for which they sought help and expressed regret. The explanation, she suggests, may lie in the extent to which the ideas that facilitate abusive actions are, in action, not subject to appraisal. While therapy may raise some of these ideas to the level of discussion, in practice the caregiver's actions may be guided essentially by "overlearned knowledge structures or . . . scripts" (Bugental, 1989, p.5). If that is the case, the challenge in intervention will be to implant the practice of some cognitive pause or some delay in action before the overlearned influences and scripts produce the same actions as in the past.

THE DEGREE OF INTENSITY OR ATTACHMENT TO AN IDEA

This fifth quality of ideas is covered by two terms: "intensity" and "attachment". The former term comes from Hoffman and Hoffman's (1973) description of the ideas parents hold about the value of children. The latter term is closer to Abelson's (1986) description of beliefs as "like possessions". Both descriptions arise in the course of comment on the ease with which people can be persuaded to give up one idea and adopt another, and on the resistance people often display to change even in the face of a greal deal of rational evidence.

The bases to attachment or intensity may be several. Those that strike us as especially extendable to the study of parents' ideas have to do with links to identity, either personal or cultural identity. Within Australia, for instance, the strongest demands that schools should foster the retention of a home language other than English come from Greek-Australian and Polish-Australian parents. In Smolicz and Secombe's (1977) analysis, these demands—and the resistance to becoming a monolingual English speaker or ending with an impoverished control of the home language—stem from the way that in both Greece and Poland the national language has long been a sign of identity, especially during long periods of occupation.

Identity that is more personal than cultural is the topic of Abelson's (1986) account of resistance to persuasion. Abelson points to the frequency of phrases that use possessions as a metaphor for beliefs. One "acquires" ideas, "borrows" opinions, "cherishes a belief", "holds onto a position", "abandons one's principles". As with "the accumulation of furniture", "one occasionally adds new beliefs to one's collection, if they do not glaringly clash with those one already has" (p.251). The old beliefs "are familar and comfortable" (p.251). "If anyone is critical of them, one feels attacked and responds defensively, as though one's appearance, taste, or judgment had been called into question" (p.251). These and other properties of beliefs, Abelson proposes, underlie the two main functions of a belief: its instrumental value (what a belief promises, either in fact or in fantasy) and its expressive value ("who the belief says you are: your groups, experiences, and feelings" [p.225]).

One last proposal from Abelson (1986) is that the degree of instrumental or expressive value that an individual attaches to an idea will be a function of several properties (attributes in his term). These attributes are the degree to which a belief is shared (especially with valued others), is unique (as long as uniqueness implies unusually good taste), is defensible (beliefs that others may readily call ridiculous have low value), is extreme (one is less attached to moderate beliefs such as "X is sort of O.K."), and is central (fits with other beliefs). To the extent that these attributes are present, it is argued, individuals will be likely to put effort into acquiring an idea and resist change once acquired. Resistance will be all the more likely when a belief is threatened, since threat gives rise to further increases in value (p.239). Few extensions to parental ideas are made by Abelson (1986) but the intuitive parallels are clear and the proposals provide a ready way of anchoring research on parents' ideas in an integrated body of research and concepts already available in social psychology.

CONNECTEDNESS OR STRUCTURE

It is extremely unlikely that all the ideas which parents hold lie about in separate pieces or are at odds with one another. On the contrary, the usual assumption is that some connections will exist, either in the form of ideas forming clusters (this set of ideas, for instance, represents a "child-centred view"), or hierarchies (the implication of terms such as "metarules" or "superordinate goals"). Nonetheless, there is surprisingly little data on the extent to which connectedness exists among parents' ideas or on the conditions that influence various degrees or forms of connectedness.

We say "surprising" for two reasons. One is that it seems intuitively reasonable to expect that a number of ideas should co-exist in parents' minds. It seems reasonable, for instance, that images of children as blank slates should co-exist with an emphasis on the importance of environmental conditions (and perhaps on parental responsibility). The other reason for surprise is the contrast between research on parents' ideas and studies of thinking by cognitive psychologists or cognitive anthropologists.

Cognitive psychologists are frequently concerned with "structure" in the sense of asking whether "information or knowledge units . . . [are] organized by having regular interrelations or interconnections among parts" (Higgins, van Cook, & Dorfman, 1988, p.178). Such connectedness is seen both as influencing the nature of information-processing and as necessary to account for phenomena such as generalisation or being reminded of one idea by another (e.g. Schank, 1982).

Cognitive anthropologists are concerned with connectedness in the sense that they "have long attempted to capture the distinctiveness of a culture . . . in concepts such as that of 'cultural themes', or 'cultural belief systems', or 'differing world views'" (Quinn & Holland, 1987, p.35). All of these are concepts implying some centrality to a variety of ideas. Quinn and Holland (1987) see the attempt to define culture in terms of an ordered set of concepts as not entirely successful. Nonetheless, the attempt is seen as essential, not only for the description of a culture but also for one possible explanation of how people come to learn a culture. If central premises exist, according to Quinn and Holland (1987, p. 35) "cultural understanding is organized into units smaller and simpler in construction and fewer in number than might have been supposed . . . . The prototypical scenarios unfolded in the simplified worlds of cultural models, the nestedness of these presupposed models within one another, and the applicability of contact of these models to multiple domains all go far to explain how individuals can learn culture and communicate it to others, or that many come to share the same understandings." One might disagree with this particular view of socialisation, regarding it as proceeding more in bottom-up than in such top-down fashion. The implications of core concepts for socialisation nonetheless remain important.

How far has this widespread concern with connectedness appeared within research on parents' ideas? We shall note in this section three studies of connections in the form of clusters or intercorrelations. Reserved for the research agenda is attention to order in the form of hierarchical patterns. The selection of the four studies is based on the investigator's reasons for asking about connections. All four, one should note, have more to do with influences on degrees of connectedness rather than with consequences. We shall, in fact, bypass the issue of consequences to this particular quality of ideas, noting only that the type commented on by Quinn and Holland (1957)—namely effects upon the next generation's learning—seem likely to be paramount.

Influences on Degree of Connectedness

The first study is by Luster, Rhoades, and Haas (1989) who have used connectedness as a check on hypotheses about links between ideas and actions. Kohn (1963), for instance, has put forward the hypothesis that goals such as self-direction or conformity will be related to differential disciplinary practices. Luster et al. (1989) ask if, even before we proceed to observing actions, we find that U.S. parents who favour particular goals also express approval of methods that are congruent with those goals. In their U.S. sample, they do. Mothers "who value self-direction ... endorse the idea that few restrictions should be placed on an infant's exploration of the home environment" (Luster et al., 1989, p.143). In contrast, mothers who value conformity "tend to believe that effective parents are strict disciplinarians who exercize considerable control over their infants' exploratory behavior" (p. 143).

The second study is by Palacios (1986; 1988), whose prime interest is in the *possibility that degrees of consistency or connectedness among ideas may reflect particular kinds of background*. We shall describe it in some detail partly because studies of clustering are rare in research on parents' ideas and partly because of the richness of this particular study.

Palacios (1986) starts by observing the lack of attention to structure or pattern within parents' ideas. The patterning of particular concern to him has to do with connections among ideas in eleven different areas dealing mainly with young children. Some of these areas have to do with parental goals (e.g. "What would you like your child to be like?"). Others have to do with the nature of the raw material and the child's early capacities or interests (e.g. "At what age do you think babies are able to .. ? "Why do you think babies put everything in their mouths?"). Some of the areas deal with the general nature-nurture balance (e.g. "Why do you think differences in intelligence exist among children?"), the effects of family (e.g. "Do you think that being an only child is a good or a bad thing?"), and the responsibilities of parents (e.g. "What do you think should be the role of the father during the first year of a child's life?"; "What positive things do you think a mother should do in order to benefit her child?"). The last set to be noted concerns ways of dealing with some specific issues and practices (e.g. "What would be your reaction if you saw your 4- or 5-year-old playing with his or her genitals?"; "What can parents do in order to stimulate their child's intelligence?").

These areas resulted in 108 questions being presented to 139 couples, mostly aged 25-30 years, and varying in residence, experience as parents, and educational level. All mothers had recently given birth to a first or second child (interviews with both parents were held in the hospital). A series of analyses then brought out the degree to which items were clustered and, of particular interest, grouped individuals in terms of their similarity to one another. We shall concentrate on the analysis that groups individuals. It yielded 7 groups of subjects, but the three of interest are the three that together account for 86% of the sample.

The first of these three groups (28% of the sample) consists of parents who are consistent in their traditionalism—in Palacios' words (1986, p.16):

people with little information about pregnancy, upbringing and education (for instance, 66% state that they have never read anything about these matters); they are not aware of the importance of the psychological aspects of pregnancy (for example 86% base their answers on physical care when asked about the things that a pregnant woman can do in order to benefit her child); they reveal innatist ideas (46% believe that the differences in linguistic competence between certain children and others are the consequence of hereditary factors); they see themselves as almost incapable of influencing the development of their child (30% believe that if a child is very timid, it is impossible for the parents to do anything to help him); they are in favour of education practices of a coercive kind (41% of the members of this class think that when a child plays with her/his genitals, she/he should be reprimanded or punished); they have stereotyped ideas with regard to the sexes (61% of this group desire their sons to be very masculine and their daughters to be very feminine); and their predisposition towards interaction with their child is very slight (72% consider that babies should be picked up as little as possible).

By and large, these parents are in rural areas and/or have the least number of years of schooling.

The second of the three groups (24% of the sample) consists of people who are consistent in a more modern orientation, holding essentially views that are the opposite of those held by the traditionals. By and large, the parents in this group are marked by tertiary education and are urban.

The third group (34% of the sample) is labelled by Palacios (1986, p.17) as "paradoxical":

> [they] reveal a high degree of search for knowledge (79% affirm having read literature concerning what children are like and how they should be brought up), although they have retained little of this information (49% recall nothing of what they have read or only recall its content very imprecisely); ... they have very optimistic expectations (50% believe that children begin to speak before they are nine months old), but it does not seem that ... their expectations lead to practices of interaction with their child ... (37% believe that things should begin to be explained to a child or the child should be reasoned with some time between 2 and 4 years of age).

What could account for such results? The villagers, Palacios argues, derive their consistency from adherence to traditions that over time have achieved some coherence. The well-educated urban parents derive their consistency from exposure to education that also has a degree of coherence to it (the views presented, for example, contain a predominantly child-centred orientation). The middle group has neither the completeness of an old view nor the exposure to an articulated alternative. They have accordingly picked up ideas in "piecemeal" fashion and have either not recognised the lack of congruence among the pieces or not acquired any concern with consistency.

A different approach to clustering and a different proposal for the source of connectedness come from Bacon and Ashmore (1986). Their main hypothesis is that the *degree of connectedness reflects the individual's roles or levels of responsibility*. They began by asking parents to provide descriptions of the social behaviours of 6- to 11-year-olds. They then reduced the material to 99 sentences that new groups of parents and siblings were asked to sort into groups "so that items within the same pile would be similar in terms of how the parent (or sibling) would think, feel, or respond if the behavior were observed in one's own child or sib" (Bacon & Ashmore, 1986, p.305). Descriptions were of boys or girls (e.g. "she picks fights" or "he picks fights"). Half of each group sorted sentences phrased for boys, the other half the same sentences describing girls.

Multidimensional scaling and hierarchical clustering analysis brought out a set of six categories used by mothers, fathers, brothers and sisters. These are labelled by Bacon and Ashmore (1986) as mature-immature, encourage-change, typical-atypical, normal vs. problem, good vs. bad, hostile vs. not hostile, sexually-oriented or not. A new set of informants was then asked to rate each descriptive statement for the degree of belongingness in these categories. Among the major findings from further clustering analyses are the following:

• For parents, the several categories are closely aligned. They form an "evaluative dimension" (p.309). At one extreme along this dimension are items such as "hits parents" or "torments a pet". Items such as "messes up the house while playing" or "puts toys away after playing" fall in the centre, while items such as "has good manners in public" or "likes to help around the house" anchor the "approved" end of behaviour.

• Mothers make stronger use of the evaluative dimension than fathers, rating more items at the extreme end of the scale than fathers.

• Parents "are much more unidimensional in the cognitive structuring of the behavior descriptions than are older siblings" (p. 236). For the latter, "cognitive organization cannot be reduced to a single continuum . . . Additional dimensions (or categorizations or schemata) are necessary" (p.336). The difference, like the difference between mothers and fathers, is attributed to differences in responsibility for young children (the siblings in this case are college age students). The test case, as Bacon and Ashmore point out, would be to determine whether a single dimension would also account adequately for categorisations by older siblings who are expected to be responsible, or whether fathers who have adopted more of the traditional "mother's role" also move to the degree of organisation around an evaluative theme displayed by mothers who have the major responsibility for child-rearing.

The differences among family members are not attributable to the gender *per se* of the person categorising. Mothers and fathers, for instance, differed but older-brother and older-sister (in this U.S. sample) did not. There were, however, interactions between the gender of the categoriser and the gender of the person being thought about. Fathers and older brothers, for instance, but not mothers, linked together behaviours that are hostile-aggressive (as distinct from simple fighting) and behaviours that might be indicative of being a "sissy": both behaviours were rated as problems (p.335). The results for fathers fit other studies in which fathers emerge as more concerned than are mothers with sex-inappropriate behaviour in a son. The effect from older brothers, however, suggests that the explanation for this effect lies less in fathers perceiving themselves as responsible for sex-role socialisation than in some general ways of thinking held by all males in a family.

The final approach to connectedness among parents' ideas comes from Main and her colleagues (Main, Kaplan, & Cassidy, 1985; Main, 1985). In brief, the proposal is that *the coherence of an account reflects the quality of the relationship*. More precisely, Main has proposed that the coherence displayed in descriptions of one's early caregivers is an indication of the degree of security experienced in the relationship with the caregiver. From interview descriptions of past and current relationships, she has characterised adults who offer disjointed, inconsistent descriptions as either "detached" or "enmeshed-conflicted", while categorising as "autonomous" those who offer a more interconnected set of memories and reflections. Classification on the basis of parents' interview descriptions has turned out to be correlated with the quality of parents' attachment relationships to their own children, as assessed in the Strange Situation procedure (Main, 1985; Crowell & Feldman, 1988). A burgeoning line of research is now applying Main's ideas to adults' relationships both with children and with other adults (e.g. with a spouse or partner). We draw attention to it here because of the challenging possibility that the degree of connectedness in parents' ideas—at least in some domains—may reflect not their exposure to others' ideas (Palacios 1986; 1988) or the kinds of responsibility they now face (Bacon & Ashmore, 1986) but the emotional quality of a past or present relationship.

RESEARCH AGENDA: CONNECTEDNESS IN THE FORM OF HIERARCHICAL ORDER

How could one go further in exploring the nature, sources, and consequences of connections among the ideas parents hold? What particular aspects of parental action or family functioning might be illuminated by paying attention to this characteristic of parents' ideas rather than to others? We shall approach these two questions by considering some analyses of parents' ideas that have paid attention to connectedness in the form of hierarchical organisation: (1) within family rules; and (2) within reference standards. We shall then ask whether general studies of cognition might provide further leads.

Family Rules: A Hierarchy?

The material in this section comes from more clinical sources than many of those covered so far. It starts with the concept of "family rule", common to a number of the theories that fall under the rubric of "family systems theory". In Walsh's description (1981, p.10): "Relationship rules, both explicit and implicit, organize family interaction and function to maintain a stable system by prescribing and limiting members' behavior. They provide expectations about roles, actions, and consequences that guide family life . . . A family tends to interact in repetitious sequences, so that family operations are governed by a small set of patterned and predictable rules."

The "small set" may be patterned in hierarchical fashion. An article by Wertheim (1975) supplies an explicit example. Wertheim describes rules as being of different orders and gives examples of first order (ground rules), second order (meta-rules) and third order (meta-meta rules). "Ground rules cover specific behavioral prescriptions, such as 'In our family, we don't fight', or 'Nobody in this house worries too much about tidiness' " (p. 290), or "If family member A is out, his task is done by member B or C or D" (p. 294). "First-order rules are governed at the next level by meta-rules, or rules about the ground rules. Meta-rules embody formal, guiding principles of systemic regulation . . . (and) can be said to reflect . . . the moral code of the family system" (p.290). Examples are: "Family members should never fight with one another"; "If people are angry at one another, it's best to talk it through"; "If people can't get on, it's best to get advice from someone more experienced"; "Family welfare is the responsibility of all members". "Meta-rules may themselves be governed at the next highest level, that of meta-meta rules (third-order rules). For example, the . . . rule 'Only kinfolk have to be protected, there is no loyalty to strangers' would determine . . . meta-rules for dealing with people within and outside the family" (p. 290).

What advantage is there to describing such a hierarchy? The primary use Wertheim (1975, pp.294-295, italics in original) suggests is as a way of distinguishing among families. "*Adaptively deficient systems*", for instance, "would be likely to have few rules. These could be expected to be global in character, interconnected loosely or not al all. *Adaptively deviant family systems* could have rule networks showing disparity in the level of complexity . . . at different parts of the network, general instability of the . . . network . . . paradoxical rule linkages etc."

One could wish for more elaboration of the consequences of position in a hierarchy, as well as of the consequences to variations in the structure of the hierarchy. Do people, for instance, feel less comfortable with one another if they agree on the ground-rules but not the meta-rules? Or is the reverse the case? Do parents pay more attention to violations of ground-rules or meta-rules? How do people feel about family members who keep the ground-rule but break the meta-rule: who do "the right thing for the wrong reason"? Does reaction vary with the age or expected understanding of the violator? The possibilities are several, but the relevant data are not yet available.

Reference Standards: A Hierarchy?

The concept is most readily illustrated by Mancuso and Lehrer's (1986) analysis of a family scenario. A 7-year-old calls her 9-year-old sister "a jerk". The name calling is at odds with the mother's standards: at odds first with her standard that siblings should not call each other names, and also with some increasingly more generalised or superordinate standards. Siblings should be polite to one another; a home should be marked by an appropriate atmosphere; the sign of a good parent is to maintain a proper atmosphere and harmonious relationships. The successive standards are regarded as being at different levels: the levels of programme (sibs should be polite to one another), principle (home atmosphere), and system (be a good parent). This division, Mancuso and Lehrer (1986) note, is drawn largely from some information-processing approaches to general cognition (e.g. Carver & Scheier, 1981).

Mancuso and Lehrer (1986) use the notion of discrepancy from standards to account for parental actions. To reduce discrepancy, for instance, the mother reprimands the child: "Robin, we don't use that kind of language in this house". The mother's statement of the rules serves also "to forestall further discrepancy . . . by creating conditions that place the 'politeness' standard—the rule—into Robin's working memory" (Mancuso & Lehrer, 1986, p.73).

The reduction of discrepancy, however, may apply to departures from any standard. Are there particular advantages to specifying whether the violation is from a programme, principle, or system standard? Is there, for instance, more affect when a superordinate standard is violated?

For Mancuso and Lehrer (1986), the main advantage to using a hierarchical analysis lies in the way it provides a breakdown of reprimands and a basis for exploring the sources and consequences of various reprimands. Reprimands, for instance, are divided into those that are "tangential" and those that are "relevant". "Tangential reprimands provide comparatively little elaboration with respect to conceptions about the rule-related event (i.e. the basis for the rule, its history, and its function" (p.74). In contrast, "relevant reprimands reference the transgressor's constructions of the event" (e.g. "maybe you think that it doesn't matter or doesn't hurt"). "Tangential", unelaborated reprimands are thought more likely to occur in situations where emotion is present (Mancuso & Lehrer, 1986, p.75), and to be used by parents who are novices in the art of reprimanding. The latter suggestion is drawn from cognitive research on expertise: research demonstrating that experts in any area have a more ordered or more principled representation of a problem, allowing them to to deal with the underlying structure of a problem rather than its surface. In an extension to parents, Mancuso and Lehrer (1986, p.77) suggest that "inexpert reprimanders may fall back on the advice of behavior change experts" rather than attempting to understand the child's schemas, to elaborate them, and to bring them more closely into line with those of the reprimanding adult.

The ultimate value of distinguishing the level of a reprimand by reference to the structure of standards is seen as lying in the possible consequences for the child. The true goal of development, Mancuso and Lehrer (1986) propose, is the child's acquisition of an elaborated or "deep structure" understanding of reprimands. This understanding may be assisted by general cognitive development (p.77). It is also seen as likely to be assisted by a parent's elaboration of the rules. What may then be shared at the end of the mother-and-Robin scenario is not only a knowledge of the rule and its violation but also some of the "mother's implicative structure about the rule" (p.75).

Once again, the material presents interesting possibilities for research on the nature, sources, and consequences of connectedness among parents' ideas, but the data are largely still to come.

Some Further Possibilities

The two approaches outlined (a hierarchy of family rules, and a hierarchy of reference standards) are by no means the only possible ways of exploring connectedness. If one were to look for a hierarchical model in studies of cognition that could offer a further (and a well established) base for exploring parents' ideas, then one is at hand in research on scripts (e.g. Schank, 1982; Schank & Abelson, 1977). In this hierarchy, scripts form the basic unit. They cover the generalised knowledge of routine sequences such as bathing the baby, going to the pediatrician or to a restaurant. They also provide ways of meeting everyday objectives. Scripts are organised in terms of higher-order units labelled "goals" and goals in turn are linked together by superordinate units known as "themes". "Getting fed", for instance, is a goal, while "being married" or "luxury living" is a theme. The advantages of this conceptualisation lie in its existing elaboration, in the way the ideas involved are stated in terms of actions (one way of avoiding the difficulty of asking how people move from ideas to actions), in the availability of data about scripts for both adults and children, and in the compatibility already seen between these concepts from psychology and the concepts of "routines" and "folk knowledge" used for the analysis of cultural differences (Quinn &

Holland, 1987). In short, if one wished to use a particular characteristic of ideas as a basis for research on the sources or consequences of hierarchical structure in parents' ideas, then the hierarchical organisation of script-goal-theme is a highly promising route, especially if allied to the priming techniques that experimental social psychologists use to order categories or establish structure (e.g. Higgins & King, 1986).

Scripts and associated concepts are, of course, not the only possibilities. By and large, research on parents' ideas may draw from four traditions in the analysis of how knowledge (everyday or social knowledge especially) is organised.

In one, the language of description looks towards schemas in the form of propositions: "To err is human", "families live together", "marriage is enduring", "money should be passed on through the family line", "daughters are more useful than sons". In one example of this approach, Quinn (1987) has dissected, from statements made by a married couple, propositions describing "marriage as a continuing journey, a durable bond, unknown at the onset, difficult, effortful, risky". In a further example, Backett (1982) notes a set that she sees as central to the views held by her Scots sample of parents: "You have to try to understand children", "Being a parent is different for everyone", "You have to learn by yourselves", "Work has to be shared between the parents". In both cases, central themes or central propositions are seen as both organising a number of other ideas and as influencing the way negotiations proceed.

The second tradition for analysing the nature and the connectedness of ideas is in terms of the images they contain: in particular, the metaphors ("children as tender plants", "post-parenting" as "empty nest"), or prototypes ("a typical two-year old", a "classic case of sibling rivalry"). Image-schemas seem especially relevant to problems that can be visualised (e.g. Johnson-Laird & Stedman, 1978) and may be especially useful for analysing ideas about relationships (images, for example, of nested relationships, of eternal triangles, or of balance among relationshps).

A third tradition, related to the image-schema type of approach, considers the organisation of ideas by noting pervasive dichotomies: dichotomies, for instance, between expert and lay, thought and action, male and female (see Goodnow, 1985b). Rosaldo (1989) provides an especially interesting example, arguing that the basic dichotomy in ideas about social life is "public/private", with other dichotomies (male/female, instrumental/expressive, strong/weak, outdoors/indoors) then becoming aligned with the public/private distinction.

The fourth and last approach to superordinate ideas is exemplified by Engstrom (1988). This approach emphasises the location of ideas or rules that are in contradiction to one another, creating a set of "dilemmas" that can then be used to characterise the nature of any work situation and to help account for discomfort or dissatisfaction. In an analysis that could well be applied to parenting, Engstrom (1988) sees physicians as caught in a situation where two general principles apply: one the principle that they need to see a certain number of patients in a day, keeping relatively close to a structured timetable, and the other emphasising the need to care and to consider the patient as a person. The relative levels of importance for these principles then need to be worked out either within the individual or by way of some form of power struggle between the groups that favour one over the other.

In effect, there is no shortage of concepts and methods to which one might turn for further studies of the way in which parents' ideas are connected with one another: an essential step if one is to describe the nature, sources, or consequences of any structure. Researchers in the parental area are essentially in the comfortable position of being presented not only with the argument that a particular topic should be pursued, but also with a world in which some baseline research has been done and some borrowable concepts and methods are already available.

CHAPTER 4

THE SOURCES OF PARENTS' IDEAS

In the previous two chapters, we have made several references to the sources and the consequences that people have proposed for either the content or the quality of parents' ideas. We are now in a position to focus directly on the issues of sources and consequences.

The chapter begins with a brief review of research on the sources of parents' ideas. It then provides an outline of two theoretical frameworks that offer conceptual and empirical leads for further research, and ends by highlighting two particular research directions. One is the need for data collected over time so that occasions and directions of change may be more directly observed. The other is the need to study the ways in which the prevailing images of parents and families affect the degree of trust that individuals feel in their own and others' ideas.

The two theoretical frameworks have appeared in the course of Chapters 2 and 3, but have not been made explicit. One is a tradition familiar to psychologists. It assumes that the major source of parents' ideas will be the individual's direct experience with children or the task of parenting. That assumption leads readily to studies that compare parents with non-parents, mothers with fathers, or parents of one child with parents of two. In this tradition, the information parents encounter is usually treated as if it were singular in kind (parents encounter, for instance, *the* reality of children) and as generally neutral (it is seldom seen as biassed, disguised, or withheld). In addition, the individual is generally seen as operating in a "scientific" mode: observing, checking, solving problems, revising ideas, possibly looking up reference books or seeking advice on a specific problem, "reality testing" to use Stolz's (1967) phrase.

The second tradition is more familiar to anthropologists, sociologists, and psychologists with an interest in cultural differences. Direct experience is still considered to be a factor. So also are the prevailing cultural images of what children, parenting or family life are like or should be like. The studies that follow are likely to compare cultural groups, generation groups, or groups with varying degrees of exposure (e.g. by way of profession) to particular cultural views. By and large—to push the two traditions apart for the moment—the information that parents encounter is likely to be seen as plural rather than singular (there is, for instance, more than one image of children) and as often not neutral (it is instead regarded as often accompanied by a demand for learning or as slanted towards the vested interests of the presenter). People are also seen as acquiring knowledge by other than the "scientific" mode. We may, for instance, absorb relatively passively the "prepackaged" knowledge presented to us. We may alertly select what suits our vested interests and resist what does not. We may also learn less from observation and analysis than we do through activity: coming to understand the qualities of others, for instance, through joint action and shared emotional experience rather than through observing the interaction as if we were outside it.

These summary descriptions are somewhat exaggerated. They will nonetheless serve to get us started, and to give some advance notice of the issues that cut across research on the way parents' ideas are acquired or come to be modified.

A LITTLE HISTORY: RESEARCH ON THE SOURCES OF PARENTS' IDEAS

Among developmental psychologists, sources were first considered in terms of the impact of direct experience with children. In what may well have been a simple extension of theory dealing with children's cognitive development, parents' ideas were expected to be constructed on the basis of experience or readily modified by experience. The prime research approach then became one of comparing groups that varied in experience with children or with the task of parenting, asking which ideas varied and whether the critical experience might be, say, the first child with a second adding little, or whether each child added new information and led to new ideas or a modification of old ones.

This approach has produced a wide range of studies. Some of the material has been reviewed (see Goodnow, 1985a; Miller, 1988). We shall summarise only the reservations that have developed about direct personal experience as the major or only source of parents' ideas:

Does personal experience really have a powerful effect? Three results give rise to this query. The first is that differences between groups varying in experience with children have been found less often than expected. The problem may lie in the methods used. Holden (1988), for instance, has been able to establish clear differences between parents and non-parents and between paediatric and non-paediatric nurses (Holden & Klingner, in press) by moving away from the usual questions about parents' views and presenting people instead with a problem to be solved. You have, for instance, just heard an infant cry. What information would you ask for in order to determine the cause of the cry? What possibilities would you consider, and how many pieces of information would you need to check before feeling fairly certain of your interpretation? The material is presented using computer simulation, and this technique in itself may engage parents' attention and lead them away from the clichés or "canned" statements that come readily to people in all groups. Holden and Ritchie (1988) offer an alternative explanation, proposing that it is only in the context of problem solving or decision making that parents make use of what they have learned during parenting. On this basis, it is the demand for goal-oriented action, rather than for statements of opinion or knowledge, that allows the effects of experience to emerge.

The second observation prompting a query about the importance of direct personal experience has to do with the way parents may make judgments based on very little experience. Within 24 hours after an infant's birth, for example, mothers often feel that they can make judgments about the infant's temperament and ability (e.g. Meares, Penman, Milgrom-Friedman, & Baker, 1982).

The third has to do with the possibility of what we shall call "second-order source effects". A father's information about children, for instance, may come by way of the mother, or his observations may be reinterpreted by her (Backett, 1982; Cohen, 1981). Over time, the ideas of two parents may also converge, as each checks with the other and begins to moderate an earlier position, not because of any new exposure to child behaviours but because of exposure to a view that the individual respects or wishes to be in agreement with. This type of experiential effect makes intuitive sense, although the argument would be stronger if one could demonstrate the nature of second-order source effects, the content areas on which they are most likely to occur, and the circumstances most likely to produce them.

When experience has an effect, is the effect temporary? De Grada and Ponzo (1971) have shown that when people are dealing with children of a particular age, their ideas about the competence of children at that age may be fairly accurate. Once the children are beyond that age, however, both parents and teachers may fall back on estimates based on general images of children as "babies" or "starting to grow up", with an accompanying increase in error. The data are substantial and the point makes intuitive sense. When the children you are dealing with are 10 years old, who recalls accurately what a 2- or 5-year-old was like? Again, the earlier knowledge or viewpoints might be reactivated by immersion into a problem-solving situation, but in readily available form they seem not to have a long shelf life.

Is direct experience relevant only at some particular times? The question is well illustrated by an account of women during a first pregnancy. During the first months of pregnancy, women sought information and formed a set of ideas about pregnancy and about themselves as mothers-to-be. After this "window" of openness, however, less new information was sought and any encountered was interpreted in the light of ideas already formed. The process had apparently shifted from influence by external sources to one of "self-socialisation" (Deutsch et al., in press).

Are experiences with children the only critical forms of personal experience? As Clarke-Stewart (1978) especially notes, information comes from experience with media images. In addition, most parents are in paid work, and the form of that work should surely have an effect upon the ideas parents hold about parenting or family life. The existence of such an effect is actually less a source of debate then the process by which it occurs. Paid work may influence parents' ideas by highlighting the importance of particular qualities such as self-direction or conformity (e.g. Kohn, 1977). It may also provide a style of relating to people that is then carried over to family life: a possibility noted by Finch (1983) in reference to fathers who encounter family resistance when they bring, to interactions with wives or children, images and expectations from their work as policemen or managers.

A similar resistance of children to mothers who bring home from school a classroom-style of interaction is reported by Molinari and Emiliani (1987; 1990). They note that mothers who are teachers, compared with mothers who are office-workers or full-time homemakers, are more impressed by how much children manage to do without being taught and by the contribution of the child's original "character". In a world that emphasises the necessity of children being taught, self-initiated learning comes as a surprise. Both effects, it is argued, stem from the tension or dialectic that can exist between the identity as worker and the identity as mother, especially in societies that contain some ambivalence about mothers being in paid work outside the home. For teachers, this tension may lead to their taking an "objectified stance" towards their own children, especially when life with children is difficult. For women in offices or factories, the tension may take the form of regret for time that cannot be spent with children, prompting an increased concern with qualities such as a child's friendliness or sense of security.

A Californian study takes the issue of potential conflict between roles a little further. It asks about the extent to which parents' views of children are influenced by their commitment to both paid work and parenting, by the experience of "role strain", and by the extent to which they perceive their spouses as supportive (Greenberger & Goldberg, 1989). For *both* mothers and fathers, higher levels of role strain were associated with more negative perceptions of children. For both also, higher levels of perceived spousal support were associated with more positive perceptions. For mothers, but *not* fathers, a joint commitment to work and parenting was associated with more positive perceptions of children. For fathers, but *not* mothers, a joint commitment was associated with high maturity demands, while a low commitment to parenting was associated with role strain. Such results are complex. They demonstrate, however, that the dynamics or dialectics between paid work and family often apply to both parents and may have differential effects upon their views of children.

Why are there such marked historical changes in concepts of children? Historical variations in ideas about children are now well documented (e.g. Ariès, 1962; Pinchbeck & Hewitt, 1969). At the least, these variations suggest that parents' ideas are influenced by conditions other than parents' direct experience or some change in the actual nature of children. It is difficult, for instance, to see either of these factors as accounting for the way images of children seesaw between images of them as angels in need of nurturance and freedom, and as creatures of strong will who need guidance: a seesaw observed in Japanese as well as European thought (Kojima, 1986).

An alternative is the argument that many of the ideas we hold are "social constructions" (Gergen, 1985), with one basis for these being the extent to which particular concepts meet the needs of the paid labour force. If economic or cultural conditions call for restrictions on the size of the paid work force, for instance, then images will be constructed —vulnerable children who need total care, incompetent older people who should retire—that justify the restriction (Gloger-Tippelt & Tippelt, 1986). In another example of such "cultural inventions", the shift of paid work from a home-base to factories and the restriction of women to unpaid work at home promotes an image of women and children as forming a unit and sharing a number of similar qualities (Kessen, 1979).

Distinguishing causes from effects can become difficult in such arguments. Worth particular note then, because of its base in historical records, is a report of the way in which changes in the prevailing ideas about the appropriateness of children working in factories or mines occurred, in one English region after another, *after* the need for children in these forms of work had declined (Rosenkrantz, 1978).

Why are differences within cultural groups often small whereas differences across groups are large? This question continues the move away from personal experience as the only source to consider, and suggests that it may in fact be a minor source. The Hess-Azuma programme (Hess et al., 1980) was among the first to present evidence of substantial differences across cultural groups. It was followed by studies that, within a single design, varied both cultural group and experience in parenting , and found that cultural differences were large while differences stemming from being an older parent or a parent of more than one child were small (e.g. Goodnow et al., 1984; Keller, Miranda, & Gauda, 1984). Parents' ideas began to appear less self-constructed than handed-down or ready-made (Goodnow et al., 1984). If so, then the concept of experience needs to include encounters with various images or ideologies of parenting and family life, either in the form of requested information or unsought advice, and research needs to be directed towards the nature of these encounters. What type of information, for instance, do parents seek? To whom do they turn? How do they react to advice?

Do parents really operate in such a "scientific" mode? For Stolz (1967), parenting was a time of "reality-testing" for a number of ideas. That type of description fits nicely with a general emphasis in psychology on the image of adult-as-scientist: noting contingencies and sequences, making inferences about what is possible or not.

The " scientist" image has been challenged in the general literature on cognition, particularly by studies noting the ease with which people use short-cuts and handy heuristics or the extent to which they are simply sloppy in their everyday thinking and problem solving. The same phenomenon applies to the study of parents' ideas, with the challenge coming especially from data showing the way in which thinking is influenced by inertia, responsibility, wishes, uncertainty, and mood. The material on mood we shall defer until the next chapter, when we consider links between ideas and feelings, but the other sources of departure from total rationality will be considered here.

Inertia.   Kohn (1977) has argued that some qualities (self-direction, conformity) may come to be seen as virtues in their own right, even if environmental conditions no longer call for them. A similar point is made more fully by LeVine (1988, p.15). Originally developed to cope with environmental risks, "the customary formulas for infant care become a cultural code that is both adaptive practice and arbitrary tradition—adaptive because it anticipates hazards and provides a practical formula for overcoming them, arbitrary because it is communicated to parents as being the natural, normal, and necessary pathway for parental action rather than a choice among several possibilities". When conditions change, a lag may then occur in the adjustment of goals to the change, and it is in this period that goals are seen as having a particularly independent or apparently sourceless status.

Responsibility.   Differences in experience are not always easy to distinguish from differences in responsibility. Parents and caregivers in full-day centres, for instance, regard young children as competent at earlier ages than do preschool teachers (e.g. Hess et al., 1984). This may be because the former have the opportunity to observe competence. It may also be because need leads people to remember any signs of competence, or to see competence in any ambiguous performance.

Wishes.   Responsibility or vested interest may increase one's skill as an accurate observer or inference-maker. The phenomenon that gives one pause, however, is the presence of data suggesting a move away from accuracy. Parents in several studies, for instance, have emerged as regarding characteristics they approve of as more stable over time than are characteristics they hope to see change (Becker and Hall, 1989; Goodnow et al., 1984; Gretarsson & Gelfand, 1988; Knight, 1986). Perhaps parents do in fact make efforts to change the less desirable. In this sense, their expectations may be accurate. The possibility also exists that parents are inclined towards ideas that help sustain hope and maintain effort with the task of parenting. Life would be extremely uncomfortable, for instance, if one were a single parent but clung to the conviction that children growing up without the sustained presence of two parents were headed for disaster.

Uncertainty.   The salience of some particular ideas about children and parenting may reflect the degree of uncertainty felt about what one can achieve. In LeVine's (1974; 1988) account, for instance, mothers in hazardous environments concentrate attention on goals that might not be achieved without their vigilance and effort. When infant mortality is high, for instance, they concentrate their attention upon the sheer survival of the infant. Kohn and Schooler (1982) make a similar point for the importance of values such as honesty, good health, avoiding drugs, a stable marriage. These values may be emphasised all the more when they are seen as desirable but not readily attained. A different hypothesis, however, comes from Richman et al. (1988), commenting on why a sample of Boston mothers emphasised goals such as independence, happiness, or generosity, and made few mentions of getting a good job, being well educated, or being self-supporting. The latter goals are by no means assured and they should be salient. The explanation offered (Richman et al., 1988, p.68 italics added) is that "parents in the United States stress general cultural values because they have so little control over the specific economic path their children will follow . . . . In *the face of this uncertainty*, mothers expressed the importance of their children acquiring other values that would contribute to their success—or at least to their happiness if their economic success were uncertain." It is as if we are dealing with some curvilinear relationship. Too much doubt, or no doubt, about an achievement being possible may reduce its salience, while some moderate degree of uncertainty may raise it.

APPROACHES: COGNITION, CULTURAL MODELS, SOCIAL REPRESENTATIONS

We have presented a capsule account of work on the sources or conditions that influence parents' ideas, noting as we proceeded some points where the parental research overlapped with or had been informed by material on the sources of ideas in general. We now wish to consider more explicitly some of the non-parental material, using it to assist in carving out and selecting some further directions and concepts for the parental research. We shall consider two approaches. One consists of turning to studies of general cognition. The other consists of turning to two overlapping literatures: one on "cultural models", the other on "social representations". These two literatures have considerable overlap but tend to exist side-by-side with little cross-reference. We shall describe them separately but recognise their similarity by drawing from both in a combined section on implications for research on parents' ideas.

For each framework, the same questions will be asked: (1) What kind of description is offered for the information or the ideas that people encounter? What properties are considered? (2) When information is encountered, what are the effects of the individual's existing knowledge or schemas? (3) Are there as well effects from the attitudes (ranging from trust to suspicion) that people take towards the new information, and its source, or towards their own ideas? (4) What routes to the acquisition or modification of ideas are considered? Are people regarded, for instance, as operating only in the "scientific" mode?

Approach 1: Research on General and Social Cognition

The Description of What is Encountered

In most experimental research on cognition, people are seen as encountering "information", with the assumption made that information represents data "out there", waiting to be discovered. The question then arises as to whether the material already contains features that assist understanding. It may, for instance, contain "affordances" (Gibson, 1966): in essence, qualities that make possible, facilitate or "afford" the ready perception of what is being encountered. It may be objectively segmented in time in the way that body movements are segmented into phases (Newtson, 1973). If one adopted such a view, then the next step is clearly to ask who is most skilled at picking up the features already present. That is, in fact, an approach which has been used in the analysis of parents' perceptions of children's actions, with parents and non-parents asked to observe videotapes of a young child's actions and to note the beginnings and ends of segments or episodes (Hayes et al., 1982; Vedeler, 1987).

What other features are considered? The most frequent references are to the quality of the signal that is provided. The information may, for instance, be described as clear, vague, weak in signal or highly redundant, with the implication that these features will alter the ease and the accuracy of picking up information. That implication has rarely been taken up in research on parents' ideas. It is present, however, in Sameroff and Feil's (1985) proposal that when experts offer only vague advice, it is less likely that parents will acquire sophisticated ideas. It is present also in data indicating that agreement between parents (one way of defining redundancy) increases the likelihoood that children will perceive the parental message accurately, even if they do not accept it (Cashmore & Goodnow, 1985).

The Effect of Existing Knowledge or Ideas

Existing ideas are generally regarded as altering both perception and memory. They alter, for instance, the likelihood of a phenomenon being noticed at all. They alter as well the salience of various pieces of information in the outside world, the way these are interpreted, and the ease with which they are remembered.

Particularly relevant to research on parents' ideas are the extent to which existing ideas predispose one towards self-confirming information, and the phenomenon of lag. One of the oddities of the parenting experience is that disconfirming information may not be abundant. As Sameroff and Feil (1985) point out, when a child is doing well, the child's state may confirm many a hypothesis, from the value of swaddling to the virtues of chicken soup. The likelihood of self-fulfilling perceptions seems in fact so high that some psychologists have wondered how ideas ever change (e.g. Miller and Turnbull, 1986). One general hypothesis is that disconfirming instances are most likely to be encountered in the course of close and sustained social interaction (Ruble et al., 1988). A more specific set of conditions concentrates on the nature of the trait being considered (Jones et al.,1984). Observers will, for instance, take more note of disconfirming information if they see the trait in question as one that is difficult to disguise or misrepresent (or the individual as relatively unable to do so). Expectancies about traits usually defined by typical behaviours (e.g. friendliness) and by external behaviours (e.g. nervousness) should also be easier to disconfirm than expectancies defined by extreme or infrequent behaviours (e.g. dishonesty) and by internal states (e.g. cunningness). Such proposals suggest that parents may more readily modify their ideas about some characteristics than others. They may also change their ideas about young children more readily than they do their ideas about older children or adults, on the grounds that the younger children are, the less their capacity to misrepresent.

Ideas That Lag Behind Changing Events.   If we tend to perceive and remember what fits with existing schemas, and if the target of thought is changing (as a child or a relationship does), then our ideas are likely to lag behind the actual existing state. Over time, it has been suggested, the individual may respond to the discrepancy by creating a new category (e.g. this is an exception or a temporary phase; the old rule still stands), by gradual revision, or by "catastrophic change" (e.g. "I used to think you would be reasonable, I now see that was an absurd expectation"). Rothbart (1981) gives an account of these three possibilities. We note them as especially relevant to parents' ideas because parents, once beyond the early days of parenting, are usually in the position of (1) holding a great deal of knowledge about the past (knowledge that has, in fact, often been effective in use) and (2) regularly finding, as a child changes, that some ideas are out of date. It is a pity that both in general psychology and in studies of parenting, studies of lag and of change over time are limited, perhaps because they do not fit well with the pressure for short-term studies. We have, in fact, starred the need for data over time in the research agenda at the end of the chapter.

What Attitudes Do People Take Towards Their Own or Others' Ideas?

Questions of attitude arise in the course of noting the extent to which people are bothered by or attentive to any lack of consistency in the ideas they hold. The general consensus in studies of experimental social cognition is that the concern is less than one might expect if people were operating in a truly scientific mode. The research questions that arise then have to do with the occasions when monitoring does take place. Who engages in "self-monitoring" (e.g. Snyder, 1974) for consistency? When does monitoring occur? How is it that we can often be so cavalier about inconsistency, even when it is pointed out to us?

The topic of attitude arises also with the observation that people do not always take a neutral view towards the information they encounter. They may discount it, regard it as less reliable than what they already know, or—if the information comes from another individual—give thought to whether the other person's interests are likely to give rise to disguised or misleading information (Jones et al., 1984). Extended to research on parents' ideas, this evaluative view of new information makes one wonder how far parents regard children as trustworthy and accurate sources of information: an issue of increasing importance in studies of child abuse (Newberger, personal communication). One is also led to wonder why there is little research on how parents view advice or comments from others about their children. A study by Keller et al. (1984) is a rare example of research on this question, and will be returned to in the research agenda at the end of the chapter.

Do People Really Operate in the Scientific Mode?

In a variety of ways, the experimental literature on social cognition points up departures from the adult-as-scientist model. People do not always give to information the weight it might be expected to have. They often come to rapid judgments on the basis of very little information. They may display quite sudden shifts in their ideas ("rapid conceptual alteration" in Gergen's [1982] phrase) even though the information base has not shown a radical shift. They are often slow to change their ideas even in the face of a great deal of information. They may set information aside because it is not palatable or does not fit their vested interests.

The literature on social cognition points also to there being more than one route by which people acquire ideas about other people. As in research on parents' ideas, the route traditionally emphasised is the scientific ideal of watching, observing, checking, revising, staying true to the evidence. Other routes are now beginning to be specified. One such route is through encounters with the ideas of others. The information that gives rise to change, for instance, may not be continued analysis and attention to the evidence, but the sharp reminder of a difference in opinion with another person. The "social conflict" emphasised by the new Genevans such as Doise and Mugny (1984) is an example of this type of position. The route to acquiring ideas about oneself and others may also be through shared experience with others: joint action, shared tasks, shared emotional experience (e.g. Shotter, 1985). The latter route seems especially appropriate to the experience of parenting and to parents' ideas, although there is little research to date on such a source.

Approach 2a: Research on Cultural Models

We have considered studies of social cognition in order to see what they offer to parental research in the way of data and concepts related to the acquisition or modification of ideas. We shall now do the same with studies of "cultural models". The people to be considered are mostly anthropologists or "cognitive anthropologists". They use a variety of terms: "folk models" (Holy & Stuchlik, 1981), "folk theories" (Reid & Valsiner, 1986), "ethnotheories" (Super & Harkness, 1986), "cultural messages" (Shweder, 1982), "cultural models" (Quinn & Holland, 1987; Holland & Valsiner, in press). We shall use the term "cultural model", and start with two overlapping definitions. One comes from D'Andrade (1987, p.112): "A cultural model is a cognitive schema that is intersubjectively shared by a social group." The other comes from Quinn and Holland (1987, p.4): "Cultural models are presupposed, taken-for-granted models of the world that are widely shared (though not to the exclusion of other alternative models) by the members of a society."

The Nature of the Information

Basically, scholars interested in cultural models emphasise three qualities to the information "out there". It is social information in the sense that it is shared with others and comes from others. It often comes with a demand for learning. And it is often not singular in form. In fact, the individual is likely to encounter a variety of views on the same topic, some contradictory to others. In a sense, one is likely to be told both " to look before you leap" and that "he who hesitates is lost" .

The Information is Essentially Social in Nature. For this point we shall draw comments from Quinn and Holland (1987) who provide a bridge to psychology through the attention they give to the account of scripts, goals, and themes provided by Schank and Abelson (1977) and by Schank (1982). Quinn and Holland (1987) see, in fact, similarities between the notion of "script" and the anthropological concept of "routine", and between the concept of "theme" and the concept of "cultural model". They object strongly, however, to psychologists' neglect of an important property of ideas (the extent to which they are shared with others). The objection arises with particular readiness because attention to the shared quality of knowledge is at the heart of cognitive anthropology, an orientation that has come "to stand for a new view of culture as shared knowledge—not a people's customs and artifacts and oral traditions, but what they must know in order to act as they do, make the things they make, and interpret their experience in the distinctive way they do" (Quinn & Holland, 1987, p.4). It is this sense of culture that is intended in the term "cultural models".

Quinn and Holland (1987 p.24) also object strongly to Schank and Abelson's assumptions about how ideas are acquired: "Schank is left with the awkward supposition that an individual's understanding of the world is accumulated through the painstaking generalization of knowledge from one first-hand experience to another. It is difficult to imagine how people could learn as much as they know, even by the time they reach adulthood, from personal experience alone." Psychologists may find the argument already made somewhat familiar by Shweder's (1982) argument for processes that go "beyond self-constructed knowledge".

Cultural Models Often Have a "Demand Quality": "Learn Me or Else".
This point is made with special clarity in D'Andrade's (1981) comments on psychological studies of cognition. What is missing, he notes, is the recognition that there is often social pressure to acquire particular items of knowledge. Learning these items is demanded as part of being a member of a culture. Not to know them is to be regarded as "immature", "ignorant", "stupid", "incompetent" or "unfit", either as a child or as a parent.

Ideas Are More Often Plural Than Singular in Form.   Psychologists are familiar with the notion that ideas may be distinguished in terms of their availability (their being present in mind or not) and their salience (their being close to the top of one's mind or not). Salience implies that we are unlikely to hold a single view or see a single aspect of events. The material on cultural models makes this point explicit. The plurality may refer to the way that cultural models often contain mixtures of "formal knowledge" (expert opinion) and "everyday knowledge". It may refer also to the presence of several viewpoints both within formal knowledge and within everyday knowledge. Formal knowledge may, for instance, contain theories that emphasise the environmental bases of ability and theories that emphasise biological bases. Informal knowledge may contain both the conviction that children should not be beaten, and that to spare the rod is to spoil the child. In one anthropologist's terms (Salzman, 1981), there are at any one time both "dominant" and "recessive" views.

Effects From the State of Existing Ideas

The main effect to be considered is in the form of the question: Does plurality matter? One consequence proposed is the feasibility of change. When people hold or have access to double theories, they may readily switch from one to the other (Kay, 1987). They may, in fact, treat them "as resources or tools, to be used when suitable and set aside when not" (Quinn & Holland, 1987, p.10). A plurality of views also facilitates a change in society. According to Salzman (1981, p. 239): "Change is less often a new society replacing the old, than it is elements of the society being shuffled into a different overall pattern with a different weighting of priorities." The essential condition for change in parents' ideas would then be seen not as a change in experience with children but a change in the social status accorded to a particular viewpoint. Changing views on the reasonableness of day care for children during the 1940s, when women were needed in the paid work force, would be one such example. Change in the value assigned to breast-feeding, and to the propriety of doing so in public, would be another.

Effects From Attitudes Towards One's Own or Others' Knowledge

From analyses of cultural models comes the proposal that it is important to consider the evaluative judgments made about the status of formal and informal knowledge. One impact of evaluation lies in the degree of interest taken in a topic such as parents' ideas of development. To Levi-Strauss, for instance, "native" models were essentially false knowledge and not appropriate topics for research: a viewpoint that may have delayed attention to them (Quinn & Holland, 1987).

One might expect also that evaluative positions would affect the view people take of their own ideas, especially when a "folk" opinion is met with "expert" scorn. A third possibility is suggested by Quinn and Holland (1987, p.13), who propose that evaluations involve perceptions of what is legitimate and what is inevitable: "among alternative versions of what is legitimate and inevitable, a given ideology is most compelling if its rightness engages the sense one has of one's own personal uprightness and worthiness, or if its inevitability engages the sense one has of one's own inherent needs and capacities." The distinction is applied primarily to the individual considering alternative social versions of reality, and would be interesting to apply to either individual or historical changes in concepts of children and parenting.

Modes of Thinking and Routes to Knowledge

If ideas are not acquired through the observations and inferences of a scientific mode, how are they acquired? To say that ideas are "received" or "handed down" is a partial answer only. What is needed is the next step of analysing how the handing down takes place.

From the material on cultural models comes first the strong argument that ideas are conveyed through language (e.g. D'Andrade, 1981). In Quinn and Holland's (1987, p.22) words, "cultural knowledge is typically acquired to the accompaniment of intermittent advice and occasional correction rather than explicit, detailed instruction; but it is learned from others, in large part from their talk". The mere naming of a person as "second cousin", for instance, brings out the fact that there is a category of people known as "cousins", and within that some subdivisions one should know about. Language and talk, however, may not be necessary. The Indian mother who withdraws from the family during menstruation, for instance, banishing herself from the preparation of food and contact with husband or children, conveys to others a powerful message of being "unclean" without using words (Shweder, Mahapatra, & Miller, 1987). The spatial segregation of children and adults—separate areas, separate activities—can convey with equal force that the interests of the two are quite different from one another. Overall, what may count most are the everyday routines: a view becoming familiar to psychologists in the form of attention to "activities" and "practices" as the basis of both academic and social knowledge (e.g. Rogoff & Lave, 1984).

More broadly, material on cultural models contains as well the argument that when people are dealing with everyday ideas the attitude towards consistency and revision may be different from that shown towards "scientific" knowledge. "There are two points here: the first is that a folk theory does not present a totally consistent whole the way a conscious, expert theory does. . . . The second point is that folk theories are not 'believed' in the way conscious theories are but are used or presupposed as the occasion of thought or communication demands" (Kay, 1987, p.76). In Quinn and Holland's (1987, p.10) examples, "individuals find it relatively easy to entertain different theories of how the thermostat works and to even abandon one theory for another; . . . to invoke conflicting proverbial advice for the solution of different problems and to adopt one or another contradictory folk theory of language depending on which one better fits the linguistic case at hand". The same perceived lack of relevance for "scientific" criteria may also mean, however, that revision is resisted. Our models of heating devices may readily flip from one metaphor to another, but, according to Quinn and Holland (1987, p.11), our models of "marital commitment, career choice, gender relations, and kinship obligations . . . are compelling in a way that does not depend on what the experts say and often seems highly resistant to revision in the face of apparent contradiction. . . . Alternative views are not even recognized, let alone considered". The challenge in parental research is then one of determining when parents' ideas are like theories of thermostats and when they are more like concepts of marital commitment.

Approach 2b: Research on Social Representations

The term "social representations" appears both in anthropology (e.g. Durkheim, 1895) and in social psychology (e.g. Farr & Moscovici, 1984; Moscovici, 1990). We shall draw from the material in social psychology, with particular attention given to work that has begun to use these general concepts for research on parents' ideas or for the analysis of socialisation. We shall also concentrate on points not already present in analyses of cultural models.

We begin with a definition from Moscovici and Hewtstone (1983, p.15). Social representations are "cognitive matrices coordinating ideas, words, images and perceptions that are all interlinked, they are commonsense theories about key aspects of the world". That definition, as Duveen and Lloyd (1990b) point out, is concerned with the content of mind. What is needed is a distinction between representations as content (systems of meanings, ideas, values, practices) and representation as a process (the process of constructing or transforming the content). For the latter, Duveen and Lloyd propose using the term representation in the singular and we shall follow that suggestion. The distinction is certainly needed.

The Nature of Information Encountered

Information is first of all seen as "social", with "social" referring to several aspects: to the way a set of ideas can come to identify a person or a group (e.g. these ideas mark you as " a true believer", or "one of the Hare Krishnas"), to the way shared ideas allow easy communication, to the importance of social life as the basis for ideas, and to the presence of differences from the logical structures presented by, say, physical or mathematical events.

The last of these meanings of "social" is the least obvious. For clarification, we shall take a contrast offered between the acquisition of academic and social knowledge. The child working on logical or mathematical problems may be regarded as encountering the "closed structures" of logical systems (Lloyd, 1987). There is a "right" and a "wrong" answer. Some implications are clearly possible and others are not. In the course of acquiring social knowledge, however, the child encounters "structured systems" of a different kind, with one essential difference being that there is "no privileged vantage point which offers an objective perspective from which to orient any investigation" (Duveen & Lloyd, 1990b, p.6). By and large, the argument runs, social representations cannot be regarded as having a propositional structure with a verifiable truth value and this difference in quality should be expected to alter the processes by which ideas are acquired.

The state of information is not singular. The main discussion of this point in the social representations literature has to do with the presence and the interplay of formal knowledge and common sense. Molinari and Emiliani (1987, p.2) provide one example, arguing that "in a modern society knowledge is derived from two sources, that is *direct experience* in everyday practice on one hand and *transformation of scientific information* on the other hand . . . . Ordinary people consume scientific knowledge and use it in their everyday communication and behavior" (italics in original). The combination of the two becomes "the contemporary version of common sense" (p.13). Their position, applied to the views of parents, is an endorsement of Moscovici and Hewstone's (1983, p.99) general view that "the disembarkation point for a common sense psychology" is optimally the investigation of connections between science and common sense. Moscovici's interest in the way psychoanalytic theory has become absorbed into everyday parlance (Moscovici, 1961) is an early illustration of using that disembarkation point. Chombart de Lauwe's (1984) analysis of the way formal theories about children are taken up in informal theory is a later example.

Effects from Existing Ideas

Where an analysis of cultural models emphasises the way that "recessive" ideas allow an easy change from one position to another, the analysis of social representations is more likely to highlight ways in which change becomes less likely to occur. One such way is by the process of anchoring: familiar categories guide the interpretation of anything unfamiliar and absorb it into an existing framework of ideas. Another is the process of objectification: the rendering into concrete examples, and into a sense of unchanging reality, of what was previously abstract and possibly diffuse. Both processes may contribute to the development of simplified images of events and of people: simplified images, for instance, of motherhood or of children (e.g. Chombart de Lauwe, 1984). The separation of these "typified" images from reality then gives rise both to unreal expectations, to a slow change of ideas in the face of contrary evidence and, Molinari and Emiliani (1990) suggest, to difficulties in accounting for individual differences and the development of distinctions between typical children and one's "own" child.

Attitudes Towards Ideas (Own and Others')

The position in social representation theory parallels that presented for cultural models, and argues again for our not expecting change in parents' ideas as the automatic result of presenting new information. In the words of Duveen and LLoyd (in press b, pp.3-4): "Because of their social psychological role, beliefs are not open to empirical validation, nor does their articulation respect the law of non-contradiction . . . . Beliefs may include inconsistent and actually contradictory elements . . . . We cannot assume . . . any primary motivation for logical consistency." In other words, the attitude taken towards one's own knowledge and towards consistency will be different from that which might be expected in a scientific mode, and parents may take the view that the issue is more a matter of faith or fashion than of evidence.

Routes to Acquisition

From the analysis of social representations come several hypotheses about the acquisition of social knowledge by routes other than scientific observation. One type of proposal is illustrated by Sarchielli's (1984) analysis of initiation into an occupational group. The individual does not simply move into a work group that provides a single message and shapes the individual towards a single goal or style. On the contrary, any work setting contains a number of social groups (from co-workers to managers). These may deliver messages that are not in agreement with one another, providing the individual with an opportunity to choose goals and to adopt a "questioning and critically active stance to the organization setting and . . . to the influencing pressures exerted within the working environment" (Sarchielli, 1984, p.263). In effect, the plurality of goals or of ways of working allows the process of acquiring ideas to be marked by some degree of choice and of resistance to ideas being pushed by others.

A second proposal emphasises the way that ideas about children are conveyed by routines, some of which involve the organisation of space. For this proposal, we shall draw from a study with a direct relevance to parenting. Emiliani, Zani, and Carugati (1981) compared two nurseries with marked differences in their daily routines: one essentially "institution-oriented" in its goals and rules, the other essentially "child-oriented". Videotaped interactions between staff and children were compared for the incidence of controlling behaviours, directive statements (commands), emphathic and affectionate behaviours, and the use of conversation to establish and maintain contact with children.

Segments from the tapes were also used as a basis for asking staff to express the goals they had in mind during these interactions. The expressed goals of the staffs differed considerably. "Respecting the routines of daily life" and "keeping the children in order", for instance, were frequently mentioned by the staff in one nursery but not by staff in the other (whose most frequent references were to providing security and developing closeness). These differences in goals, and in the views held about the needs of children, are seen as strongly influenced by the way in which the everyday routines reinforce one of the two views of children that are always present in a society.

Implications for Research on Parents' Ideas

Some implications have been noted in the course of describing the analysis of cultural models and of social representations. We draw together here some suggestions that arise from both analyses: suggestions for studying the content of parents' ideas and the processes involved in either acquisition or change.

The Content of Ideas.   One of the simplest implications has to do with the need to ask how far ideas are shared. To what extent do people from various occupational or experiential groups share the same ideas about children, parenting, or the nature of development? That type of question has been asked by Reid and Valsiner (1986), starting from an interest in cultural models and concentrating on parents' ideas about punishment. At least in the United States, what emerges is considerable consensus on such aspects as the importance of a public vs. private setting. Infractions (e.g. being rude to a parent) are more serious if they occur in public. Discipline is more suitably administered in private than in public. Questions about the extent to which ideas are shared have also been asked by Emiliani and Molinari (1990), starting from an interest in social representations and concentrating on the values and practices that mothers see as important in the rearing of young children. What emerged was a shared concern with order, cleanliness, toilet training, and the divisions of labour between mothers and fathers. Mothers either endorsed traditional views, or used these as a basis for expressing dissent without, however, being able to state a well-articulated alternative.

Content may also be explored by asking whether parents hold singular or plural views and whether their ideas parallel those of formal psychologists. Both implications have been taken up by Mugny and Carugati (1985) in their investigation of the concepts people hold of intelligence. Their study brings out the fact that people do not hold a single view of intelligence. Instead, they consider at least three kinds:

knowledge about things, abstract problem-solving ability, and social intelligence. Moreover, they endorse more than one view, even while giving temporary priority to one rather than another on the basis of their experience as parents or their professional socialisation as teachers.

The same study brings out as well the extent to which parents may disagree with propositions that are contained in today's formal accounts of cognitive development: propositions, for instance, about discovery, activity, the benefits of play and of encounters with discrepant opinions. As Carugati (in press) points out with particular clarity, research along these dimensions differs in two ways from the analysis of popular concepts of intelligence by Sternberg and his colleagues (Sternberg, Conway, Ketron, & Bernstein, 1981). One difference is in the emphasis on people being able to hold more than one view. The other lies in the way the design allows people to endorse opposing views. Both features, Carugati argues, need to be incorporated into any research on parents' ideas.

The Processes of Acquisition and Change. We shall use Carugati's (1990) critique to pursue another point of difference from standard approaches. Carugati's concern in this case is with the extent to which psychologists see social cognition as an understanding of some single objective reality or as a construction based on encounters with that one reality. What are the alternatives? And how would these alter the research one does?

One alternative sees the critical encounters as being with representations of the way the world is, and the critical cognitive processes as consisting of choosing among these, attempting to reconcile them, or transforming them so that they fit more comfortably with one's own experience. To use a transformation sentence we have often heard from mothers, "Oh, I know they say you should always explain to them and never spank them, but it doesn't work with my children." We could well use more thorough analyses of the ways in which parents demonstrate an awareness of formal theory but either evade its application or challenge its validity. Conscious evasion or challenge may, in fact, not even occur. In a provocative experimental study Triana and Rodrigo (1989) have divided parents into those taking a more environment-centred and those taking a more child-centred view of development. The two groups could be shown to be familiar with both views. Each read more easily, however, and made greater sense of, the material similar to the view preferred.

A further alternative consists of turning attention to alternate routes for the acquisition of ideas. We are, for instance, impressed by the extent to which ideas may be acquired through nonverbal routes. The organisation of space and of routines in baby clinics, preschools, and schools must all convey to parents a number of ideas about what children are supposed to need or what parents are supposed to be like. We would like to see an extension of such possibilities into the way people are inducted into the concepts of "mother" , "father", or "parent". Fathers, for instance, may well acquire a sense of lesser importance as parents as a result of practices varying from "ladies' lunches" during pregnancy to exclusion from the moment of birth and condescending demonstrations of how to hold a baby.

The third and last alternative has to do with the analysis of change. Parent's ideas may display both the "rapid conceptual alteration" that intrigues Gergen (1982) and the resistance to change that leads Abelson (1986) to propose that some ideas are like cherished possessions, abandoned only with reluctance. Suppose, for instance, that rapid change is made possible by people holding in mind two different ways of looking at the world. One should be able to test that type of possibility by taking an instance where marked change seems to occasion no disquiet. The people who believe before the first child arrives that child care will be shared, and then accept easily that it is not, should be people who have in mind before the birth both the view that "sharing is the right way" and the view that "mothers are best with infants". In related fashion, the people who do not shift readily, who are in fact dissatisfied with a lack of sharing—as a number were in the study by Ruble et al. (1988)—should be people who hold before birth a less plural view of how events should be and a stronger attachment to one particular position. In effect, it should be possible to translate the notion of plurality of views into an analysis of change not only at the historical or group level often emphasised by analysts of cultural models and social representations but also at the level of individual parents.

RESEARCH AGENDA: IDEAS OVER TIME, THE PLACE OF ADVICE

From a number of possible research directions, we select two. One has to do with the need for data gathered over time or with some regard for changes over time. The other has to do with conditions that influence the attitude taken toward one's own ideas and those of others, with particular attention to feelings of trust, confidence, or suspicion. To some degree, the first research area stems primarily from the emphasis on ideas as acquired from one's own direct experience, while the second stems more from the kind of approach represented by studies of cultural models or social representations. Both research problems, however, are relevant to both traditions and may be informed by both.

Ideas Over Time

Most studies of parents' ideas, like most research on adults' social cognition, involve one-time observations. That approach, however, does not fit well with two features of parenting. One is that parents have relatively complete knowledge of their children's past behaviour and consequently base many of their ideas on the history of their interactions with them. The second is that ideas about specific children are peculiarly subject to becoming wholly or partly obsolete. The third is that parents expect children, and their ideas about a child, to change simply by virtue of a child's age and perhaps even before change has been observed.

How might issues of data across time be approached? Three ways may be suggested:

Inserting material about the past into a vignette about the present. This suggestion is based on a study by Mancuso and Lehrer (1986). They asked adults to judge the effectiveness of various disciplinary actions, described as taken by parents on a specific occasion. The vignette contained as well a brief statement about the parent's usual approach, and this information swayed judgment more than did the one-time action. This type of design would appear to be hightly adaptable for other research purposes.

Variations in parents' ideas as a function of a child's age. One example comes from an analysis of longitudinal data by Roberts, Block, and Block (1984). During the period in which their children grew from age 3 to age 12, parents increasingly emphasised child-rearing values and goals related to achievement and independent behaviours. From a further longitudinal study, Poresky and Hendrix (1989) add the information that changes in goals and in methods are more pronounced over the 3-24 month span of a child's life than over the 36-60 month span.

Such variations suggest the value of adding information about age to any description of a child's behaviour: a procedure illustrated in the study by Dix et al. (1986) of adults' responses to hypothetical misbehaviours by children and adolescents. The older the child, the more likely parents were to infer that that child understood that certain behaviours are wrong, that the transgression was intentional, and that the behaviour indicated negative dispositions in the child. Furthermore, when parents inferred that the child was capable of self-control and that the misbehaviour was intentional, they were more upset with the child, and they thought punishment, rather than discussion and explanation, was a more appropriate response.

In an interesting variant of this type of design, presented by Zebrowitz-Macarthur and Kendall-Tackett (1989), photographs have been added to vignettes describing various transgressions, so that the children now vary not only in age (4 years vs. 11 years old) but also in the extent to which they are "baby-faced" or "mature-faced". The parents are parents of 10- to 12-year-olds, and the results show intriguing effects from both the gender of parent and child, and from the child's age. Mothers and fathers perceived less intentionality for misdeeds of baby-faced children of the opposite gender, regardless of whether the children were 4 or 11 years old. Gender was the critical variable rather than age. In contrast, age influenced the severity of punishment recommended. Parents recommended more severe punishments for mature-faced than for baby-faced 4-year-olds. The reverse was true for 11-year-olds, especially for acts of commission. The result may have something to do with the current age of the parents' own children (10 to 12 years). What is proposed, prompted largely by the importance of whether the action was one of omission as against commission, is that some actions are sharp violations of the expectation that baby-faced adolescents (and adults) will have "benign" dispositions. They may be forgiven for forgetting to act in approved fashion, but not for acting "out of character".

A third, more extended example comes from research examining the hypothesis that parents' ideas about their children function as expectancies about the way the children will behave under particular conditions. The term "expectancies", as used by Collins (in press, p.4) refers to "complex schemata of thought, action, and emotion that affect the perception and interpretation of other persons' behavior and that, therefore, guide actions and reactions in relationships". In a first phase of this research, the judgments have to do with children in general and the sample of interest has been adults who were not parents of adolescents (the age-group being judged). These adults were given a Behavioural Expectancies Inventory that listed 28 behaviours commonly thought to change between the ages of 11 and 16, and asked to indicate whether each item was "characteristic" or "not characteristic" of each of three age groups: 11- to 12-year-olds, 13- to 14-year-olds, and 15- to 16-year-olds. Each group of adults rated only one sex. Generally, expectancies for 11- to 12-year-olds and 15- to 16-year-olds were at the extremes and expectancies for 13- to 14-year-olds in the middle. In some categories, however, the older two groups were thought to be similar, but different from the youngest group. For example, behaviours having to do with communication and sensitivity, such as "is moody" and "responds in a surly way to parents' comments", were thought to be characteristic of the older two groups, but not of the younger. In a third type of pattern, a few items were expected for 15- to 16-year-olds but not the younger two groups. In short, there was considerable differentiation on the basis of age alone, divorced from any cues about individual physical or personal characteristics (Collins, in press).

Collins (in press) has also considered whether parents' perceptions of their own children were discrepant from their expectancies regarding "ideal" youngsters of the same age and gender. Discrepancies between perceived behaviour and idealised expectancies were greater for parents of 14-year-olds than for parents of 11- or 17-year-olds, suggesting that violations of expectancies occur more commonly during the rapid physical and social changes of early adolescence.

Suppose we assume that in periods of rapid developmental change, parents' expectancies are frequently violated. Why do such violations occur? Collins (in press) has proposed two reasons. One is that parents' ideas may have stabilised during periods of relatively slower developmental change, so that when pronounced changes occur (e.g. during puberty, or in the shift from elementary to junior-high school), discrepancies between actual and expected behaviour are especially noticeable. As an instance, children who have previously been compliant may begin to question parental demands, which parents may perceive as resistance or insolence. A second reason is that parents may prematurely form new expectancies, based on signs of incipient maturity in one area that are not matched by maturity in other aspects of a child's behavior. For example, more mature physical appearance may not be matched by an increased sense of responsibility for schoolwork or for work around the house.

Both processes provoke the question: How do changes in a child become apparent to mothers and fathers in the course of daily interactions? Some changes—physical changes, for instance—may be easy to detect. Others—changes in attitude, for instance—may be less so. For these, one interesting possibility is that the awareness of change may come partly at an emotional rather than a cognitive level (R. Collins, 1981). Parents may sense and respond emotionally to a change in a common routine (e.g. no longer going out to a Saturday movie with parents and siblings) or to a shift in attitudes toward the routine, before they recognise a more general need to be autonomous or a preference for spending time with friends.

Both processes also provoke the question: What are the outcomes of observing change in a child or of discrepancies between the image one holds and what one observes? One effect is likely to be on parents' sense of well-being and satisfaction (Silverberg & Steinberg, 1987). Discrepancies may also prompt parents to adapt or realign their ideas so that they are in better accord with children's developmental status (Collins, in press; Steinberg, in press). That hypothesis is certainly consistent with the finding that discrepancies between parents' expectancies of the "ideal" child and perceptions of their own child are less pronounced in middle adolescence than in early adolescence (Collins, in press). The pattern suggests that parents' ideas become realigned with the altered characteristics of adolescents, following the discrepancies in early adolescence.

Longitudinal studies of change. Information is needed about the direction of effects in times of change, and for this longitudinal material is essential. We shall single out first a study by Silverberg (1989). Silverberg starts by noting that in several cross-sectional studies, parents' sense of self-esteem and well-being have been linked to a sense of increased distance and challenge within the parent-child relationship. A one year longitudinal design with mothers and fathers allowed her to establish that the flow of effects was from changes in perceived distance to a diminished sense of life satisfaction and a reappraisal of one's life, that the perceived distance was primarily in the areas of the child's amenability to guidance and control rather than in the seeking of emotional support, and that the most pronounced links between changes in perceived distance and psychological change in a parent occurred with mothers of sons. The question now being pursued is whether similar results apply in mother-headed (single parent) households.

More generally, the result underscores again the benefits of choosing major developmental transitions as occasions for exploring links between parents' ideas and changes in children. The advantages are twofold: the changes in children are highly visible, and the implications of change are likely to be significant to both parents and children and to the relationship between them.

The second study to be singled out is by Mills and Rubin (in press), reported in a chapter that describes their extensive programme of research on children's social competence. The original testing was when the children were four years old (Mills & Rubin, 1990); the second when the children were six. At both times, mothers were asked to rank-order their preferred strategies for dealing with acts of aggression and acts of withdrawal, to give their attributions for these behaviours, to state how they felt about the child's actions (concerned, puzzled, angry, disappointed, etc.), and to indicate what they thought they would do in each case.

At issue are three central questions. One is whether stability varies with the nature of the child's actions. Overall, the correlations across the two year period were significant for withdrawal but not for aggression, suggesting that stability reflects the view that the behaviour being considered is a trait, as shyness is often thought to be. The second question has to do with whether stability over time varies with the nature of the strategy being commented upon. Beliefs about preferred strategies (relying on the child's personal experience and observational learning) showed more continuity than beliefs about the less preferred strategies (adult explanations and directive teaching). The third question—the one that yielded surprising results—has to do with whether changes in beliefs are correlated with shifts in the mothers' general perceptions of the child's personality/disposition/social skills. These correlations were unexpectedly low, raising doubts about the extent to which changes in parents' ideas reflect a sensitive monitoring of changes in the child. The higher correlations were with the mothers' socio-economic status and perceptions of social support. The result suggests that, at least for ideas about the use of coercive versus gentle methods of treating a child, changes in ideas may reflect changes in the mother's well being rather than in the child. Measures of continuity or change in the parents' state, as well as the child's, will clearly be in order for future research.

The Place of Advice

This section starts with an interest in the attitudes that parents take towards their own ideas and those of others. One reason for doing so is theoretical. If ideas are acquired from others, the process is not likely to be one of entirely passive absorption, especially if the ideas presented are plural in form, allow some degree of choice, and contain some judgmental qualities (some ideas, for instance, are more "expert" or "up-to-date" than others). To explore the less passive aspects to acquisition, however, we need a substantive topic. The attitude taken towards one's own ideas and those of others offers some feasible research possibilities.

The second reason is practical. A mother's confidence in her ability to parent has powerful effects. The data comes from a longitudinal Canadian study (Williams et al., in press) of the transition to parenthood: " the mother's experience with infants and her prenatal expectations regarding her ability to understand her infant's signals predicted not only her confidence postpartum, but also predicted postpartum attachments . . . and postpartum emotional state . . . . Moreover, prenatal parenting confidence predicted postpartum adaptation to motherhood."

How might we explore views of one's own and others' ideas or expectancies? The following steps seem possible: (1) at the level of general or textual analysis, consider the nature of advice given to parents and of debates over the validity of the prevailing images of family, women, and children; (2) at the individual level, consider the correlates of confidence, the use of advice, and the response to advice.

Research Approach 1: Analyses of Texts and Their Effects

To be noted first is Clarke-Stewart's (1978) analysis of primers-for-parents: books of advice in which, she notes, parents largely emerge as incompetent and as in need of expert guidance. More specific to women, and to differentiations between mothers and fathers, are feminist analyses of the extent to which women are presented in many texts as incompetent, as victims, as like children, or as inextricably tied in their identity and their fate to children. Thorne (1987), for instance, points to a variety of ways in which "womanhood has been linked to motherhood in a mixing of identities that simply does not occur for men and fatherhood" (p.96). Definitions of "the day-care child", for instance, are regularly linked to definitions of "the working mother". Discussions of social policy for children typically assume that the major responsibilities for children will rest with women, and the increasing autonomy of women is presented as at the expense of children (e.g. at the cost of the "loss" or the "erosion" of childhood). More subtly, and more directly damaging to a sense of competence, women are often likened to children. Both tend to be seen as falling short of complete adulthood, to be less than fully responsible or competent. Both may also be seen, even within some feminist analyses, as victims rather than as agents or actors who have some capacity for independent action and who may resist the images held out for them (Goodnow, 1985 b).

Do such images of "women and children" matter? Thorne (1987) proposes that they alter the direction of research, the nature of social policy, and the capacity of women to see themselves as competent and able to act. We would add a further possibility. Such proposals may affect the readiness of fathers to accept proposals about the importance and the feasibility of their being fully involved in parenting (or as involved as their wives are). As Thorne (1987) and several other social scientists have pointed out, adults use children to define themselves. Adults are responsible, dominant, and sexual; children are not. Adults are independent, children are dependent. If the images of women and children overlap, it seems reasonable that fathers will be doubly reluctant to take on a nurturing role, since to do so moves them not only towards greater similarity to women but also towards similarity with children. It would certainly be of value, and feasible, to determine whether the degree of reluctance to take on a nurturing role, or a "mother-like" commitment to parenting, is correlated with the extent to which fathers also hold the perception of women and children as like one another and as incomplete adults.

Research Approach 2 : Explorations at the Individual Level
    We might start by noting some further data from the Williams et al. (in press) study related to changes in confidence. The happiness and confidence of mothers postpartum were correlated with the extent to which they felt that they and their partners shared similar feelings about the pregnancy, and with the extent to which they consulted their partners about their concerns regarding the child. Confidence, however, was not a stable phenomenon: Confidence postpartum did not predict confidence in oneself as a parent at the toddler phase. In effect, if we are to explore parents' confidence in themselves, we should expect it to change as the tasks of parenting change, and to involve feelings not only about oneself and the child, but also feelings about one's partner or other sources of support.

    A second possible route is to look at *variations among people in the use of advice*. Who, for instance, turns most readily to other family members (spouse or grandparent) or to agencies outside the family? One interesting possibility is that looking to sources outside the family is especially likely to occur when a break in tradition makes family sources—even when available—seem less reliable than outside experts are. The suggestion is based on results reported by Frankel and Roer-Bornstein (1982). Their study deals with two ethnic groups in Israel (Yemenite and Kurdish in background). The former turn more readily to clinics and hospitals, often for minor complaints, and make less use of advice from their own parents or grandparents. The difference appears to reflect the extent to which the expert advice is compatible with the general form of advice given within the family. The Kurdish tradition is compatible with it. For events such as miscarriage or difficulty in childbirth, for instance, their emphasis has always fallen on physical explanations. The new explanations they took on board might direct attention to different physical causes, but the type of explanation was similar. In contrast, the emphasis on magical, spiritual, and phenomenological factors within Yemenite tradition is far less compatible with the style of modern medicine. In the course of becoming "modern" in the new land, this particular group of immigrants ends with an uneasy amalgamation of old and new ideas (they have a clear understanding of neither) and, it appears, a loss as well in confidence about their own competence as parents and their own knowledge.

    The third route that we suggest consists again of attention to expert advice, noting especially *the selective use of expert advice*. This is not an easy research route. As several analysts of books of advice to parents have observed, it is one thing to note that the books have been written and to locate the number printed or the number of editions. It is less easy, however, to determine whether the books are read or used (Schütze, 1987).

One way to proceed is to concentrate on situations where parents put themselves in the path of new advice, and note the points at which their accceptance ends. Two studies point to this possibility. One is by Cohen (1981), reporting on a group of English mothers, newly moved to a housing estate and on the way to becoming firmly middle-class. These mothers formed a group, discussed books of advice about preschoolers, and divided among themselves a number of the activities suggested (e.g. taking children to galleries, encouraging finger-painting or water play), with the allocation of activities influenced by the degree to which particular women found the arguments for them convincing. The study brings out as well another example of plurality and of variable acceptance of both views. The plurality in this case consists of two views about how to help children achieve in school: one view arguing for play, discovery, and expanded activities, the other for practice, effort, and attention to adult-assigned tasks. The mothers in Cohen's study started from a preference for the "practice and effort" orientation. They turned out to be ready to suspend it and go along with the "play and discovery" theme but only while the children were in preschool or in the early grades of primary school. For children in fifth and sixth grade, these same mothers were not ready to continue with a "progressive" approach and they worked for school changes to see that their original orientation was implemented. In effect, they were willing to apply the new orientation to young children, where the consequences might be good and were not seen as in any case major. The original orientation remained in force, however, for "real" or "serious" phases of life. In Salzman's (1981) terms, it was briefly "recessive" but it had certainly not been eliminated.

The fourth and last route we suggest consists of analysing *responses to advice or comment about one's chidren*. We may not be able to make many quantitative analyses of the way people use books written for parents, but the response to direct face-to-face comment may be more amenable to analysis and to some degree of experimental variation. Oddly enough, there seems little available data. A study by Keller et al. (1984), however, suggests some interesting possibilities. They included in their interviews with mothers in West Germany and in Costa Rica two kinds of question about sources of information on child development: questions about whom they would ask, and questions about how they felt about advice or comment. It is the latter type of question on which we shall focus. The two samples were very different in educational level (e.g. 40% of the Costa Rican sample had attended school for only 6 years or less). Nonetheless, in both samples, "less than half of all women liked people commenting on the child's rate of development" (p.174). In both also, advice was more likely to be "judged positively if those persons (the advice givers) are estimated as experienced, well-informed, or giving orientation or teaching to the relatively uninformed mothers" (48% FRG vs 71% Costa Rica) (p.175). Where the two samples differed most sharply was in the view of advice. German mothers were *more* likely to:

● Accept advice only if they agreed with its content (FRG 39%; Costa Rica, 6%).

● Distrust comments from others (22% vs 2%).

● Be uninterested in the views of others (32% vs 18%) "because they (the parents) stress the individuality of each child" (40% vs 16%) (p.175).

The data do not tell us how far, within samples, the answer to one question is linked to the answer to another, so that the presence of some core or central ideas about advice is difficult to determine. What the study does suggest, however, is the importance of ideas about the individuality of children. As in Backett's (1982) Scots sample, the appeal to a child's individuality appears to be a highly acceptable basis for turning away from advice, providing a useful buffer to intrusive advice and perhaps a way of accounting for the failure to use it. It is possible, for instance, both to endorse and to reject advice by making such statements as "it's a good idea but it just wouldn't work with my child". We need now analyses that will determine whether a belief in individuality predicts to a distrust of advice based upon normative data, or whether the distrust has other sources and is then socially justified by an appeal to the individuality of each child or each parent-child relationship.

More broadly, the nature and expression of trust or suspicion towards advice, along with confidence or doubt towards one's own ideas, would provide a way of exploring links between the ideas of individuals and the ideas of others. It represents a concrete way of exploring the implications of cultural models or social representations for the ideas held by parents, just as observing change over the course of parenting—with particular attention to transition points—represents a concrete way of exploring several implications contained in more experimental studies of social cognition. Ideally, research on either problem, along with the general analysis of acquisitions and changes in parents' ideas, will be informed by an awareness of both theoretical positions and an interest in bringing the two together rather than in forcing a choice between them.

CHAPTER 5

CONSEQUENCES: EMPHASIS ON PARENTS

In Chapter 4, we concentrated on the sources of parents' ideas. In Chapters 5 and 6, we turn to consequences. Chapter 5 picks up consequences related primarily to parents: the way they feel about children and parenting, and the actions they take. Chapter 6 emphasises consequences related primarily to children: the nature or level of their academic and social development and the ideas they come to hold about parents, parenting, and families.

This chapter begins with attention to affect and then considers parental actions. As in the previous chapter on sources, we shall provide a brief account both of research on parents' ideas and of some broader traditions within which the parental work can be situated: traditions that allow both borrowing and contributing. We shall also end again with some selected issues for a research agenda, supplementing the research possibilities and directions noted throughout the chapter.

We begin with affect for two reasons:

1. It has a complex place in any chain of events constructed for parents' ideas. It has been seen, for example, as both a consequence of ideas (satisfaction results, for instance, when expectancies are met) and a source (e.g. mood alters our perception of children). It has also been seen as a consequence and a source of action (relief follows the release of anger, for instance, and feeling may be the spur or the energy source for action).

2. There is a lack of balance between the extent to which research takes note of the affective side of parenting and the extent to which both positive and negative feelings are a major part of parenting. There is perhaps no other kind of work in which feeling is so constant a component or swings through such a wide range. An emphasis on parents' ideas might seem to make the balance even more out-of-kilter. In fact, as we shall see, it is providing a route back into the nature of parental affect, and into the apparently simple question: Why is parenting marked by such pervasive, variable, and often extreme feeling?

AFFECT

We shall use the term affect rather than emotion, in agreement with the argument that the term affect covers not only emotions (anger, joy, etc.) but also preferences, desires, and mood states (Bradbury & Fincham, 1987).

The first point to note is that the amount of parental research to date is far from large. To present it, and to place it in terms of research on affect and ideas outside the parental area, we shall reverse the sequence used in Chapter 4: namely, the sequence of presenting first the parental research and then the possible settings. Instead, we shall note first the large lines of research and then place within each of these some particular studies with parents. The large lines have to do with:

Affect as an influence on ideas and actions, altering what one perceives, how one remembers it, and the degree of effort put into problem-solving.

Affect as a consequence. Most of this material deals with the impact of ideas on the sense of satisfaction with self, work, marriage, motherhood, or parenting. Satisfaction, or its lack, is related to particular attribution patterns, to whether expectancies have been met or violated, and to the sense of success being difficult to define or achieve.

Affect as a social phenomenon, or a socially constructed phenomenon. This approach comes mainly from social psychologists. The general argument is that emotions are not givens, identified by universally agreed-upon cues. Instead, we come to learn not only display rules but also the socially understood names for the way we feel, with learning taking place by way of shared experience with others and their help with naming ("You must have felt proud", "No wonder you felt indignant", "Weren't you embarrassed?" etc.)

Affect as a Source of Ideas or Actions

Within cognitive psychology, affect increasingly emerges as an influence upon the way thinking proceeds. Hoffman's (1986, p.200) statement provides a summary of the effects already established: "Affect may initiate, terminate, accelerate, or disrupt information processing; it may determine which sector of the environment is processed and which processing modes operate; it may organize recall and influence category accessibility; it may contribute to the formation of emotionally charged schemata and categories; it may provide input for social cognition; and it may influence decision-making".

How is all this material related to research with parents? The links we shall single out have to do with the extent to which parents (1) seek for information or for meanings in their child's behaviour, and (2) perceive their children as in difficulty.

Seeking Information and Meaning.   Psychologists (and parent educators of many kinds) have long been interested in the amenability of parents to information about children and about parenting. At issue throughout are questions both about when information is sought or accepted, and who is most likely to seek it. One way of framing such issues is to link them to studies of the influence of affect on the extent to which an individual engages in problem solving (Isen, Means, Patrick, & Nowicki, 1982) or in "causal search" (Weiner, 1986). Isen et al. (1982) propose that low to moderate levels of affect lead to simple problem solving and to fewer checks on information than do high levels of affect. Weiner (1986, p.292) proposes that a search for further information or causes "is most evident when there has been an unexpected outcome (e.g. failure where success was anticipated), when a desire has not been fulfilled (e.g. there is interpersonal rejection) . . . and/or when the outcome is important". Such possibilities may help account for why it is the middle-class that is most active in seeking information (Seginer, 1983). They may hold higher expectations, and experience both more frequent encounters with discrepancy and higher levels of concern.

The Perception of Problems in Children   Among children referred by parents to clinics, there turn out to be a number whom the clinicians see as having no particular problems. The phenomenon has been noted by several clinicians. We single out a report by Rickard et al. (1981) which took the further step of asking whether the mother's affective state might be a major factor. In their sample, the paradoxical referrals were in fact associated with mothers' high scores on a depression inventory.

A study that directly compares depressed with non-depressed mothers adds further information (Kochanska & Radke-Yarrow, in press). Affect emerges as both a condition influencing perceptions of children and as an outcome of particular expectations. The effect on perceptions is not surprising. It seems reasonable that the depressed mothers would be less happy about their child's development. It is more intriguing to find that the depressed mothers set the stage for disappointment by regarding parental input as the major influence on development. The non-depressed gave equal weight to biological and parental factors, and gave as well—for positive outcomes—some credit to caregivers other than parents.

The differences also varied with the domain of development. For non-depressed mothers, the significant correlations between perceived causality and satisfaction with a child's development were all in the affective area (not in the cognitive or social area). In contrast, the significant correlations for depressed mothers had to do with cognitive and social development but not with affective development (essentially how happy a child is). Why a domain difference should occur is far from clear. The difference was large, however, and it serves as a reminder that research in this area will need to proceed with some care and some consideration to specific expectations and specific rather than generalised influences from affect. That conclusion from parental research, one should note, is very much in keeping with the conclusion, from more experimental studies of mood, that the effects are often target and context specific, with a great deal still to be learned about when effects occur and when they are cancelled out by some effort at "controlled processing" (Forgas, Bower, & Krantz, 1984). Efforts at controlling or counteracting the effects of mood are not readily observed in laboratory situations (the main goal so far has been to induce effects) and it may well be that situations of real concern to people—parenting situations, for example—will be needed if we are to observe efforts at corrective thought.

Affect as a Consequence of Ideas

We shall pull out three particular hypotheses that are readily extended to parents or have begun to be extended. These have to do with consequences that stem from: (1) particular patterns of attribution; (2) expectancies not being met; and (3) the nature of the work of parenting.

Affect and Particular Attribution Patterns. The material most relevant to parenting comes from studies of couple relationships, summarised by Bradbury and Fincham (1987):

● High levels of satisfaction are associated with generous attribution patterns: more specifically, with rating, as higher than one's own, a partner's contribution to positive events and, as lower than one's own, a partner's contribution to negative events.

• Lower levels of satisfaction are associated with the tendency to see the causes of positive events as situational and unstable, but the causes of difficulty or conflict as global (affecting many areas of the marriage), and as reflecting a partner's stable disposition. In contrast, partners more satisfied with their marriage display the reverse pattern. Positive events are seen as likely to be caused by global, stable factors; negative events by situational, unstable factors.

As Bradbury and Fincham (1987, p.66) comment, "little is known about how attributions are generated, the extent to which they are private versus public events . . . , and their effects on interpersonal behavior". Nonetheless, the material provides a general background for some specific findings from parental research. One of these is that the degree to which a parent would feel upset by a child's misbehaviours increases with the child's age and with the parent's attributions of the behaviour to the child's stable disposition rather than to circumstance or a passing phase (e.g. Dix et al., 1986). The other has to do with feelings associated with actions of aggression and withdrawal. In a study described by Rubin , Mills, and Krasnor (in press) mothers of 4-year-olds were given two stories describing acts of aggression (in a peer-group or at home), and two describing acts of withdrawal (at preschool or at a party). They were asked how they would feel if their child acted this way several times in a row. Nine possible emotions were offered, each for rating on a 3-point scale: angry, embarrassed, amused, disappointed, concerned, pleased, surprised, puzzled and guilty. Concern was the predominant emotion for each type of act, accompanied by anger and disappointment for acts of aggression, and puzzlement and surprise for acts of withdrawal. The authors suggest that the differential response to aggression and withdrawal reflects the amount of information available to parents from media sources about the two kinds of behaviour in childhood (more available on aggression than on withdrawal). The same source is also suggested for the way mothers are more likely, for withdrawal compared with aggressive acts, to use low power strategies and to seek information about the behaviour.

Affect Stemming from Violated Expectancies and Departures from Standards.   Affect may be generated by expectancies met or not met. This type of hypothesis often carries a particular emphasis on depression as a response to a perceived discrepancy from standards or expectancies. Beck (1967) is the best known theorist. Higgins and his colleagues offer an expansion, relating different types of depression to particular departures from one's own and others' standards (e.g. Higgins, Klein, & Strauman, 1985).

Is parenting especially likely to be a situation where standards or expectations will not be met? Schütze's (1987) analysis of standards for "the good mother" is an example of concern with this question. Her general argument is that the standards advocated by experts make success more and more difficult to achieve. A case in point is an account of mother-love which insists that the essential prerequisite for a child's healthy development is a warm, confident attitude during pregnancy, conveyed to the child in utero. Schütze (1987) notes that this kind of thesis moves influence away from fathers at any point and away from mothers' later feelings (if feelings "in utero" are critical, the mother clearly cannot recover from an ambivalent start and become a good mother after the birth is over). The standards become all the more unattainable, Schütze (1987) points out, if one adds, to the requirement of proper attitudes during pregnancy or during the first hour, a "boundless giving of oneself" (p.61), and a sense of personal enrichment. "The mother of the second half of the twentieth century can carry out her duties until she drops from exhaustion, and yet she is culpable if she does not have the feeling of personal enrichment, or if she has even unconscious negative feelings" (p.61).

Three further studies of parents add to the picture. The first of these asks about occasions of dissatisfaction. Dissatisfaction with oneself as a parent turns out to be highest when a child's characteristic is seen as open to influence in principle, influenced by others in practice, but—for one reason or another—not being influenced by one's own efforts (Emmerich, 1969). In effect, the unhappiness springs both from not meeting one's own standards and from an attribution pattern that provides little comfort for not doing so.

The other two studies are longitudinal and focus on feelings in relation to "violated expectations" in the course of the transition to parenthood. They are by Belsky and his colleagues (Belsky, Lang, &Huston, 1986; Belsky, Ward, & Rovine, 1986), and by Ruble and her colleagues (Ruble et al., 1988). We shall concentrate on the latter group. They start from an interest in why marital satisfaction seems to decline for so many new mothers. They note the presence of literature indicating the general importance of departures from expectations, and the presence of results (Belsky et al., 1986) indicating that violated expectations led to a drop in marital satisfaction among mothers but not among fathers, three months after the birth of a first child. Their concern is that the data analysis in the study by Belsky et al. (1986) does not indicate which violated expectations were the most important. In particular, the data and its analysis do not allow a check on the hypothesis that the critical expectation may have to do with divisions of labour (the labour of caring for the child and for housekeeping).

The sample in the Ruble et al. (1988) study came from Toronto, Seattle, and New York. The design was both cross-cultural and longitudinal. The results make clear first of all that expectations are not always met. Pregnant women, for instance, expected to share child-care tasks equally (33%) or at least not to do much more than their husbands (12%). Postpartum women reported a low incidence of equal shares (12%) and a high incidence of doing much more that their husbands (46%). As Ruble et al. (1988) note, it is not clear why the women had such high expectations, in the face of the usual norms. They offer the intriguing suggestion that each couple expects to be "different": that is, with them, the ideal will be met. For whatever reason, the stage is set for discrepancy of a negative kind.

The results also bring out sharply the links between departures from expectations and various aspects of satisfaction. Discrepancy in the direction of doing more than one expected was significantly associated with negative feelings about the husband's involvement and about the influence of the baby on the marital relationship, but not with the mother's sense of closeness to her partner, perhaps because the mother sees the difficulty as a situational issue rather than as a global problem for the marriage. It is clearly critical not only to ask which violated expectations are important, but also to consider a variety of aspects of satisfaction and of feelings about the child and the marriage.

One final point needs to be added to the links between affect and standards or expectations. This has to do with *parenting as a public performance.* It is carried out under the eyes of children, partners, relatives, friends, and "the state", all of whom feel the right to judge and, with varying degrees of openness, to comment. The standards applied are not simply one's own. Such a feature suggests that one way to consider ideas about parenting is to ask when parents feel the need to explain or to justify family events, and whether mothers, fathers, or siblings feel equal needs to do so. It also suggests that one way to describe a social context—for parents or children—is in terms of the people who perceive themselves as having the right or the obligation to judge, praise, criticise, and perhaps over-ride a parent's decision, and who are accepted by parents as having this role. The extent to which others do the judging should alter the extent to which one's self-concept as a parent and one's sense of satisfaction is based on one's own actions or on the reactions of others. It may alter as well the extent to which children see parents as powerful, a perception important both for the children and for the parent's sense of satisfaction.

Parental Affect as a Consequence of the Nature of the Job.   This aspect of affect has been foreshadowed in Schütze's (1987) comments on impossible standards. It appears also in a great deal of feminist writing on motherhood , covering the nature of the task, its status, and its sufficiency as an identity. Thorne (1987) provides an example. In her analysis, a number of feelings—confusion, anxiety, resentment, and depression—are the result of some particular aspects to the status and conditions of motherhood. To start with, mothering is a job with a contradictory status: on the one hand, held out as the highest or noblest role to which women may aspire, on the other so low in prestige that no man would wish to take it on and little government money or social support needs to be provided. It is also a job with very difficult conditions: long hours, uncertain rewards, indefinite completion dates (when does parenting end?), a great deal of ambiguity as to what constitutes success, and the temptation to feel that the job done, however successful, could perhaps have been done better still.

A further example is Ruddick's (1982) analysis of "maternal thinking". The central proposal is that a number of ways of feeling and thinking (summarised under the label "maternal thinking") go with the task of being responsible for a young child. The phrase applies to any person, male or female, who has primary responsibility for a child but, since this person is usually the mother, Ruddick prefers the phrase "maternal thinking".

In Ruddick's (1982) analysis, the job of mothering is characterised, on the one hand, by three responsibilities (responsibility for the child's preservation, its growth, and its acceptability to herself and others) and, on the other, by three sets of conditions. One set is related to the nature of children. They are vulnerable to damage or death, they are imperfect, their "acts are irregular, unpredictable, often mysterious" (p.82), and they constantly present the mother with conflicting goals. At one and the same time, how can she, for instance, both preserve and let go, encourage independence and physical skill but guarantee safety, promote achievement but keep competitiveness below whatever level is judged to be unacceptable?

The second set of conditions is related to the demands of the job. It requires a great deal of one's attention, a mixture of "loving, self-restraining, and empathy", which often has to be learned and practised. The third set has to do with the conditions of the world in which children are raised, presenting the mother often with "the insupportable difficulty of passionately loving a fragile creature in a physically threatening, socially violent, pervasively uncaring and competitive world" (Ruddick, 1982, p.81).

The result, Ruddick (1982) argues, is that the mother comes to feel and to value a particular set of feelings and ideas. The child's vulnerability, for instance, encourages in her an attitude of protection, a sense of humility, and the placing of value on particular qualities in herself (humility, for instance, and "resilient cheerfulness" rather than assertiveness or the "melancholy" that could easily arise "in the face of danger, disappointment, and unpredictability" [p.81]). In related fashion, the changes constantly occurring in children encourage a respect for growth (more a respect for others' growth than for her own), while the demand to accept "the uses to which others put her children" (turning them into soldiers or into submissive creatures are examples) promotes a sense of powerlessness, a demand for double-thinking, and, at times, an easy slide into unhealthy denial or "anguished confusion" (p.86).

Ruddick's (1982) view of maternal feeling and thinking is openly acknowledged as her own view, based upon her own experiences in U.S. culture. Its emphasis on feelings as stemming from the nature of the parenting task, however, fit well with other observations. One of these has to do with analyses of work in terms of dissatisfaction arising from conflicting demands: the demands of caring for patients, for example, and at the same time coping with the bureaucratic requirements of a health service (Engstrom, 1988). A second has to do with mothers' comments on the pleasure of being told that their children were especially helpful or courteous when at someone else's house (Goodnow & Delaney, 1989). Contributing to the pleasure was not only the relief of being told that one's children have behaved in publicly acceptable ways, but also the sense that "they do know", that "the message has got through". In the normal course of life at home, feedback about the success of one's teaching may be equivocal.

The final observation comes from Roth's (1963) analysis of how people respond to situations where the length of a task or project is indefinite, and benchmarks are few. His interest in such situations began with a stay in a TB sanitarium before the advent of pharmacological treatment. For him, and for others, this indeterminate sentence provoked extraordinary efforts to set some benchmarks and to invent signs of progress. Roth proceeds to point out the indeterminate length of parenthood and the similarity between doctor-patient negotiations and parent-child negotiations, as both try to set benchmarks that allow flexibility and some assurance about signposts: "When you've had two weeks without fever . . . "; "when you're old enough", "when you're 12 or 21". The essential features to both situations are the unease felt when signposts or benchmarks are lacking and the resulting effort to create or invent some. We suspect that these features will be even more marked when children depart from the usual timetable (when they have a developmental disability, for instance) and parents can less readily turn to the observation of other children in order to estimate progress.

Affect as a Social Phenomenon or a Social Construction

Studies of emotion have long contained an interest in the way emotions are expressed and recognised by way of facial or bodily cues, with attention often given to the extent to which these cues can be recognised across cultures and by children as well as adults. The ethological orientation that has prevailed may be contrasted with a position such as Averill's (1982, p.25): "The person who says I am angry with you or I love you is not simply labeling a state of physiological arousal; he is entering into a complex relationship with another person. The meaning of the relationship, not only for the individuals involved but also for the larger society, is embodied in the feeling rules (social norms) for that emotion".

Emotions as socially constructed or socially identified are of particular interest for research on parenting, since it is quickly apparent that one of the tasks of parenting is to teach children the display rules for emotion: the occasions when its expression is appropriate, the forms it should take, the desirability of open or "leaked" display, the limits of expression. This kind of teaching is at least as widespread as teaching about cognitive skills, but the amount of research on such affective training is scarce.

What is contained in studies of parents? We shall note first that families vary considerably in the views they take about the expression of emotion. The extent to which both disagreement and signs of caring are openly expressed, for instance, is much higher in Greek-Australian than in Anglo-Australian families (Rosenthal, 1984). The bases to the difference are yet to be determined, but we suspect that beneath the differences in overt display are ideas about the signals which demonstrate one "cares" and, more subtly, ideas about the place of rationality in family life. The definition of family in all cultural groups appears to contain some expectation that rationality may be suspended. It is "natural" to see one's children or one's partner as better than they are, or even as "the best". It is, for children, a justifiable complaint if their parents do not find them especially attractive, do not lean towards their point of view, do not "support" them regardless of what they do, or act towards them as if they were other than parents ("don't be my teacher", to quote a child's comment to its mother—a schoolteacher—in a report by Molinari and Emiliani, 1987). The expectations, by parents or children, as to when rationality and when emotionality should be the dominant mode have yet to be determined but we suspect they are a substantial part of differences among families and among cultural groups.

The second point to be noted comes from research on the way parents define emotions for children and introduce them to the actions and expressions required. The research is by Semin and Papadopoulou (1990) and deals with embarrassment (the emotion one may feel, for instance, when a child drops a jar of pickles in a supermarket or, in a restaurant, spills its milkshake over itself or others). In addition to data, the report contains an interesting theoretical concept. At the base of the mother's embarrassment, it is proposed, lies a mother's sense of "joint identity" with the child. She is not only embarrassed by the child, but also *for* the child. If one adds the further possibility that children also may be embarrassed by their parents (because of a sense of joint identity?), and that the outside world is, to varying degrees, ready to judge one family member by the actions of another, the concept is an interesting step towards understanding why affect seems so pervasive in family life. At the very least, joint identity must increase the number of occasions on which mothers sense a discrepancy from expectations or standards.

PARENTS' ACTIONS AND INTERACTIONS

We turn now to the consequences that have been for many psychologists the starting point to an interest in parents' ideas: namely, the actions parents take towards children. We shall proceed by noting (1) two possible directions of effect (from ideas to actions, and from actions to ideas), (2) some examples of parental research in the two directions, and (3) moves towards more conceptual approaches, drawing both from research with parents and from research in social psychology on links between ideas and actions.

The Possible Directions of Effects

The direction most often considered goes from ideas to actions. This is the direction of interest when parents' ideas are considered as "cognitive mediators" between the stimuli that children's actions provide and the actions parents take (e.g. Parke, 1978). It is also the direction of interest in much of experimental social psychology, both in studies of congruence or consistency between attitudes and actions, and in studies of the ways in which expectancies influence our perceptions of others and our interactions with them. (For reviews of this material, Fazio, 1986, and Miller and Turnbull, 1986, are useful sources).

There is, however, an alternate direction of effect: one yet to be considered strongly in parental research. This direction appears in the proposal that actions can come about without much grounding in thought (e.g. they can occur without thinking, or on the basis of feeling or habit). Thought comes later, when people are prompted by their actions to develop rationales or justifications. They may, for instance, use actions already taken to define themselves or to determine what their views must be (Bem, 1972). In a sense, one says to oneself, "I must be a good parent after all, or I would not have gone to so much effort."

Some Examples of Parental Research

Ideas Following Actions.   We have been able to locate one example of a study where parental actions are noted as preceding thought. It is a study by Niemala (1981) in Finland, covering the views taken by three groups of women towards combining motherhood with paid work. The women were interviewed when their youngest child was 8 years old, and again when the child was 11. At the time of the second interview, mothers were regarded as falling into three groups, based on the extent to which they defined themselves only as mothers. For one group, being a mother was still the main source of identity. For these women paid work was a distinctly secondary part to their lives, and few changes in their life pattern were expected. A second group were openly ambivalent about motherhood being a sufficient reward, but were conflicted about making changes in the direction of entering paid work or increasing their commitment to it. The third group considered that they had already made changes and worked through them. For this group especially, the investigators (Niemala, 1981, p.4) had expected that "first the mother would think and ponder about changes in her life and about going to work, second she would work through the changes emotionally, and third, finally, she would be ready to take a job. This, however, was not the typical pattern . . . . It seems that many long-time mothers first go to work without pondering much and then start thinking and working through the changes brought about by the changed life situation." It seems likely that a number of other aspects of parenting—from becoming pregnant to striking one's child—involve a similar pattern of act first, think later, and fit the ideas to the action already taken.

Ideas Considered as Leading to Actions.   More readily available are studies where parents' ideas on various topics have been correlated with their actions in experimental situations or, more naturalistically, with the way they structure the child's environment. These studies fall into several sets:

• Correlating ideas about the way children learn or reason with actions in teaching situations or with educational aspects of the home environment (e.g. Hess et al., 1986; McGillicuddy-DeLisi, 1982; Schaefer, 1987; Skinner, 1985).

• Correlating ideas about children's competence, dispositions or power with actions of a more "social" kind: reprimanding, disciplining, encouraging, asserting, praising (e.g. Antill, 1987; Bugental & Shennum, 1984; Dix et al., 1986).

• Correlating ideas about relative areas of responsibility or jurisdiction with negotiations and interactions (e.g. Smetana, 1988).

The first two sets have been the basis for conclusions by Miller (1988) and by Sigel (1986) to the effect that the evidence for forward effects from parents' ideas has so far been less than overwhelming. More specifically, it may be said that the results are similar to those found in the literature on attitude–action consistency, and that the critical issue is not whether congruence occurs but *when*. We do know, for instance, that congruence is more marked for some people than for others. Fathers, for instance, show a higher congruence between stated principle and teaching actions than do mothers (McGillicuddy-DeLisi, 1982). We also know that congruence is higher for some actions than for others. In Skinner's (1985) study, for instance, mothers' views about the way children learn corresponded well with the way mothers handled a child's off-task behaviours, but not the child's on-task behaviours. Established also is the presence of higher correlations when the actions being predicted to are not "one-off" or relatively insignificant situations: when they are, for instance, a composite of actions taken over several occasions (Kochanska, Kuczynski, & Radke-Yarrow, in press) or an action that will have consequences for the way the child's and the parents' day will be organised (the decision to send a child to preschool, for instance, and the choice of preschool or day-care centre [Toussaint, 1986]). The challenge now is to make the most conceptual sense of why congruence sometimes occurs, and sometimes does not.

Conceptual Moves

Both within and outside parental research, there have been moves to make greater sense of consistency data by laying out alternative models, and by analysing the nature of research designs, the nature of action, and the assumption that ideas and actions form a special kind of dichotomy.

Developing Alternative Models.   Ideally a study should check not only whether one model fits the data but also whether some other model might fit even better. An example in practice comes from Conger et al. (1984). They wished to predict the affective quality of mothers' interactions with their young children. Most of the children were preschoolers. Interactions were coded as positive, neutral, or negative, and the outcome measures dealt with both the frequency and the relative proportions of these. The models considered all started from environmental stress as an initial variable, with stress defined mainly in terms of demographic conditions: income and/or dependence on public support, family structure (number of children, single-parent head of household), educational achievement and mother's age at first birth. These stressors might be considered as having a direct effect on maternal behaviour. Their influence might also be by way of such mediating variables as the degree to which mothers value obedience and approve of external control rather than reasoning as a disciplinary strategy, the extent to which they see the child in a positive or negative light, and the general level of emotional distress.

Conger and his colleagues (1984) then proceed to lay out three possible models and to check these against the data. In Model A, the demographic variables have an impact only by way of the mediating variables. This model turns out not to fit. In a second model (Model B), the demographic variables alter both mothers' actions and mothers' ideas and mood, but the latter have no impact on actions. This model also turns out not to fit. In a third (Model C), the demographic variables predict to actions and to mother's ideas and mood, and both sets of variables (demographic and mediating) have an influence on actions. This model fits the data. So also, the authors note, might a model in which the mediating variables drive the demographic variables (e.g. the mother's values and emotional distress contribute to her level of income or education, number of children, etc.). This fourth model, in their view, cannot be ruled out on statistical grounds but appears less plausible to them than does Model C.

Determining the Effect of Experimental Designs.   The sharpest comments come from Miller and Turnbull (1986) in a review of research on the effects of expectancies upon interpersonal processes. Expectancies, they note, have long been demonstrated as having self-fulfilling or self-confirming effects. Parents' and teachers' expectations alter students' achievements. Expectations of friendliness alter the social approaches people make to others. Information about an opponent's cooperativeness, gender, or age alters bargaining and negotiation behaviours. Knowing the other person's gender or age can alter the assignment of tasks. Being told that a performance can be improved by practice alters the degree of help given.

The difficulty is that these effects seem easiest to demonstrate in "stripped-down" situations that are rather remote from everyday life. The effect is more likely to appear, for instance, when relatively little is known about the other person, and at the start of an interaction than at later points. Knowledge about a child's age, for instance, alters the initial selection of a task to be worked on jointly but not the interactions after that (Brody, Graziano, & Musser, 1983). In the later interactions, the other person's actions and the knowledge they provide presumably override the original expectancies based on knowing only about age. In addition, self-confirming effects seem most likely to occur in situations where the person being perceived is uninformed about the perceiver and is in no position to challenge or to counter the other's preconceptions. In fact, according to Miller and Turnbull (1986, p.241), "a reader of the expectancy literature might be forgiven for concluding that targets of erroneous expectations are powerless to alter or to resist the behavioral confirmation sequence once it has begun. Neither the phenomenology nor the resources of the target have generated much interest among psychologists."

There are some changes in design that move the person who is the target of perception or action from a state of complete ignorance or powerlessness. In some studies, for instance, the target has been given information about the perceiver (e.g. told that he or she is a "normal" or "ordinary" person, a homosexual, or a former mental patient) and the perceiver has been told that this is the information held by the target. In others, the target has been instructed to act in ways that would fit or challenge the perceiver's ideas. To choose an example from parental research, children have been trained to act in responsive or difficult ways towards women who have varying ideas about their ability to control children (Bugental & Shennum, 1984). Such changes in design help bring experimental studies closer to the conditions of real life parenting: conditions likely to involve the complexities of a history of information about past actions, knowledge by one person of what the other's perceptions may be, and some possibility of action to counter a perception felt to be invalid or unflattering.

Analysing the Nature of Actions.   Part of the difficulty in relating ideas to actions is that the move is often made without a theory or a framework that describes how action comes about and how ideas fit into this picture. Within research on parenting there are now several proposals that begin to meet these needs, suggesting both some particular ways of regarding actions and some particular facets of ideas that are likely to be relevant:

Parental actions as structuring a child's environment rather than directly framing a particular action. This view of parental action comes mainly from anthropologists, with Beatrice Whiting as one particular advocate. As she points out, the most significant actions parents may take concern the assignment of children to various niches, areas, or habitats: from playgroups to sports clubs, ethnic associations, private schools, or work settings. Many of the child's activities and friendship groups are then constrained by these settings rather than by continued parental action. Whiting's (1980) proposal has been incorporated by Super and Harkness (1986) into their concept of "developmental niche". Both approaches would certainly argue for attention to parents' ideas about the impact of various settings on children and to parents' actions in selecting some settings rather than others.

Actions that reflect prescriptive as against proscriptive rules. The distinction comes from Hanson (1988). Prescriptive rules cover possible actions, proscriptive rules cover actions that are not to be used. In families, Hanson (1988) suggests, the latter may be more explicit than the former. For our purposes, that possibility and the distinction itself suggests that links between proscriptive rules and actions may be relatively straightforward. The links between prescriptive rules and actions, however, may be more difficult to locate.

Actions as a sequence of decisions. Actions seldom require a single choice. They may, in fact, be thought of as a branching tree, starting from the decision to act at all and then moving to the choice of particular actions. The first decision—the decision to act—may be the easier to predict from ideas determined before a study. It may also reflect ideas with a different content (e.g. ideas about the likelihood of having any impact, regardless of the specific action taken) from those that influence later actions. If this argument is correct, then data analyses will need to avoid aggregating actions over time, and instead will need to distinguish among first and later moves: a step clearly useful in the study already mentioned by Brody et al. (1983).

Actions as contingencies. In addition to involving more than a single choice, actions by one person display varying degrees of linkage to the actions of another. This feature of actions has been used effectively by Kindermann and Skinner (1989) in a longitudinal study demonstrating that, as mothers began to regard their young children as more competent in the areas of walking, eating, and dressing, they altered the kind of response they made to their children's actions (e.g. their response to actions indicating dependency) and the extent to which they responded at all.

Actions as choices or as selections from a repertoire. The proposal that actions are choices comes from Eccles (1986) and frames her long-term research on factors that influence the choice of mathematics vs. other school subjects, particularly by girls. When action is seen as choice rather than avoidance, Eccles (1986) proposes, then attention is drawn to ideas about goals, options, feasibility, value and relevance. In addition, a sizeable literature on planning, decision making, and compromise among competing goals is at the researcher's disposal. The emphasis on selections from a repertoire is best illustrated by two studies in progress. In one, Grusec has asked mothers how comfortable or how "good" they felt about using a particular way of responding to a child's misdemeanours. In the other, Goodnow and Warton have asked parents to rate whether they regarded various actions (e.g. paying a child for jobs around the house) as highly acceptable, acceptable but not a first choice, O.K. as a last resort, or unacceptable under any circumstances. In both studies, the results to date point to parents regarding actions as part of a repertoire, with actions low in preference drawn upon as earlier moves prove unsuccessful. In one mother's words, "When you get desperate, you try almost anything." When actions display this feature, then clearly the ideas to look for will need to deal with principles that determine the order of selection from the repertoire.

Actions as everyday routines, with little processing in thought. The notion that ideas lie behind all actions leaves untouched a useful distinction among actions in terms of the amount of thought that may be involved. Some actions may be relatively automatised, while others are given deliberate thought. The distinction is a basic one in cognitive psychology. It has been extended to the analysis of child abuse by Bugental (1989) who suggests that abusive actions are often undertaken with little processing and that this feature may account for why the lessons learned in therapeutic sessions, where the level of processing is high, may not transfer to everyday situations.

Action as a public performance. Attention to this aspect of action is prompted by the work of Reid and Valsiner (1986), who have explored the ideas that mothers hold about appropriate reprimands or punishments (e.g. verbal vs. nonverbal) for children in various situations. One of the striking results has to do with the importance of whether the setting is public or private. To hit a parent, or to be rude to a parent, in a supermarket or when guests are present is a more serious transgression than the same act carried out in private. What is more, U.S. parents hold strong ideas about the appropriateness of punishing a child in public, even though punishing in private usually means a delay, and parents consider that punishment should follow the transgression as quickly as possible and not be "in cold blood". The material draws attention again to an aspect of parental action that we see as neglected (namely, its public vs. private nature) and to the need for considerably more data than we have at present on parents' ideas about the significance of public acts by either parents or by their children. At the moment, we are a long way from understanding why parents are at times tempted to act as if their children did not really belong to them or why they make such comments as "just wait until we get home". We suspect that public acts increase in significance when parents see children as representing the family, when the child's act undercuts a precarious public image, and/or when a society offers few explanations for children's actions other than the quality of parenting. Relevant data, however, are not available.

Also in short supply is information about what we may call "speech day rhetoric". On certain kinds of occasions or in certain settings—speech days, political platforms, family celebrations, funerals—it is expected that people will speak in terms of the way things are supposed to be rather than in terms of the way they really are. What we have yet to learn, especially within families, are the means by which parents signal that they are now speaking "for the book" or "in principle" and the ways in which children come to understand that some forms of statement are to be interpreted more as rhetoric than as a binding contract. They are not intended to be followed by deeds, and the audience (including the researcher) is expected to anticipate and understand the lack of connection.

Beyond the Dichotomy of Thought and Action.   We have been proceeding on the assumption that thought and action are to be distinguished, with the relevant questions having to do with the directions of effect and the conditions that may influence the direction and the degree of connection. These conditions primarily have to do with types of thought, types of action and—in proposals by Bem (1972) and by Snyder (1974)—types of people, in the sense that some individuals are more concerned with consistency than are others.

It is critical to note, however, that the usual dichotomy between thought and action is not without its difficulties. To start with, the measure of thought—the indicator of an "idea"—is often a verbal statement. Verbal statements, however, are actions. We may contrast "word" and "deed" on the grounds that the verbal action may often cost less than some other form of action, but both are actions. In essence, we are often asking not whether ideas and actions go together but whether one action is consistent with another kind, given that the two may be undertaken at different times, in different settings, at different costs, and with different significance for the individual.

In addition, the usual dichotomy between ideas and actions often overlooks the fact that many ideas are themselves about actions. What we term the "concept" of something is often defined by what it does or by the actions we may take towards it. Chairs are more "things to sit on" than they are "items of furniture" (although even "furniture" consists of "things to put in your house"). Children are people who "belong" to parents, are in need of protection, deserve love, provide joy, sorrow, and annoyance. Parents are people who should love and protect their children. These definitions by action may not be the formal or legal definitions of objects and people but they appear to be the definitions we live by and they suggest that the usual chasm between "word" and "deed" or between "thought" and "action" may be more misleading than useful. We may do well to abandon the dichotomy or, at the least, to ask whether it does not represent a shorthand way of referring to distinctions that we have yet to properly unravel.

RESEARCH AGENDA: AFFECT, "MUTUAL COGNITIONS"

From the several possibilities noted in the course of the chapter, we pull out two for special consideration. One is related to the understanding of parental affect, the other to actions (more specifically, to interactions between parents and children).

Understanding Affect

We have suggested that a great deal remains to be done in terms of parental affect as a response to violated expectations, to the nature of parenting as a form of work, and to expected displays of emotions in various family settings or on various family occasions. Each of these possibilities suggests avenues for further research, linked to some general hypotheses about the place of affect in cognition and action. To bring out the qualities specific to parental affect, however, we suggest taking first the relatively exploratory step of locating and dissecting occasions when parental affect is marked.

One example of such an approach is Semin and Papadopoulou's (in press) account of developmental change in the response of embarrassment. They propose that mothers' embarrassment be divided into feelings of embarrassment for herself and for the child, and they combine this distinction with a Vygotskian description of the mothers' actions. At the younger ages, for instance, the mother acts out embarrassment and repair moves for both herself and the child. At later ages, she transfers more of this responsibility to the child.

A second example comes from research on divisions of labour. We single it out for its indications that some of the special sources for parental affect are the ambiguity of feedback, the ambiguity of one's status, and the hazards inherent in any enterprise where someone else's actions and expressions of feelings define whether a project—constructing a sense of family, for instance—has been successful.

These features emerge first in the strength of feeling among mothers about family members being "willing to help". The importance of willingness emerges both in mothers' descriptions of children as their children as "not doing much, but they are very good if I ask them", and in the bitterness with which a small number of those interviewed by Goodnow and Delaney (1989) said that, if they were to become ill, "everything would be left until I got better". Similar comments have been reported for wives describing husbands in England (Julia Brannen, personal communication). One has the sense that willingness is often left untested, perhaps because to test and find it absent would be devastating to the relationship. What is not clear is why a lack of willingness would be so upsetting. We suggest, extending an argument by Goodnow and Delaney (1989), that the significance of willingness lies in the way people perceive approaches to work around the house (one's own work and the work of others) as a sign of the state of a relationship. On this basis, to be unwilling denies the sense of family. It suggests that one feels no sense of reciprocity towards a person who does something for you, and implies that this work is not a gift to be appreciated but a job that others have managed to avoid. To entertain such feelings would certainly make it difficult to sustain the illusion of a family unit or the rhetoric of being cared for.

The hazards of using particular markers in assessing the state of a relationship emerge also in mothers' comments about "good moments" and "low moments" related to children's work about the house. The good moments turned out to be almost always occasions when children acted without being reminded. When probed, these occasions had two meanings for mothers. First, they meant that "the message was getting through." One would not, in the words of one mother, "have to spend all your life sounding like a broken record." The other significance lay in the implication that children "cared", that they "recognised what we do for them", and they were "not just thinking about themselves".

The low moments turned out to be occasions when mothers felt more like servants than they felt like members of the family. In the pilot interviews, the references to servants and drudges were so frequent that in the full sample, mothers were asked to recall the last occasion when they felt treated as if they were a servant or the family drudge, or when they had said something about not being the maid or the home not being a hotel. All but one mother quickly agreed that they had experienced such feelings and they volunteered their own "favourite sayings": "the maid didn't come today, is on strike, hasn't been paid"; "who was your last slave?"; "what do you pay these days?"; "this is a house, not a laundromat, restaurant, hotel, boarding-house, delicatessen". Overall, work around the house emerged as containing a particular kind of ambiguity. The overt actions of mothers and maids are often similar. Their status is not supposed to be. The distinction lies, however, in the intentions behind the action (for love vs. for money) and in the expected reward of appreciation. If the intentions are not recognised, and the reward is not forthcoming, the thin line between mothers and maids, or between homes and boarding-houses, no longer holds. Small wonder that the stage is set for strong feelings.

The Analysis of "Mutual Cognitions"

The phrase "mutual cognitions" comes from Maccoby and Martin (1983), who rightly note that if we are to study the effect of ideas on parenting and on parent-child interactions, we shall need to come to terms with the ideas held by both parents and children. If we are to do so, we shall certainly need to ask about the causes and consequences of departures from a match between the two.

A lack of match may arise from differences in conceptual level. Both Damon (1977) and Selman (1980), for instance, have argued that the child's lower level of conceptual development contributes to a mismatch between adults' and children's concepts of relationships and, thus, to their scripts for how interactions should proceed. The sources of difference may lie also in a child's changing sense of what he or she is entitled to. For example, a script whereby children make self-disclosing statements to parents, but parents do not disclose private information about themselves to children, may be typical and tacitly shared during early and middle childhood, but not in adolescence. At this older age, children are likely to withhold certain information about themselves and to recognise parents' right to do the same. Parents may also move to a script of mutual privacy, or they may continue to expect the one-sided self-disclosure of earlier years (Miller, 1988; Selman, 1980).

For the consequences of a lack of match in ideas about the way a relationship should proceed, the majority view is that smooth interactions require that both parent and child must act from the same script (Hinde, 1979; Kelley et al., 1983; Maccoby, 1984). Mismatches are thought to promote conflict, with the implication in some analyses (e.g. Collins, in press; Damon, 1977; Selman, 1980) that the conflicting views gradually result in the views of one or both people changing and ending in realignment with one another. That such realignment may be the eventual outcome is certainly suggested by Collins' (in press) finding that discrepancies between parents' ideas and children's positions are less pronounced at ages 11 and 17, than when childen are 14 years old. This cross-sectional comparison implies that an initial agreement (11-year-olds) may be followed by disagreement (14-year-olds) and then by a process of adaptation (when children are 17). The hypothesised change needs to be examined directly by a longitudinal design.

To the general expectation that discrepancy prompts conflict, we would add two promising research leads. One comes from a study by MacKinnon and Arbuckle (1989). Mothers and their 7- to 9-year-old sons were observed while working together on an Etch-a-Sketch task (each controlling one of the two knobs). Interactions were rated for their overall coerciveness. Mothers and sons were also asked, when presented with stories where the intent of one party was ambiguous, to describe how the situation may have come about. These descriptions, and other comments, were then coded for the extent to which the situation was seen as brought about by the other's negative intentions (as against a prosocial intention or an accidental outcome). The highest incidence of coercive interactions occurred with dyads where both parties were inclined, on the vignettes, to attribute negative intent to each other. The next highest incidence of coerciveness occurred with dyads where the mother's attributions—but not the son's—were predominantly negative. Analysis is continuing of the nature and sequence of coercive moves, and of the way these are linked to other aspects of attributions (e.g. perceiving the other's behaviour as internally caused, global, and stable).

A further promising lead comes from research by Smetana (1988) on the nature and degree of match between parents and adolescents of different ages regarding judgments of responsibility for the adolescents' behaviour. In this research, parents and their children (in school grades 5 to 12) were given an interview that dealt with three topics. One (Hypothetical Authority Situations) was concerned with judgments and justifications with regard to the legitimacy of parents' authority in three domains. The domain could be moral (e.g. would it be O.K. for parents to make a rule about lying to parents or hitting brothers and sisters?), conventional (e.g. a rule about calling parents by their first names), personal (e.g. a rule about sleeping late on weekends), or multifaceted (e.g. a rule about not going on a picnic with the family, wearing punk clothes, or not cleaning one's room). In all, 15 situations were presented. The critical scores dealt with whether parental authority was seen as legitimate or not, and with the type of justification offered. Justifications were categorised as moral (e.g. appeals to fairness), conventional (e.g. appeals to politeness, authority, or responsibility), psychological (e.g. referrals to autonomy or disposition), or personal (personal choice).

In the second topic area (Occasions of Conflict) parents and children were asked to generate lists of disagreements and conflicts with each other. They were then interviewed in depth about these areas, with attention to both the degree of conflict and the nature of reasoning. As part of this interview, parents and adolescents were asked to rate their degree of agreement with the other's perspective, and the seriousness of conflict. They were also asked first to reason about an issue from their own perspective ("justifications") and from the other's perspective ("counter- arguments").

Of particular interest are four results. First, differences occurred between parents and adolescents in the justifications offered, especially for personal and multifaceted issues. "Parents most frequently viewed the issues causing conflicts as of a conventional nature. In contrast, children most frequently saw conflicts to occur over jurisdiction" (Smetana, 1988, p.96). In effect, "parents and adolescents were arguing over fundamentally different issues" (p.102). Second, differences also occurred between mothers and fathers in justifications, with fathers the more likely to offer moral justifications, whereas mothers appealed to social norms or to psychological reasons. Third, both parents and adolescents were able to reason from the other's point of view when asked to do so. Although the data are not from within-family comparisons, as a group adolescents presented parents' arguments as predominantly conventional while parents showed an awareness of the adolescents' appeal to personal jurisdiction.

The fourth and last result has to do with the severity of conflict reported. This varied with the degree of sophistication that adolescents brought to their disagreements with social conventions. The more sophisticated the argument (the higher the level of reasoning about conventions in the Turiel–Smetana hierarchy), the lower the frequency of conflict and the lower the importance given to disagreements, probably because parents perceived at least an agreement in style of argument even when the final verdict was not shared. The use of a sophisticated style of argument presumably signals to the parent that, although the adolescent disagrees, the reasoning is essentially "adult" and, accordingly, treatment as an adult is appropriate.

The study by Smetana (1988) is a major step towards considering mutual cognitions and a provocative base for further research. It would now be feasible, for instance, to put together dyads with different ideas about the same issues and to observe the sequences of argument or negotiation as children or parents proceed to ignore or to build upon the other person's reasons. To any such study, we would wish as well to add information from each family member as to how they thought negotiations should proceed (e.g. the amount of argument that is reasonable, the points at which one party should capitulate or both "agree to disagree"). With such steps, we would be moving closer to the ideal of observing links between ideas and interactions in a situation where the ideas have to do with interactions, where both parties have some knowledge of each others' ideas, where there is some opportunity to challenge or resist the ideas of the other, and where the actions are from more than one family member and involve more than a single act: in effect, where the conditions are closer to those that obtain in everyday parenting.

CHAPTER 6

CONSEQUENCES: EMPHASIS ON CHILDREN

In the previous chapter, we considered consequences for parents, with particular attention to parental affect, parental actions, and interactions between parents and children. In this chapter, we turn to consequences framed primarily in terms of children.

The chapter begins by outlining some of the main bases for interest in children's ideas, and the way these lead to differences in the questions explored. The second section provides a way of grouping the diverse studies in this area, primarily by noting the kinds of ideas and consequences that have usually been studied and the types of hypothesis offered for a connection between the two. The third and fourth sections consider several moves towards strengthening research findings. These cover finer specifications of outcome, the use of multiple measures, and the development of procedures for testing hypotheses about conditions or processes. The final section of the chapter notes two special items for the research agenda. One of these has to do with taking account of children's encounters with the ideas of people outside the family. The other is the question: Can material on consequences for one generation be used to help understand consequences for the other? Do children and parents acquire their ideas about parenting and about families in comparable ways? To the extent that they do, studies of acquisition for the one generation may highlight gaps and possibilities in research with the other.

One general point needs to be noted before we begin. This is that, overall, research on consequences for children is not as yet well integrated, at either the level of data collection or of theory. In part, this is the result of an especially high degree of diversity in the form of research. Some studies, for instance, consider only the correlations between parents' ideas and child outcomes while others consider a number of features (e.g. parents' ideas, actions, education, income, mental health) and ask about their relative contributions. There is, as well, diversity in the measures chosen to cover parents' ideas and child outcomes. Few studies use the same measures, so that replications are scarce. Moreover, measures that would appear similar do not always yield the same results, even within a single study. In a challenging study by Miller (1986), for instance, children's cognitive development was measured by items drawn from I.Q. tests and from Piagetian tasks. Correlations with the accuracy of parents' assessments (predicting whether their children would succeed on a task) were considerably higher for the I.Q. items than for the Piagetian tasks.

Diversity is the case also when one considers hypotheses or assumptions about processes that might underlie a link between ideas and outcomes. In a very broad sense, there is one common hypothesis: A child's acquisition of particular viewpoints or skills is promoted to the extent that parents' ideas give rise to conditions that facilitate acquisition. The conditions seen as facilitating, however, run the whole gamut of theories in developmental psychology: from good fit or low risk to the modeling of strategies, the provision of intellectual challenge in a Piagetian style, and the supply of supports and guided learning in a Vygotskian manner.

Under such circumstances, it is all the more important to be cautious in expecting any simple links between parental ideas and child outcomes. We noted in Chapter 5 that parents' actions are likely to be influenced by multiple factors, with parents' ideas being one of these rather than the sole factor. The status of being a contributing factor is even more pronounced when one comes to linking parents' ideas with child outcomes. Multiple factors and a variety of paths to an outcome must be expected rather than single causes and any simple translation of one idea to one outcome.

REASONS FOR INTEREST IN
CONSEQUENCES FOR CHILDREN

Three general lines of interest need to be distinguished, each giving rise to some particular research designs. The first starts from an *interest in differences among children.* Why, for instance, do Japanese children, even in kindergarten, achieve higher scores on mathematics tests than U.S. children do? Why do males more often choose mathematics as an elective subject in high school than females do? The relevant conditions may then be sought either in the schools or in the expectations and teaching styles of parents. Less cognitive versions of the same starting point may ask: Why are some children abused whereas others are not? Why are some popular and others rejected? Why do some display poor mental health whereas others are more sturdy or less vulnerable? The relevant conditions may be sought in the expectations and standards that parents apply to children or to themselves, or—in the case of popularity—in the ideas that parents have about the way to make friends and the advice they give their children.

This type of approach assumes that parents (usually mothers) make a major difference to a child's development. It also assumes that an important aspect of parents is their view of a child: their definition of a child as a problem, their perception of a child as competent, their sense of the standards a child should reach. On this basis, parents' expectations and perceptions are readily included in the set of conditions considered. Aspects of parenting may, in fact, be the only condition considered, with little data gathered about additional conditions.

The second route starts from *an interest in demographic factors and their effects*. The assumption is that "demographic" or "social" factors make a difference to outcomes for children. These factors may refer to conditions within the family: e.g. the number or spacing of children; the level of income, years of schooling, or type of occupation for mother, father, or the two combined. Increasingly, they refer also to conditions outside the family: e.g. to the opportunities and hazards in particular regions, or to the economic conditions prevailing at a particular time. Attention to demographic factors (e.g. to the occupational level of parents) may be relatively routine, almost an aside in a research report. For some researchers, however, demonstrating and understanding the effects of class, culture, or geographic setting are the primary goals. Attention then turns to the questions: *How* do these demographic factors have an effect upon children? What are the steps or the mediating processes that would account for correlations between, say, socio-economic status (SES) and school achievement? Parents' ideas and actions quickly emerge as possibilities.

Does it matter whether one starts from an interest in demographic factors as against an interest in differences among children? An interest in demographic factors is the more likely to lead to the inclusion of factors outside the family. It is also likely to prompt questions about relative contributions: Do parents' ideas add information that the demographic factors alone would not supply? Is there now more effective prediction to the child outcome than one would gain from, say, considering only socio-economic status or parental education?

The third and final starting point is *an interest in the nature of "transmission", either "cultural transmission" or "inter-generational transmission"*. The starting assumption is that many of our ideas or life-styles are absorbed from others, rather than being entirely constructions from personal experience. The questions then arise: What does "transmission" involve? How does it proceed? By now, the reader will recognise that transmission is especially likely to be of interest to those who take a "social" or a "cultural" view of development. The reader may also anticipate that this line of interest leads to particular attention being given to agreement or lack of agreement between the positions of children and their parents.

SOME WAYS OF GROUPING STUDIES

We have noted that research in this area takes a diversity of forms. We shall produce some order by noting that studies can be grouped in terms of the aspects considered when looking at parents' ideas or child consequences, and the nature of the hypotheses that underlie the research. These groupings help introduce the area and make possible the later and larger section on promising ways forward.

The Kinds of Ideas or Outcomes Considered

Suppose we ignore for the moment the question of whether studies include measures of parents' actions or demographic factors and concentrate upon the two constants: measures of ideas and measures of child outcomes.

On the side of *parents' ideas*, there are essentially two variations. Researchers consider either *content* (e.g. parents' goals or standards for children) or *quality* (e.g. the degree of agreement between parents or the extent to which the information provided by parents is the only information available to a child). Attention to both content and quality within a single study is less common than attention to one or the other.

On the side of *child outcomes*, we may again group measures into two large sets and then distinguish within these. One set deals with *relational outcomes*: e.g. the accuracy of a child's perception of a parent's position, the degree of agreement (perceived or actual) between the child's and the parent's views, or the degree of conflict between parent and child. The larger set of measures considers *outcomes for the child as an individual*. The outlook is essentially child-centred. Within this group, the measures may deal primarily with cognition, social cognition or social adjustment. These three are not necessarily intrinsically different (we would, in fact, argue for interdependence). They have, however, tended to lead to varying measures and to bring out some different hypotheses about the bases of effects.

In research emphasising cognitive effects, for instance, the outcome measures are most often achievement scores (scores on I.Q. tests, Piagetian tasks, or tests for literacy or school achievement) or choices of school subjects (e.g. the choice of mathematics as an elective). Research considering these measures is generally linked to parents' expectations, attributions for success, knowledge about cognitive development, or accuracy in assessing a child's competence. The most frequent assumption is that parents' ideas make a difference by way of actions that match a child's skills or needs, and/or by values and attributions that children internalise and then use to regulate their own actions.

In research emphasising social cognition as an outcome, the outcome measures have to do with a child's understanding of, say, concepts of authority, the difference between rules and social conventions, ways to solve interpersonal problems with peers, or the nature of gender schemas. Research on gender schemas illustrates some common hypotheses about processes, with effects attributed to the models that parents provide by way of their own gender-marked actions or to parents' "social marking" of gender by way of different nouns, pronouns, names, games, activities or dress for boys vs. girls.

In research emphasising social development as the outcome, the measures have to do with social adjustment or with the social skills children display when joining a group or attempting to persuade others to one's point of view. The area has attracted hypotheses about the importance of flexibility in parents' thinking about parental strategies for dealing with social situations. The child may, for instance, benefit from the guidance of mothers who can describe helpful strategies for joining a group and demonstrate their use, or a child may carry over to the classroom—to interactions with teachers especially—approaches used at home and originally practised with parents.

Single or Multiple Hypotheses?

We have noted that research may vary in the original source of interest, in the aspects of parents' ideas considered, in the types of consequences for children that are explored, and in the kind of hypothesis (implicit or explicit) that underlies research. In addition, research in this area varies in the extent to which it is built around a single hypothesis. Studies of cognitive outcomes will provide the examples.

One single-factor hypothesis is the proposal that the optimal condition for cognitive development is the presence of a match between what a parent or teacher expects of a child and what the child can do.

Given this hypothesis, interest then comes to focus on the accuracy of a parent's assessment and the effects of a bias towards expecting more or less than a child can do. The hypothesis is represented in an early study by Hunt and Pareskovopoulos (1980) and a series of later projects summarised by Miller (1988).

A single central hypothesis also underlies a more complex U.S. programme of research (e.g. McGillicuddy-DeLisi, 1982; Sigel & McGillicuddy-DeLisi, 1984). The hypothesis is that children's level of cognitive competence (their representational skill especially) is influenced by the extent to which parents take a "child-centred" view of learning, regarding the child as acquiring knowledge less by direct instruction than by discovery, by the active construction and generalisation of ideas, and by questions that encourage children to take their own knowledge one step further rather than rely on being given an answer. This central hypothesis governs the selection of particular measures for parents' ideas and actions. The analysis is then supplemented by the comparative analysis of predictions from ideas and from actions (e.g. McGillicuddy-DeLisi, 1982), and by attention to several demographic factors such as SES and the number and spacing of children within a family.

In contrast, a more eclectic set of hypotheses underlies two further large programmes. The outcome of concern in both is the child's scholastic achievement, particularly in the area of mathematics. One of these programmes brings together scholars from the U.S. and Japan (the research is summarised in an article by Hess et al., 1980, and is connected also to work in Mexico by Holloway, Gorman, & Fuller, in press). The other brings together scholars from the U.S., China, and Japan (e.g. Bacon & Ichigawa 1988; Chen & Uttal, 1988; Stevenson et al., 1985; Stigler, Lee, Lucker, & Stevenson, 1982). It is connected also to research in Peru by Barber (1988). In both of these large programmes, the decision to consider families is based on the observation that differences in achievement are observed in the earliest grades of school (pointing to effects from sources other than schools). The decision to consider a number of aspects of families and of parents stems from drawing together several viewpoints in developmental psychology: viewpoints describing families as contributing to school success by providing standards, practice in interaction skills that will be useful in school (e.g. ways of dealing with questions or of asking them), direct help (e.g. with homework), and/or attributions that may be internalised and used by the children to regulate their own efforts. The measures used then reflect all these possibilities. Price and Hatano (in press) demonstrate a somewhat similar diversity in their proposal that families may alter cognitive or academic outcomes by serving as forum and audience, by providing apprenticeship or instruction, or by acting on bottlenecks (either removing or mitigating them).

Does it matter whether research uses a single hypothesis about connections or a multiple set? If the goal is to test or extend a particular theory, then working from the single hypothesis will indicate whether or not this theory is relevant. It will also probably add to our understanding of the theory and its range. It will not, however, tell us whether some other theory, or some other factors, might be equally relevant or allow an even stronger prediction. There may be larger fish in the sea.

MOVES TOWARDS STRENGTHENING RESEARCH

We have suggested that research on connections between parents' ideas and child outcomes presents a number of difficulties. To spell them out: (1) the effects, when found, are often not strong, in part because any child outcome is likely to have multiple factors contributing to it; (2) if only one antecedent is considered, the relative strength of the contribution cannot be assessed; (3) if only one outcome is considered, we cannot determine whether the contribution of parents' ideas is unique to that outcome or has a broader impact; (4) the processes by which effects occur are often difficult to establish. These difficulties are similar to some of the problems that in the past have marked the study of intervention programmes, where the designs and measures used have often made it difficult to identify the components of a programme or the processes that have contributed to pupil improvement.

If difficulties were the only story to be told, this chapter would not be a hopeful one. There have, in fact, been a number of moves towards strengthening research.

Attention to the Description of An Antecedent or An Outcome

The antecedent or the outcome considered may be of a single kind. The concern about antecedents, for instance, may be restricted to parents' expectations. The concern about outcomes may be restricted to a child's school achievement or the degree of agreement between a parent's viewpoint and a child's. There are now moves towards making the description both less bald and more amenable to specifying how an outcome comes about or why results may vary from study to study.

Changing the description of parental ideas.   A first kind of change refers to tightening the description. As Price and Hatano (in press) point out, the success of a programme designed to teach children to swim cannot be determined until we know whether the goal is to "drown-proof" a child, turn out a "journeyman swimmer", or produce an Olympic star. One illustration of the value of such tightening comes from a study of the effects of locus of control and the extent to which it predicts mothers' use of health resources and the health of their infants. It turns out that such prediction is possible, but only if the items testing for a sense of control are made highly specific. It is not enough, for instance, to take general control scales or even health control scales. The items need to deal with the control mothers perceive themselves to have over the specific outcomes of pregnancy and birth (Tinsley, 1989; Tinsley & Holtgrave, 1988).

The analysis of parents' "expectations" provides an even sharper example, together with a second move towards changes in description: namely, a move towards asking about the precise nature of expectations and the extent to which a particular idea is represented in a culture. The material comes from comparisons of school achievement in China, Japan, and the U.S.A.

The importance of asking about the precise nature of expectations is brought out especially in a study by Chen and Uttal (1988). Their comparison of mothers in Beijing and in Chicago covered the following measures, each contributing to a more complete picture of cultural differences and a more effective check on factors contributing to achievement:

Attributions for a child's performance at school (mothers rated the relative importance of teachers and parents). The groups differed on this measure: 60% of Chinese mothers believed that the teacher was more important than the parents, compared with 19% of U.S. mothers.

The level of performance that mothers expected from their first, third, and fifth grade children. On a test for which the maximum score is 100, for instance, what score would you expect your child to get? The two groups did not differ in what they expected a child to achieve. On the question asking for an estimate out of 100, for example, both groups expected their child to get a score of 80 to 85.

The mothers' satisfaction with the child's performance at school and, on the hypothetical test, the score she would be satisfied with. The groups differed markedly on this measure. U.S. mothers would be satisfied with a score that averaged 7 points lower than the expected score, Chinese mothers with a score 10 points higher than the score expected. The groups differed also on whether they were satisfied with their child's current performance in school. "Among American mothers, 76% were either very satisfied or satisfied, compared to 36% of the Chinese mothers" (Chen & Uttal, 1988, p.355).

The extent to which mothers perceived their children as liking school or as satisfied with school (a check on whether the only expectations that matter are the mother's). The groups differed again on this measure. Beijing mothers perceived children as more satisfied than did Chicago mothers. In addition, a difference appeared in the extent to which the perception of a child's satisfaction was correlated with the mother's satisfaction (significant for the Chicago mothers, but not for those in Beijing).

The point at which mothers would become concerned if their child's performance was below the average for children at that grade level. Here again a difference emerged. In first grade, Chinese mothers expressed concern about a performance that fell slightly below the mean. In contrast, U.S. mothers were dissatisfied "only when their children's performance was almost one standard deviation lower than the average" (Chen & Uttal, 1988, p.355). By fifth grade, mothers in both samples were alike (they became concerned when their children fell slightly below the average). Mothers in the U.S. sample were apparently willing to accept a slower start. The Chinese mothers were more concerned with children doing well from the start.

In short, different measures of parents' expectations yielded different links to the achievement outcome. As the same kind of array begins to be used in further studies, we shall find ourselves moving towards being more certain about which aspects are critical and what the underlying processes may be.

A different kind of benefit stems from asking about the degree to which a particular expectation is shared by many people in the culture. The clarification in this case has to do with the processes that may account for effects on children. The widespread presence of a viewpoint may not only reinforce parents' views (a "cumulative voice" effect) but also give rise to the child's encountering views that are not the parents' and that offer the child a choice of ways to look at events. The "cumulative voice" effect is the more often emphasised. For students in China, for instance, it is pointed out that performance in competitive examinations has long been the route to positions in the civil service, and that the culture emphasises the importance and the feasibility of improving oneself. In Chen and Uttal's (1988) analysis, one of the basic tenets of Confucianism is the importance of self-regulation: "The Confucian doctrine was cultivate yourself, regulate your family, govern well your state, then govern well the kingdom" (Chen & Uttal, 1988, p.354). When combined with an emphasis on making a start, even if only in a small way, the overall cultural climate presents to the child a picture of the importance both of doing well at school and of the child taking a sizeable degree of reponsibility, by way of effort, for doing so.

Similar general analyses have been offered for Japan. Some of the emphases are the same (Confucianism is common to both). In addition, however, Japanese scholars (e.g. Azuma, 1982; Bacon & Ichikawa, 1988; Hatano, 1982) have pointed to the widespread presence of expectations that each person (adult or child) will aim at the faithful and diligent performance of an assigned task and will accept two particular approaches to learning. One is the view that "from practice comes understanding", a viewpoint that places less value on "advance organisers" than on emerging understanding. The other is the importance given, within and outside the family, to developing habits of concentration and persistence with a task. These expectations and habits, one suspects, might make a particular difference to content areas that do not yield quick rewards, require extensive practice, and can be less driven by an appeal to students being "interested". Mathematics could be such an area.

Changing the Description of a Particular Child Outcome.   We have been dealing with ways to change the description of parental ideas. A second way forward lies in looking carefully at the description of outcomes. Let us stay for the moment with outcomes that have to do with a child's cognitive or social achievements. For examples, we shall turn to a set of studies that contain an interest in gender.

One provocative change comes from Eccles (1986), summarising a programme of research on factors that contribute to the choice of particular school subjects (mathematics especially). The contributing factors explored have been of several kinds: parents' expectations, knowledge, and level of skill in mathematics; parents' and adolescents' perceptions of the relevance, appropriateness and degree of effort required for boys vs. girls; and the actual level of achievement in mathematics (often more similar for boys and girls than are the perceptions of relevance or the need for effort). Eccles (1986) argues that it is essential to consider females' infrequent specialisation in mathematics as *choice* rather than as avoidance (the usual interpretation). This re-interpretation directs attention to students' goals, to the options that are available, and to the attractiveness of some school subjects. English, for instance, may appeal not only because it is seen as more appropriate or easier for females, but also because it is the more effective route to the goal of a high aggregate mark. On such grounds, attention to the choice of mathematics only, without attention to other choices, is likely to be insufficient (Eccles, 1986).

The child's acquisition of gender schemas supplies the second example of expansions to descriptions of a particular kind of outcome. The expansion is from Lloyd and Duveen (1990). It takes the interesting form of distinguishing among steps towards an outcome, rather than taking an outcome (social skill, school achievement, etc.) as varying only in degree. In essence, Lloyd and Duveen regard a child as entering into a social system that calls for coming to know a variety of signs and signals and for demonstrating one's understanding. Entry is first achieved in contexts which offer the child some "scaffolding" and then demonstrated "independently of context" (Lloyd & Duveen, 1990, p. 43). The research considers the extent to which children aged 18 months to 4 years display gender-marking in their use of toys in action play (regarded as a scaffolded situation) and in tasks such as pretend play or sorting photographs of people and toys into groups: "settings which offer little or no perceptual support" (p. 42). Gender differentiation was far more marked in action play than in pretend play or in sorting. In action play, apparently, the actual toys remind children of the difference between boys' and girls' activities, and boys especially come to feel that "it is imperative . . . to mark a difference" (Lloyd & Duveen , 1990, p. 43)

Changing the Description of Agreement Outcomes.   The simplest approach to studies of agreement is to ask if parents and their children give the same answers when asked for their views on important qualities to acquire, the best occupations to choose, or the sources of success either socially or academically. One may then elaborate by asking whether the agreement is greater or less for attributions for success vs. failure, for some school subjects rather than others, for same-sex vs. opposite sex pairs, for pre-adolescent vs. adolescent children. For some representative studies, the reader may note research by Alessandri and Wozniak (1987), Cashmore and Goodnow (1985), Holloway, Hess, Azuma, and Kashiwagi (in press), and Miyamoto (1984). Similarity between parents and grandparents—a less explored pairing—is represented in research by Frankel and Roer-Bornstein (1982).

The value of considering more than one form of agreement is brought out with particular clarity by a study by Block (1972). The younger generation consisted of students who joined protest marches or freedom rides, took part in industrial action and were, in general, "activists", often at cost to other interests. On the surface, there was no correspondence between this life-style and that of their parents. There was often, however, agreement between the two generations at a more general level. Though the area of commitment varied, both generations valued being involved and "full-on" rather than being lukewarm, staying on the sidelines, or limiting oneself to some average degree of effort or concern. In effect, the two generations shared a quality of commitment.

A similar lesson may be learned from a study by Smetana (1988). The surface agreement in this case has to do with whether parents and adolescents agree on whether parents have the right to make rules about moral issues (e.g. stealing) and about more personal issues (e.g. one's choice of friends, or cleaning one's room). Agreement occurred for moral issues, but not for personal issues (Smetana, 1988). The same study, however, added attention to agreement in the form or level of reasoning used to reach a decision. Where the two generations both used fairly sophisticated reasoning, there was less conflict within the family even though the two generations held different views.

An aspect of description to which we would draw particular attention consists of a distinction between actual agreement and perceived agreement. In actual agreement, the two parties in fact hold the same views. In perceived agreement, one or both assumes agreement when this is not actually the case. The distinction is accompanied by the argument that actual agreement involves two steps (an accurate perception of the other's position and its acceptance), and by the proposal that different conditions and processes may be involved in the two forms of agreement or in the two steps (Furstenberg, 1971; Cashmore & Goodnow, 1985). Accurate perception, for instance, may be most strongly influenced by the clarity of the signal being given by the other. Cashmore and Goodnow (1985), for example, note that children's accurate knowledge of parents' positions (but not their actual agreement) is predicted by agreement between parents, and by the issue being one that parents are likely to have verbalised (e.g. the importance of being neat or obedient as against the importance of being honest, considerate, or anxious about how things work). In similar fashion, Alessandri and Wozniak (1987) find that the accuracy with which fathers can predict a child's response in a number of hypothetical situations increases when children—sons especially—move into adolescence. They suggest that the increase in accuracy stems from the father's becoming more involved in the adolescent's challenge to the mother's authority or to family rules.

The strength or clarity of the signal, the redundancy in a parental message, the salience of the issue, the extent to which information is managed or kept from either generation—all these seem likely to affect the accuracy of perception. What then affects actual agreement, after perception is accurate? The answer, it is proposed, lies in conditions such as the individual's vested interest in agreeing, in the warmth of the relationship, or the closeness of identification (Furstenberg, 1971; Cashmore & Goodnow, 1985). These conditions, warmth especially, have often been proposed as influencing actual agreement, but the empirical data have not been supportive. The distinctions between perceived and actual agreement may point to part of the problem. No matter how warm the relationship, actual agreement will not occur unless the position one adopts is based on an accurate perception of the other person's views. In effect, the finer definition of what agreement refers to not only produces clearer data but also helps bring out new hypotheses about the nature of the processes involved.

Using Multiple Measures of Antecedents and Outcomes

We turn now to a second way in which research on child outcomes is being strengthened. Since we have given the larger share of attention to cognitive development to date, let us take our examples in this section from studies that concentrate on social development or combine attention to both cognitive and social outcomes.

For Social Skills as Outcomes.   As an example, we shall take a study by Krasnor (cited by Rubin et al., in press). Outcome measures came from observing children's interactions in preschools to determine their goals, their strategies, and the outcomes of their strategies, and from asking teachers to rate each child's social competence. Mothers' ideas were checked by first distinguishing three kinds of social skill (making friends, sharing possessions, and leading or influencing others). For each of these, mothers were asked for ratings of importance and attributions for difficulty. Each attribution for failure was followed by a question about how difficult it would be for parents to change that state of affairs. Finally, mothers were asked what they should or should not do to help their child learn the three social skills, with the main coding of strategies being in terms of whether they involved information seeking or planning vs. power assertion (low, medium, or high).

From the complex matrix of results that this study allows, we select the following:

● Children rated by observers and teachers as socially competent were likely to have mothers who rated all three social skills as important, and who attributed occasions of low social competence to factors external to the child (e.g lack of previous opportunity or of parental teaching). The combination of these aspects, rather than any of them singly, seems to provide the optimal prediction.

● The analysis of observed strategies suggested that children were carrying over strategies developed with mothers. The children of mothers who suggested the use of high-power strategies to improve children's social skills, for instance, tended to be rated as fearful and anxious by teachers and, in their interactions with others, to use strategies that were unassertive and adult-oriented (for the majority of their classroom interactions the teachers were the target). In contrast, children who were more sensitive and independent in classroom interactions tended to have mothers who proposed effective strategies for themselves. These children also chose peers as targets for interaction more often than they did teachers. By and large, what appears to be carried over is not so much the model that the mother provides but the kind of behaviour, and the expectations of influence, that the child has practised with the mother. These classroom interactions, it should be noted, hold the potential of allowing still further elaboration. The analysis to date combines interactions with teachers and with peers, and the appearance of carry-over may reflect the high frequency, for several groups of children, of interactions with teacher as the target. A different type of carry-over could emerge when classroom interactions with peers are separated from interactions with teachers, and when data become available on children's usual interactions with siblings as well as mothers.

For Cognitive and Social Outcomes.   Two large research programmes, both longitudinal in design, will provide examples of what can be learned from using multiple measures. In essence, both these programs bring out the greater predictability to date of cognitive as against social competence. The second adds as well the need to consider parents' ideas as influencing child development by virtue of their adding to the weight of a set of risk factors rather than by some unique role.

The greater predictability of academic vs. social competence appears first of all in a programme directed by Earl Schaefer (Schaefer, 1987, provides a summary). The antecedent measures cover mothers' interactions with children (observed when the children are aged 4 and 12 months), the mother's ideas about child-rearing and education, her values, and her "parental modernity" (essentially a willingness to grant rights and self-direction to children), and measures of mother's intelligence and, for both parents if present, education and occupation. The intercorrelations among these measures (a necessary check but one not always made) are significant, suggesting that they are "each indicators of the cultural or psychosocial environment of the family" (Schaefer, 1987, p. 378).

The measures of child development come from teacher ratings when the children are in kindergarten. Factor analyses of the several scales showed the need to differentiate two forms of competence: academic and social. The former covers not only verbal intelligence but also curiosity/creativity, task-orientation (e.g. distractibility), and dependency when faced with tasks. The latter covers behaviours oriented more directly towards people (withdrawal/sociability, extraversion/introversion, considerateness/hostility). Academic competence but not social competence at age 5 years was predicted by the mother's ideas and behaviours when children were aged 12 months. Predictability, one may note, was also higher for white than for black children in the sample, for whom the psychosocial environment was also less stable than for white children ($r = 0.57$ from infancy to kindergarten vs. $r = 0.72$).

A similar result appears in a report by Sameroff and Feil (1985) of results emerging from a large longitudinal study . The starting point of the research was an interest in the nature of "risk" in development. This led to considering both cognitive and social outcomes, and to considering a variety of factors such as mother's mental health and SES, along with family size, race, and the sex of the child. Mothers' ideas were considered in terms of their quality, on the assumption that the most effective parent may be the one who can think in "perspectivistic" fashion about a child's behavior. In essence, perspectivistic thinking involves seeing a problem as having several causes rather than a single base such as "all my fault", "all the child's fault", or "all the fault of the other parent". Such thinking is regarded as allowing the parent to achieve both some emotional distance from an immediate interaction and some flexibility in action through being able to frame a problem in several ways. In a first analysis, academic and social competence emerged as having different predictors. Parents' ideas made an independent contribution to intelligence scores but not to social competence scores, while parental mental health made an independent contribution to social competence scores but not to child intelligence scores.

A later report by Sameroff et al. (1987) restricts itself to intelligence test scores but includes the quality of parents' ideas within a more complete set of regression analyses. The analyses cover 10 risk factors: mothers' quality of thought ("parents' perspectives"), mental health, anxiety, education, occupation, minority status, and observed interactions with the child (scored mainly for spontaneity), together with family size, family support (father present or not), and the number of stressful life events encountered during the past four years.

The first major result is a linear trend between *the number of risk factors* and a child's score. The second is that the risk factors fall into five clusters, each with 2, 3, or 4 risk factors. The factor of mothers' perspectives is represented in only one of these clusters, linked to minority status and mother's education. This particular cluster, however, is no more strongly linked to a difference in IQ scores than is any other cluster, pointing once more to its being "not any single variable but the combination of multiple variables that reduced the child's intellectual performance" (Sameroff et al., 1987, p.347). For anyone planning research in links between parents' ideas and child outcomes, the challenge is now to determine not only the relative contribution of parents' ideas in relation to other factors but also to determine whether this contribution is unique in kind as against achieving its effects by being an addition to a set of factors already present.

So far, we have emphasised statistical analysis as a way of dealing with a multiplicity of antecedents and outcomes. An alternative or additional procedure is the exploration of typologies. We shall take as an example some proposals from Elias and Ubriaco (1986). They consider a complex set of antecedents (covering parents' ideas, parents' practices, and family interactions) and two main outcomes: the child's adjustment in second grade (rated by teachers) and the child's ability to solve a number of social-cognitive problems described by the researchers (e.g. coping with rejection by peers or wanting something that a peer has).

The several antecedents are seen as giving rise to some general family styles that then influence outcomes (styles labelled "firm", "warm", "agree", and "apart"). The child of the prototypical "firm" family, for instance, was rated as extremely well-adjusted in school, but she emerged as relatively weak on the interpersonal problems and displayed an external locus of control. The child of the "warm" family was rated as satisfactory in social behaviour by teachers but scored high on the social problem-solving tasks: tasks in which she focussed on feelings and on solutions by way of mutual compromise. The child of the "agree" family (few guidelines were made explicit and an appearance of consensus was imposed) was rated by teachers as poor in self-control and low on positive mood. He was, however, above average on social problem solving with peers. The child of the "apart" family (highly discordant beliefs and little "togetherness" in actions) was rated as adequate in general behaviour by teachers but received a very low score on the social problem-solving tasks, largely because of a preference for wishful or magical thinking.

This type of approach brings out again the value of using more than one measure of outcome and the need to ask why predictions might be better to one outcome than to another. The teachers' ratings and the child's scores on the problem-solving tasks could clearly be discrepant, and hypotheses can now be constructed as to why and when the two measures might coincide or be different. The approach brings out as well the need to locate some ways of describing the general ambience or quality of a family, either by noting the degree to which parents agree in their ideas, the kinds of problem solution they model or allow the child to practise, the orientation that one or both parents take towards the outside world (e.g. Reiss et al., 1983), or, as Hess and Handel (1959) proposed in an earlier approach to family analysis and typologies, by isolating some particular family themes around which parents build images, activities, family myths and family stories.

Testing the Nature of the Connection

The previous two sections dealt with ways to strengthen the measures of antecedents and outcomes. We turn now to ways of strengthening tests for the nature of the connection between parental ideas and child outcomes. One way of doing so has already emerged in the previous section: namely, testing the nature of the connection by asking: Is the contribution of parents' ideas unique or additive and exchangeable? We now wish to follow that question with others. Two of these follow from the first: What are the effects of factors outside the family? What is the nature of the child's contribution? The remaining questions are especially concerned with testing the validity or the range of a proposed connection: Are the results artefacts? Do test cases or contrasting cases provide support or challenge? Do experimental variations or longitudinal studies support the connection indicated by correlations?

Checking Additive Effects: Cumulative Risk, Cumulative Voice.   The results reported by Sameroff et al. (1987) point to parents' ideas influencing child outcomes more by their quantitative contribution to the weight of a set of factors than by the unique influence of ideas.

This kind of contribution warrants careful consideration and inclusion in future analyses. To it, we would add a hypothesis, which we shall label "cumulative voice". It refers to the possibility that parents' ideas gain power by virtue of being one of a set of viewpoints that reinforce or supplement one another. This type of connection underlies the concern of Holloway et al. (1988) that some groups of Mexican children may be exposed to two views of the world: one from their parents, one from their teachers. The result need not be that so often feared: namely, confusion on the child's part. Children seem to be adept, as many adults also are, at living in more than one social world. What seems likely to happen, however, is that the strength of the parents' message may be diminished, leading to its lesser acceptance, or to its acceptance as relevant only for some domains (e.g. parents are seen as having something reasonable to say about family life, but teachers know about school life, and peers know about social relationships).

Is there any empirical data on the effects of cumulative voice upon the ideas children come to hold? An interesting example of what may happen when parents' positions lose their monopoly status is provided by Siegal and Storey (1985). Among children in a day-care centre, the "old hands" (those who had for a longer period received a mixture of home-care and centre-care) displayed an earlier understanding of the difference between moral rules and social conventions than did the "new arrivals". The former group had apparently benefited from the range of information provided by parents, centre staff, and peers. Processes related to the monopoly vs. plurality status of an idea, it should be noted, are not limited to social cognition. We suspect that they are especially important for any achievement that is particularly helped by exposure to more than one point of view. Learning to take the perspective of another is such an achievement. So also, in a more classically cognitive outcome, is breaking up an old way of looking at a problem. In both cases, one might anticipate that exposure only to parents' ideas—only to situations where parents' ideas have the quality of being a monopoly—will lead to a lower level of understanding on the child's side.

A second and quite different example of considering agreement among several voices comes from Deal, Halvorson, and Wampler (1989). They start by noting that agreement between parents is often regarded as having a positive effect on family dynamics and child outcomes. Seldom considered, however, is the extent to which parents who agree with one another are likely to be also effective parents and—the point of particular interest to us—parents who hold ideas similar to those of many other parents. Parents who agree with one another turn out to display both these features, with the latter (agreement with the group) suggesting that "parental agreement is not so much a within-family variable . . . but rather an issue of agreement to the (common) standard. The couple agrees not just with each other, but with a common culture that goes beyond the couple" (Deal et al., 1989, p.1032). This wider agreement may then also be a critical factor in accounting for why the children of agreeing parents in this sample displayed fewer behavioural problems. The test sample, as the authors note, would be parents who agree with one another but not with the general culture: a sample less easy to find than most, especially when a sample consists of volunteers. The design and the results nonetheless open a novel and a larger way of considering agreement or cumulative voice within the family and beyond it.

Considering Factors Within and Outside the Family.   Are parental or family factors always critical? The concepts of cumulative risk and cumulative voice have already suggested that parents and their characteristics may not be the only factors that should be considered if we are to build a satisfactory account of child outcomes. Conditions outside the family—from support systems to economic conditions—are increasingly recognised in the developmental literature as influencing development. How does this type of recognition emerge in research on parents' ideas and consequences for children?

One kind of recognition takes the form of including a parent's tie to the outside world as a factor that influences ideas and/or outcomes. This recognition is particularly sharp in studies that explore settings where children may be exposed to conditions that are outside the knowledge of parents, and beyond their expertise. What happens when children's experiences go beyond their parents, when the children, for instance, speak the language of the new country but the parents do not, or when the children are literate and the parents are not? Wagner and Spratt (1988) provide an example. Conditions in Morocco, they note, provide a way of testing the possibility that "since most of the children . . . were engaged in an endeavor unfamiliar to their non-literate and little-educated parents, the attitudes they acquired from their parents might be especially susceptible to experiences encountered outside the family" (p. 365). The lack of overlap in experience undoubtedly contributed to the lack of agreement between first-grade children and their parents (mothers or fathers) when asked about the characteristics and habits likely to produce a good reader of Arabic (characteristics such as speaking Berber or Arabic at home, habits such as reading silently or aloud, alone or in a group). The difference in experience probably contributed also to the finding that parents' ideas about the characteristics of a good reader were less strong as predictors of a child's reading level than were children's ideas.

Exploring the Child's Contribution.   Considering factors outside the family is one way of acting on the possibility that parents' ideas may not be the only critical factor influencing children. A further expression of the same possibility lies in attention to the child's own contribution. The ways that are particularly relevant to the influence of parents' ideas probably have to do with children's perceptions of their parents' ideas or intentions, and their evaluations of these as reasonably justified, accurate, or comprehensible: perceptions and evaluations that may be influenced by the child's general cognitive capacity, his or her direct experience, and the presence of cultural stereotypes.

A nice example of a contribution from the general quality of a child's thinking is reported by Pederson and Gilby (1986) for the concepts of family reported by parents (mothers and fathers) and their preschool children (aged 3 or 4). Ideas about what constituted a family were tested by asking children to name the people in their family, to construct an imaginary family by putting together various figures, and to say whether a given grouping of people was considered to be family. We shall concentrate on the last measure. It generated only one item showing clear agreement: Mr. Smith, living alone, was not a family for either parents or children. In the children's eyes, to be a family required a common residence, two parents, a child, and—for a number of children—more than one child. Pederson and Gilby (1986) attribute the lack of agreement with parents' judgments as based on the child's lower level of cognitive skill. These children, however, were all in two-parent families: an experiential factor that may have contributed to their sense that being a family requires two parents.

Experience is certainly suggested by a report showing that Australian third-graders hold views both like and unlike those of their parents about many aspects of work around the house. The two generations agreed, for instance, about which jobs you should not ask others to do (it is O.K., for instance, to ask another to set the table when it is usually your job, but it is not reasonable to ask them to make your bed or put away toys or books you have used). They did not agree, however, on whether it is reasonable to be paid for making one's bed. Parents did not consider money payments as appropriate. Third-graders (but not sixth- or ninth-graders) considered it reasonable, mainly on the grounds that this is "a big job". Australian third-graders, unlike children in later grades, are seldom involved in any negotiations with parents about money for jobs, and even pocket money at this age is often a non-event. In effect, the children's experience with money and its connections with work is extremely limited, and the family rules have not yet been made explicit to them. Under these circumstances, children's ideas may well be based on criteria quite different from those of their parents (Warton & Goodnow, in press).

The third and last factor to be noted with regard to the child's interpretation and the factors influencing it has to do with cultural stereotypes. The data with most impact come from studies of abuse: an area where parents' actions and the justifications they offer would seem both difficult to comprehend and especially likely to invite negative interpretations on the child's part. In fact, children may find physical abuse or emotional coldness more comprehensible if such action comes from the father than from the mother, and may find reasonable from fathers but not from mothers the justification that distance and lack of involvement in the family are a result of a positive concern for contributing by involvement in paid work (Herzberger & Tennen, 1986).

Testing for Artefacts   Especially in areas where odd distributions of scores are likely to be encountered, concern about artefacts is inevitable. A cautionary tale comes from Miller (1986). After noting some sizeable correlations between the accuracy of mother's assessments of children and children's actual performance (the r values ranged from 0.47 to 0.85), he took the exemplary precaution of asking what the size of the correlations would be if one constructed random mother-child pairs. The step was based on noting mother's tendencies towards giving optimistic appraisals. The result is neatly stated by Miller (1986, p.283): "The fact that the correlations for randomised mother-child pairs were as high as those for actual mother-child pairs certainly suggests caution in interpreting the accuracy scores as measures of maternal insight."

Searching for Test Cases or Contrasting Cases. Hypotheses about connections invite, very appropriately, attention to test cases. These may not disconfirm a hypothesis but they may indicate limits to the range of ages or settings to which a particular hypothesis applies. Two ways of proceeding may be noted. In one, school grade is varied to provide a test case. In the other, geographic region is varied.

One test case highlights the possibility that particular conditions will have varying effects in different school grades. The study by Wagner and Spratt (1988) tests for the effects of parental characteristics on children in first, third, and fifth grade. It asks for parents' opinions about the duties of parents and children, the involvement of parents in helping with school work, and the place of traditional values about marriage or the involvement of women in paid work. In regression analyses (parental opinions entered first), these attitudes accounted for a fairly steady proportion of the variance in reading scores (10% in first grade, 12% in third grade, 8% in fifth grade). In contrast, school grade brought changes in the size of the additional variance explained by background factors (region, home language, SES, parental education). In the three grades, these accounted respectively for 9%, 1%, and 1% of the additional variance. Parental positions emerge as having the more steady influence.

Varying school grades is a technique employed also in another case (Bacon & Ichikawa, 1988), designed to test whether Japanese students' superiority in school performance (as compared with students in the U.S.A.) stems from family factors (high maternal expectations, parental insistence on work rather than play) and/or from more structured classrooms. Both types of hypothesis, the researchers note, derive from studies of children in primary school, but none of them seems to fit well with the case of kindergarteners. They do not fit, for instance, reports of Japanese mothers as especially indulgent of their children up to the age of 6 years, or reports of Japanese kindergartens as relaxed and play-oriented. Nonetheless, Japanese kindergarteners outperform U.S. children in mathematics (but not in reading).

The Bacon and Ichikawa (1988) study proceeds to verify the difference in achievement scores for children in Sendai and Minneapolis-St.Paul and, by observation techniques, the less structured and more play-oriented approach of Sendai kindergartens. It also proceeds to an analysis of parental expectations, finding differences between the two groups. The differences in expectations, however, are not in line with earlier hypotheses about the bases to superiority in mathematics. For instance, more U.S. mothers consider that kindergartens should supply academic experience (18% vs. 3%); fewer U.S. mothers mention the importance of kindergartens assisting children's social and emotional development (55% vs. 92%); more of the U.S. mothers also consider it appropriate to reward kindergarten children for doing well in school (83% vs. 11%) and to have homework assigned (60% of U.S. mothers would object vs. 93% of Japanese mothers).

Overall, Bacon, and Ichikawa (1988, p.381) comment, "what emerges . . . is a picture of Japanese mothers with lower expectations and lower levels of involvement in their children's education than their American counterparts." What could then account for the Japanese children's superiority in mathematics? Bacon and Ichikawa (1988) suggest that the answer may lie in the more realistic expectations of Japanese mothers. When asked, in a study by Stevenson, Lee, and Stigler (1988) to rate their children's cognitive abilities in comparison with other children of the same ages, Japanese mothers were closer to the average than were those of U.S. mothers. These more realistic expectations, Bacon and Ichikawa (1988) suggest, may produce a more effective style of mother-child interaction. Alternately, they propose, Japanese mothers may be particularly skilled at "sustaining a child's interest in a task", a hypothesis emphasised by Hess et al. (1986) and applicable to the difference between mathematics and reading skills if one assumes that mathematics calls for more sustained interest than reading does. The extension to kindergarten has clearly provided a major challenge to hypotheses that fitted very well the first round of results from higher grades in school.

Changing the geographic region provides another way of testing the limits for any particular hypothesis about the influence of parental factors. As an example, we shall take research by Barber (1988). Peru, she notes, provides "a unique opportunity . . . to examine families with similar genetic and cultural heritage in vastly different environmental contexts" (Barber, 1988, p. 370). The one group of Indians (Quechua-speakers) may be found in their native highlands and in two regions to which they have migrated: the jungle and the shanty towns of Lima.

The measures of outcome were the children's scores on reading and mathematics achievement tests, given in Spanish (the language of school instruction) to children in two age groups (6-8 years, 9-12 years). The antecedent measures covered parental expectations for the child and parental teaching practices. Further measures covered parents' descriptions of the child's daily life. The results of particular interest for this section have to do with the extent to which the three regions fit an expected statistical path for effects on the child's achievement scores. In this path, home quality and father's education affect achievement both directly and also indirectly through parental teaching style and help with homework. The model holds only for one region: the highlands. In this region, the combined factors account for 16% of the variance in achievement, compared with 5% for the Lamas jungle setting and 2% for Lima. In the highlands region also, home quality (often considered as a summary expression of expectations and resources) had a direct effect on parent teaching behaviour and parental help with schoolwork, as well as on achievement (Barber, 1988, p. 375). These differential effects by region are attributed to the place parental factors occupy in relation to other influences. In Lamas, parental factors are offset by the poor conditions for learning (the families spend most of the week on distant farms and return to the village on weekends, with the children expected to help from a young age). In Lima, parental factors are offset by the children's wide exposure to "numerous socialising agents and situations in addition to those provided by their parents" (Barber, 1988, p.376).

Going Beyond Correlations: Longitudinal and Experimental Variations. This is the sixth and final way by which researchers are attempting to test the nature of connections between parents' ideas and child outcomes. Correlations, as is well known, do not tell us about the direction of effects. One move towards overcoming this limitation consists of longitudinal studies. We have noted some of these throughout this chapter and in Chapter 4. Others are underway in several places (Minneapolis: Collins; North Carolina: McCubbin; Seville: Palacios, Gonzalez, and Moreno; Sydney: Antill, Russell, and Goodnow; Waterloo: Rubin and Mills).

A further move away from correlations is to determine whether altering parents' ideas makes a difference to children's development. Parent education programmes, for instance, have aimed at changing parents' sense of being able to influence a child's academic or cognitive skills and the methods they then use to do so (e.g. Radin, 1972). Interventions within therapy have aimed at persuading parents that they are capable of coping with a problem (the child need not be completely turned over to professionals), "normalising" a child's behaviour (e.g. demonstrating that it is part of normal growth), and bringing parents to see a child as a new life rather than as a reminder of their past experiences as children (Sameroff & Fiese, in press). Such interventions are not usually seen as experimental studies. They do, however, provide a way of going beyond correlational data in order to test hypotheses about connections between the ideas parents hold and the way children develop.

RESEARCH AGENDA: FROM PARENT TO CHILD?

The items selected for special attention are related to ways of including influences other than parents' ideas, and to the question noted at the start of the chapter: namely, what does the analysis of consequences for children suggest for research on consequences for parents? Both questions are ways of breaking away from some standard features to the analysis of consequences, namely: restricting the analysis only to influences within the family, and considering effects only in terms of one person's direct impact upon another.

Combining Encounters with Ideas Within and Outside the Family

The importance of parents' ideas for children should not obscure the presence of children's experiences outside the family and to people other than parents. Attention to parents' ideas seems often to be based on the assumption that children's encounters with the social world always involve parents acting as gate-keepers, introducers, interpreters or buffers. Parents often do act in these ways. There are also circumstances, however, in which the child's experience is not filtered through the family and may exceed that of its parents. We noted earlier in the chapter settings where the child is literate or speaks the language of the new country while the parent does not. In addition, children may readily become more computer-literate than their parents are, and more knowledgeable about current forms of slang, popular music, sport, dress, or dating behaviour. In effect, the circumstances for child expertise being greater than that of parents' are not limited to exotic cultures.

How could one proceed to take account of encounters within and outside the family? The first step we would advocate has to do with adding to the metaphor most often used to describe any interweaving: namely, the metaphor of "embedding". By "embedding" we refer to concepts that place children at the centre of a series of expanding circles: child in family, family in community, community in a larger region or culture etc. That metaphor may fit a number of circumstances. It does not, however, fit all of them, and it provides little place for the child's direct contacts outside the family. Are there then alternatives to the concept or metaphor of embedding? One consists of substituting, at the level of metaphor, the image of "triangles", with the three points representing children, parents and the community. This image might better represent the child's direct access to people and institutions outside the family, with events then interpreted without the filtering views of parents (Goodnow, 1979). A second possiblity, already suggested in this chapter, lies in asking whether the ideas of people inside and outside the family amount to a "cumulative voice", operating in a fashion similar to that proposed for cumulative risk.

A further possibility consists of exploring parents' ideas about the child's outside experiences, or about the place of the community and state. Whiting (1980), for instance, has suggested that the most important actions taken by parents—important in the sense of having the most impact on children—have to do with the assignment of children to various niches or settings in a society: from creches and centres to private schools, apprenticeships, helping sell produce in the market, or tending animals. Each of these settings has flow-on effects upon the people children encounter, their opportunities for play with peers, and their opportunities to acquire informal cognitive skills. What we do not know are the expectations parents have of these various settings, the degree of influence they feel they have over what happens in them, and the way parents respond to a lack of match between their expectations and what they perceive as happening. Nor do we know much about the inferences children draw from a parent's approach to placement in settings: approaches that may vary from a quick throw into the deep end to a cautious series of transitional activities and transitional placements.

In related fashion, it would be of value to consider the ideas people hold about their responsibilities in comparison with those of the neighbourhood, the school, or the state. We bring up this point because of the concern that parents often feel about the state's direct access to children (medical advice for minors, separate legal representation, sex education at schools), and because of the tension implicit in the right of the state to essentially repossess a child by declaring the child neglected or abused, or the parent as unfit. We bring it up also because this is an area where the child's experiences outside the family may result in an altered view of the importance of parents and the validity or force of their ideas. To take an example provided by Margaret Steward (personal communication), clinicians often feel that one of the most damaging consequences to experience in Family Courts is the child's recognition that parents have more limited power than the children thought they had. That kind of consequence to a particular interweaving of experiences within and outside the family is well worth pursuing.

Consequences for Children and for Parents: Comparable Processes?

In many ways, the appeal of considering consequences for children, and the tendency to see parents as defined only by a concern with children, have led to more research attention to consequences for children than to consequences for parents. Where consequences for both have been considered, the emphasis has fallen on the effects that parents and children have upon one another. We would certainly argue that children affect parents just as much as parents affect children, and that there is a need to develop an effective account of interaction effects, especially as they change over time. We would also propose a question that sidesteps the issue of direct impact, and takes the more conceptual form. Do consequences for parents and children take similar forms? Do they come about by the same routes? Among the specific questions one might ask are these:

1. *Does departing from the mainstream have a similar impact?* The specific case for children has to do with behaviour that follows the choice of mathematics as an elective. For adolescent girls, the choice of mathematics at any advanced level is often accompanied by a choice of friends who are academically average (Buescher & Olzewski, 1987). These associates apparently confer a "normal" or "average" quality on the maths-elector. Maths-electing boys, in contrast, tend to associate with boys who are at their same level in other areas. Male stars can freely associate with other stars, without attracting the label of "freak". The study is based on a U.S. sample and it would be of interest to see if the same forms of outcome occur in countries (China, for instance) where the gender-marking of mathematics is reported to be less strong than it is for adolescents in the U.S.A.

Do similar ripple effects or cover-up effects apply also to parents? We might well expect, for instance, that similar effects may be found for parents who "dare to be different": fathers who take over the "maternal" role, for instance, mothers who are the economic mainstays of their families, or mothers who voluntarily "yield" the custody of children to the father. Research on the consequences of parents taking a different view or a different direction from the mainstream appears to be scarce.

2. *Do similar routes or processes occur in the acquisition or modification of ideas?* Children and adults certainly vary in several ways: in their exposure to cumulative voice effects, for instance, and in

the likelihood of past experience (e.g. the experience of having been part of an earlier family) influencing the interpretation of a present situation.

There are, however, similarities that need exploring. One is the presence of second-order sources. Fathers have several times been noted as possibly gaining their ideas about children through mothers (e.g. Backett, 1982; Klein, 1965). However, at least one observer, Cohen (1981), has commented on a similar effect for children. They may gain, she notes, many of their ideas about fathers from their mothers' interpretations of a father's behaviour, especially when the father is absent for long parts of the day or for months at a time. Cohen's (1981) report takes special note of the "father-gilding" that often occurs in such circumstances, with the child being assured that the father will certainly be interested in hearing what is happening to the child in addition to the father being briefed on questions to ask.

The similarity that we regard as least explored has to do with socialisation into a role or into an identity. There is an odd difference between the amount of attention given to a child's socialisation into the family, or into the role of child, and that given to a parent's socialisation into the role of parent. Except in a legal sense, we do not "become" parents overnight. It is a developmental process, inevitably influenced by experiences with children (our own and others') and by the way other adults prepare us for the role and remind us of what is expected. Nonethless, there is not, for instance, the close attention given to the processs of acquiring notions about being a mother, or a father, or a generic parent that scholars have given, say, to a child's acquisition of gender identities and gender schemas.

Where could one start? One possibility is to begin with the accounts offered by Lloyd and Duveen for the young child's acquisition of gender schemas (e.g. Lloyd, 1987; Lloyd & Duveen, 1990; Duveen & Lloyd, in press). Their analysis, as we noted earlier, pays particular attention to (1) the ways in which adults (mothers and teachers) mark gender for children by their choice of toys, the way they respond to the infant's activity, the styles of play they choose; and (2) the steps by which the child comes to participate in the gender system (e.g. their choice and use of toys or clothing, their use of names). Children demonstrate gender marking in their practical activities, for instance, before they come to describe themselves in terms of gender or before they can easily apply gender differentiations to all the people they meet or to photographs of people.

What are the equivalent steps into the acceptance and use of mother/father distinctions or parent/non-parent distinctions? On becoming a parent, does one immediately become more interested than before in knowing whether other people are parents or not? Does this salience develop slowly? Does it develop differentially, in the sense that, say, mothers use a parent/non-parent schema more readily than fathers do (who wants more to know if a person newly met has children or not?), or in the sense that for all people the characteristic of having children or not is more salient when women, rather than men, are considered?

Some of the steps towards becoming a parent may be found in relatively anecdotal accounts of how people (mostly women) experience, at different points in their lives, the sense of being a parent (e.g. Gravenhorst, 1988). What we would particularly like to find is evidence of the way other people mark for new parents the difference between being a parent or non-parent, or being a mother vs. being a father, in the way that has been done for children being inducted into the gender system. Others do mark the differences for us, not only by the way they treat us but also by their comments about the future ("Wait until your children . . .", "This is just the calm before the storm" etc.). The sharpest signs of such marking, however, may need to be sought in circumstances where becoming a parent does not follow the route so often noted in stories, television, or observations of one's own parents. That comment is based on the account provided to us of the experiences of a woman whose child was born with Down's Syndrome. She was promptly innundated by visits from special nurses, social workers, and members of various helping associations. Both before and after leaving the hospital, she received invitations to join various groups so that she would know what to expect and how to cope with it. The crowning point came when someone actually said, "Now that you're a Down's Syndrome mother . . ." with the implication that this was now the woman's one and only identity. The process of induction into the identity of parent and into schemas about parenting may need first to be observed in such special cases, or in cases where parents depart from the established roles and schemas. Induction and change—for becoming the kind of parent or child one is supposed to be and for holding the kinds of ideas that one is supposed to hold—apply, however, to all parents and all children, and need to be studied for both generations if we are to understand the processes involved, for either generation, in the acquisition or modification of ideas about individual development or family life.

CHAPTER 7

CONCLUDING COMMENTS

In this brief closing chapter we set ourselves two aims. One is to pick up some methodological issues likely to be faced regardless of whether the concern is with the nature, the sources, or the consequences of parents' ideas. These are issues related to choosing measures and to sampling informants. The other is to outline some perspectives that cut across all issues. We feel that the time has not yet come for any single grand theory of parental ideas. As in developmental psychology in general, however, it is possible to propose some promising general orientations or, as they have come to be called, "perspectives".

METHODOLOGICAL ISSUES
Selecting Measures

Measures for assessing parents' ideas have typically been devised for research on specific topics. Researchers have developed, for instance, measures of implicit developmental timetables to assess maturity demands, measures of reasons for valuing children to explore fertility decisions, measures of attributions for children's transgressions to understand parents' approaches to discipline. Few measures will serve a broad range of goals.

In addition, there will frequently be no readily available tool for one's particular questions. That difficulty makes all the more important a comment by Holden and Edwards (1989), to the effect that inventories of parents' attitudes, knowledge, or beliefs—often generated for specific questions—have not been examined for the extent to which they form scales. In the absence of information about how separate items are related to one another, it is impossible to draw inferences about the structure of parents' ideas. In addition, one can only make limited comparisons across parents or across groups. Time spent on instrument development would be well spent.

A further issue to be faced in choosing measures involves the target of questioning. Shall we ask for ideas about children generally, typical children of a particular age group, "ideal" children, or the parent's own child? These different possible targets vary in the concreteness of the referent (although in getting ideas about children generally, one may actually be getting parents' perceptions of their own child). They may vary also in the effects of experience. Ideas about one's own child, for instance, are likely to show the effects of experience more strongly than ideas about "ideal" children or even "typical" children. In addition, the connections among the several judgments and types of judgment may vary from one family member to another. In a study by Collins (in press), for example, the degree of discrepancy between perceptions of one's own child and descriptions of "ideal" youngsters at 11, 14, and 17 years of age varied as a function of age for mothers, but was a constant for fathers.

The easy implication of such results is that the researcher needs to give thought to the consequences and benefits of choosing particular targets, or combinations of targets (e.g. asking about "own" and "typical" child). The less obvious implication is the need for research on the way judgments about one target affect judgments about another. A provocative case in point is provided by Eccles, Harold-Goldsmith, and Miller (1989). Parents who make the category-based judgment that talent in mathematics comes more naturally to males than to females (success for females requires more effort) are likely to overestimate the ability of their sons but not of their daughters. In effect, these two types of judgment do not simply have independent paths. They influence one another in ways that we still need to explore.

Sampling People

Two kinds of decisions confront the researcher. One has to do with sampling from among families. The other has to do with sampling within families. In both cases, the knowledge now available provides the beginnings for a guided rather than a completely exploratory approach.

Sampling Among Families. The ideal of a representative sample is as essential to research on parent's ideas as in any problem in the social and behavioural sciences. The issue to be faced is when to aim at such a sample. A representative sample is ideal, for example, for questions about the value of children in a given society or nation, or questions about the extent to which ideas are shared. For many other problems, however, more selective samples are preferable. If one wishes, for instance, to study the links between parental affect and judgments of a child, or between parental expectations and abuse, then specific groups are needed, with any variations within them as controlled as is possible. By and large, homogeneous samples are preferable for addressing questions about processes related to parents' ideas. Even apparently homogeneous groups, however, may turn out to contain unexpected variations. Abusive parents, for instance, may need to be distinguished in terms of the extent and the type of abuse (physical, sexual, psychological) before any clear picture of connections emerges (Emery, 1989). The point we wish to underline is that a thoughtful approach to sampling is required not only to decide whether to seek relatively extreme, homogeneous or stratified groups instead of representative samples of parents, but also to assure that less apparent variations do not threaten the assumption of homogeneity that guides the choice of participants.

Sampling Within Families.   Once the decision is made regarding which families to sample, there is still the question of which members of the family shall be included as participants. The study of parents' ideas—and, indeed, the study of family functioning generally—has been based mostly on the reports of mothers, or on children's or adolescents' reports about mothers' behaviour. There have been notable exceptions. Hess and Goldblatt (1957), for instance, obtained from both parents their views of their adolescent children and their perceptions of the adolescents' ideas about the parents' positions. The multiple foci permitted a more extensive analysis of the interrelations of ideas than any one focus alone would have. By and large, however, seeking information from and about fathers is a relatively recent addition. So also is attention to information from and about siblings (e.g. Dunn & Munn, 1985) or grandparents (e.g. Tinsley & Parke, 1987).

The problem is to decide when and why to concentrate upon a particular view (e.g. mother only), when to seek other informants, and, if the latter step is taken, how to put them together. Suppose, for instance, the aim is to develop an understanding of parents' views on a particular topic or their response to experience. Is there then some reason to include fathers as well as mothers? In many ways, it is as incorrect to assume that mothers represent all parents as it is to assume, as psychologists once did, that one can generalise from samples of males to people in general. Including fathers wherever possible is a step towards both generalisability and social justice.

Nonetheless, we do need to ask: *When* are fathers likely to yield information that differs from the information gained from mothers? And can we fit these differences into some general concepts about the nature of thinking or judgment? We know, for instance, that fathers perceive changes in their adolescent children less readily than do mothers, perhaps because the initial changes in routine or challenges to authority do not impinge upon them as much as they do on the parent with the stronger responsibility for everyday family life (Alessandri & Wozniak, 1987; Collins, in press; Silverberg, 1989). We also know that fathers show the larger degree of consistency between statements of principle about the way children learn and the nature of interactions on a teaching/learning task (McGillicuddy-DeLisi, 1982), perhaps because their lesser experience with a specific child leads them to operate more from principle than from a past history of teaching experiences with that child. To take one last example, we also know that intervention programmes with parents (family therapy, parent education) are likely to change fathers' views and actions more than they do mothers' (Larsen & Harris, 1989; Watson & Russell, 1988). In these several instances, it is as if fathers often start more from the position of observer than the position of prime actor in child-rearing. If that is so, then we should be able to predict that mother–father differences will be similar to the actor–observer differences found, for instance, in many attribution studies. We would not expect this type of difference to be the only source of mother–father differences. There are likely to be as well differences in the interplay between paid work and family life, and in the extent to which males and females generally are expected to be responsible for the emotional state of any relationship. The goal, however, should be one not of collecting mother–father differences willy-nilly, but of linking them to some general hypotheses about the sources or consequences of ideas and then using these to test for the conditions that affect generalisability.

Developing a generalised account of parents' ideas, however, is not the only reason for including the viewpoints of people other than mothers. Multiple viewpoints are automatically called for whenever the issue is one of the degree of actual or perceived agreement between parent and parent, or between parent and child. Less obviously, multiple viewpoints are also called for whenever one wishes to characterise a family. Just as it is inappropriate to characterise a family in terms of one member's occupation, income, or political opinion, so also is it a distortion to take one person's viewpoint and then regard this as "the family's" view of the world or "the family's" account of the past.

Recognising that one person's view is an insufficient account, however, is only a first step. How are we to put together several perspectives? It is possible to ask whose view is dominant or which people agree, just as it is possible to ask how family members form hierarchies or alliances of various kinds. It is also possible, as Reiss et al. (1983) have demonstrated, to use degree of agreement among family members as a way of characterising families. In fact, Reiss et al's characterisation of some families as "consensus-sensitive" captures not only the presence of agreement but the degree of concern felt by the several family members for being in agreement with one another. The latter aspect of agreement is one we would wish to underline. In some families, disagreement is highly threatening; in others, good-natured verbal jousting is the norm; in still others, dramatic disputes are commonplace. In some families, periods of change, disagreement and conflict represent crises. In others, these represent the norm: periods of calm and stability are the aberrations. We shall need to know how a lack of agreement on specific issues is interpreted before being able to develop any clear picture of the impact of departures from complete family agreement upon the ideas or actions of any one family member.

GENERAL PERSPECTIVES

In many ways, the perspectives that have pervaded our approach to parents' ideas and to research priorities might be labelled "socio-historical", "contextualist" and "transactionalist". Those terms, borrowed largely from discussions of life-span development, help place our general views but do not entirely fit them or specify them.

It is clear, for instance, that we are in sympathy with what has been called a "socio-historical" perspective: a perspective that argues for the need to consider the particular cultures and the particular times when behaviours such as parenting occur. To this general recognition, however, we would add the need to ask more precisely about the difference that a particular socio-historical period makes and the aspects of parenting or parental thought that are particularly affected. The kind of theory being developed in the course of exploring "cultural models" or "social representations" (Chapter 4) is attractive precisely because it is addressed to the need for such specification. To the usual general references to periods or cohort effects, these two frameworks add an emphasis on variations in the several ideas available and dominant in a particular group. To the usual psychological emphasis on the individual operating in timeless and rational fashion on neutral, faceless information, these two frameworks add also an emphasis on people as belonging to social groups, as building social identities marked by the ideas they hold and share with others, and as choosing, "appropriating", or resisting ideas from a range presented with varying degrees of coherence, pressure and availability.

It is clear also that we are in sympathy with what has been called a "contextualist" perspective. Parents think and act within particular settings or situations, and in the face of particular responsibilities. "Context", however, is a term again in need of specification. We would prefer to argue for two variants of it: one that we shall call a "relational" perspective, the other a "public" perspective. The former refers to the way individuals think and act within relationships with others. It gives rise to our particular emphasis, as in Chapter 5, on the need to explore interactions and mutual cognitions rather than concentrate only on parents' actions and parents' ideas. It underlies also our emphasis, as in Chapter 2, on the value of asking not only about parents' views of children or of themselves but also of asking about views of relationships, the meaning of "family", and ideas about the way various family members should divide responsibilities or combine to present a united front to the world.

The "public" perspective might be fitted under a "relational" umbrella. We mark it out as separate, however, because it highlights a general feature of parenting and of behaviour that we see as neglected. In the course of psychology's emphasis on the individual, it has been a natural move to ask about internal processes, with self-monitoring included as one of these. Ideas and actions, however, also involve monitoring from others: a monitoring that is perhaps especially marked in areas such as parenting where the larger group feels it has some investment and some responsibility. The implications of a "public" perspective are yet to be explored in detail, but we have used it to draw attention to the way definitions of "private" and "public" areas of responsibility vary among families and among social groups. As discussions of "domestic violence" continually underline, some parents regard what happens in the home or between parent and child as "no one's business but their own" whereas others outside the family feel a moral obligation to act when certain boundaries are crossed. We have also used the public/private dimension of parenting to draw attention, as in Chapter 4, to the need for research on the way parents respond to advice given by various observers of parents' ideas or actions: observers · whose comments may be seen by parents as more vs. less legitimate and to whom parents may feel various degrees of need to explain their ideas, actions, and feelings.

Finally, it wil be clear that we are in sympathy with what has been called a "transactionalist" or a "dialectic" perspective. More precisely, we agree with the argument that progress in the understanding of parenting or family functioning calls for moving away from unidirectional models and considering instead mutual influences and multidirectional processes. A parent's developmental timetable, for instance, may be altered by the signs of early competence that a child displays. The altered view may then affect the way the child's environment is structured, leading in turn to a change in subsequent displays of competence. To take another example, premature infants who flourish when caregivers provide responsive care may confirm the caregiver's implicit view that the quality of care overrides biological factors and increase the likelihood of later responsive care (Sameroff & Chandler, 1975).

To date, psychologists have tended to apply a transactional perspective mainly to the interplay of one individual with another. The result has often been illuminating. Bugental (1989), for example, has been able to chart the way in which a child's avoiding eye contact (looking away or down) may lead to negative affect and an interpretation of "difficult" child, especially among adults who have a low sense of their own capacity to influence children. In turn, the negative affect and the lack of positive approach by the adult may itself increase the likelihood that the child will look away, cease to smile, or withdraw, confirming the adult's original interpretation and perhaps escalating the negative quality of the interaction. The specific interaction would be expected to be different in a culture that regards direct eye-contact as inappropriate for a child, as indicating a lack of respect for the adult. An interweaving of effects, however, would still be expected.

These applications of a transactional perspective to parents' ideas are essentially an extension of approaches to other aspects of parent–child relationships (e.g. Patterson, 1982). We would wish to add to them the argument that transactions refer also to the interplay between the views of individuals and the views of the social group (the "social representations" or "cultural models"). To take an example from the sociological literature, Foucault (1980) has proposed that the knowledge present in any society contains both "formal" and "informal" varieties. Formal theory often moves into informal theory. The concepts and terms of psychoanalysis, for instance, become part of popular language (Moscovici, 1961). As Foucault (1980) points out, it is also true that "alternative medicine" and "alternative education" act as vehicles for criticising formal theory and can come to modify it. Once again, the processes involved are not one way.

Does such an emphasis on transactional effects, especially when we invoke the large social group, mean that we no longer pay attention to the individual and to internal processes? Far from it. Without a concern for internal processes, for instance, we could not come to emphasise, as we did in Chapter 3, the importance of asking how ideas form clusters or hierarchies. The individual ultimately has to do the work of abstracting, choosing, combining, discarding and generalising, bringing to the task a range of skills, tools, and established schemas. We have simply tried to rectify the balance, arguing for attention also to the state of the world that the individual deals with.

Does an emphasis on transactional effects, to ask a last question, perhaps lead us into more complexity than we can handle? It may certainly seem so, especially if we wish to combine attention to multiple directions with an interest in the way ideas, actions, affect, and child outcomes are interrelated, and with an interest in changes over time. Part of the answer to such complexity lies in effective statistical analysis. Part of it also, however, lies in developing hypotheses about the nature of the connections among components in any complex chain or net. It is to meet that aim that in our dissection of several components and connections we have argued for the need to know not only the past research on a topic but also the conceptual frameworks from which one may draw in order to frame alternative hypotheses.

The conceptual frameworks, we note as our final point, serve a further purpose. In the long run, our hope is not only to clarify the nature of parenting and parental thought, but also to place questions about parents and families within the larger setting of how it is that people of all kinds come to acquire and share some ideas rather than others, come to cherish or to change some rather than others, come to act or feel more readily on the basis of some rather than others. Parents' ideas have a double significance. They are worth studying for the light they throw on the nature of parenting and family life. They warrant our attention also for the way that an understanding of parents' ideas increases our understanding of the general nature, sources, and consequences of thinking in the course of adulthood and the course of everyday life.

REFERENCES

Abelson, R.P. (1986). Beliefs are like possessions. *Journal for the Theory of Social Behavior, 16,* 223–250.

Alessandri, S.M., & Wozniak, R.H. (1987). Parental beliefs about the personality of their children and children's awareness of those beliefs: A developmental and family constellations study. *Child Development, 58,* 316–323.

Antill, J.K. (1987). Parents' beliefs and values about sex roles, sex differences, and sexuality. Their sources and implications. In P. Shaver & C. Hendrick (Eds), *Sex and gender: Review of personality and social psychology,* (Vol. 7), pp.294–328. Beverley Hills, California: Sage.

Argyle, M., & Henderson, J.K. (1985). *The anatomy of relationships.* Harmondsworth: Penguin.

Ariès, P. (1962). *Centuries of childhood.* New York: Vintage Books.

Ashmore, R.D., & Brodzinsky, D.M. (1986). *Thinking about family: Views of parents and children.* Hillsdale, N.J.: Lawrence Erlbaum Associates Inc.

Austin, J. (1979). Other minds. In J. Austin (Ed.), *Philosophical papers* (3rd Edition), pp.44-84. Oxford: Oxford University Press.

Averill, J. (1982). *Anger and aggression: An essay on emotion.* New York: Springer-Verlag.

Azuma, H. (1982). *Two models of teachability: U.S. and Japan.* Paper presented at meeting of Australia Psychological Society, 1982.

Backett, K.C. (1982). *Mothers and fathers: The development and negotiation of parental behaviour.* London: Macmillan.

Bacon, M.K., & Ashmore, R.D. (1986). A consideration of the activities of parents and their role in the socialization process. In R.D. Ashmore & D.M. Brodzinsky (Eds), *Thinking about the family: Views of parents and children,* pp.3–34. Hillsdale, N.J.: Lawrence Erlbaum Asociates Inc.

Bacon, W.F., & Ichikawa, V. (1988). Maternal expectations, classroom experiences, and achievement among kindergartners in the United States and Japan. *Human Development, 31,* 378–383.

Baldwin, A. (1965). A is happy—B is not. *Child Development, 36,*, 583–600.

Barber, B.L. (1988). The influence of family demographics and parental teaching practices on Peruvian children's academic achievement. *Human Development, 31,* 370–377.

Bargh, J.A. (1982). Automatic and conscious processing of social information. In R.S. Wyer, Jr., & T.K. Srull (Eds), *Handbook of social cognition* (Vol.3), pp.1–43. Hillsdale, N.J.: Lawrence Erlbaum Associates Inc.

Bar-Tal, D., & Guttman, J. (1981). A comparison of teachers', pupils', and parents' attributions regarding parents' academic achievements. *British Journal of Educational Psychology, 51,* 301–311.

Baszormenyi-Nagy, I., & Spark, G. (1973). *Invisible loyalties: Reciprocity in intergenerational family therapy.* New York: Harper & Row.

Beck, A.T. (1967). *Depression: Causes and treatment.* Philadelphia: University of Pennsylvania Press.

Becker, J.A., & Hall, M.S. (1989). Adult beliefs about pragmatic development. *Journal of Applied Developmental Psychology, 10,* 1–18.

Bell, R.Q. (1979). Parent, child, and reciprocal influences. *American Psychologist, 34,* 821–826.

Belsky, J. (1984). The determinants of parenting: A process model. *Child Development, 55,* 83–96.

Belsky, J. (1985). Exploring individual differences in marital change across the transition to parenthood: The role of violated expectations. *Journal of Marriage and the Family, 47,* 1037–1044.

Belsky, J., Lang, M., & Huston, T.L. (1986). Sex-typing and division of labor as determinants of marital change across the transition to parenthood. *Journal of Personality and Social Psychology, 50,* 517–522.

Belsky, J., Rovine, M., & Fish, M. (1989). The developing family system. In M. Gunnar (Ed.), *Systems and development, Minnesota Symposium on Child Psychology* (Vol.22), pp.119–166. Hillsdale, N.J.: Lawrence Erlbaum Associates Inc.

Belsky, J., Ward, M.J., & Rovine, M. (1986). Prenatal expectations, postnatal experiences, and the transition to parenthood. In R.D. Ashmore & D.M. Brodzinsky (Eds), *Thinking about the family: Views of parents and children*, pp.119–145. Hillsdale, N.J.: Lawrence Erlbaum Associates Inc.

Bem, D.J. (1972). Self-perception theory. In L. Berkowitz (Ed.), *Advances in experimental social psychology* (Vol.6), pp.1–21. New York: Academic Press.

Benedict, R. (1938). Continuities and discontinuities in cultural conditioning. *Psychiatry, 1,* 161–167.

Berkowitz, M.W. (1985). The role of discussion in moral education. In M.W. Berkowitz & F. Oser (Eds), *Moral education: Theory and application*, pp.68–93. Hillsdale N.J.: Lawrence Erlbaum Associates Inc.

Block, J.H. (1972). Generational continuity and discontinuity in the understanding of societal rejection. *Journal of Personality and Social Psychology, 22,* 333–345.

Blount, B.G. (1972). Parental speech and language acquisition. Some Luo and Samoan examples. *Anthropological Linguistics, 14,* 119–130.

Bogdan, R.J. (1986). The importance of belief. In R.J. Bogdan (Ed.), *Belief: Form, content and function*, pp.1–16. Oxford: Oxford University Press.

Bott, E. (1957). *Family and social network: Roles, norms and external relationships in ordinary urban families.* London: Tavistock.

Bourdieu, P. (1977). *Outline of a theory of practice*. Cambridge: Cambridge University Press.

Bradbury, T.N., & Fincham, F.D. (1987). Affect and cognition in close relationships: Towards an integrative model. *Cognition and Emotion, 1*, 59–87.

Brody, G.H., Graziano, W.G., & Musser, L.M. (1983). Familiarity and children's behavior in same-age and mixed-age peer groups. *Developmental Psychology, 19*, 568–576.

Bronfenbrenner, U. (1958). Socialization and social class through time and space. In E.E. Maccoby, T.M. Newcomb, & E.L. Hartley (Eds), *Readings in social psychology*, pp.406–425. New York: Holt, Rinehart, & Winston.

Brooks-Gunn, J. (1985). Maternal beliefs about children's sex-typed characteristics as they relate to maternal behavior. In I. Sigel (Ed.), *Parental belief systems*, pp.319–343. Hillsdale, N.J.: Lawrence Erlbaum Associates Inc.

Buescher, T.M., & Olzewski, P. (1987, April). *Influences on strategies children use to cope with their own recognized talents*. Paper presented at meeting of the Society for Research in Child Development, Baltimore.

Bugental, D.B. (1989, April). *Caregiver cognitions as moderators of affect in abusive families*. Paper presented at meeting of the Society for Research in Child Development, Kansas City.

Bugental, D.B., Blue, J., & Cruzcosa, M. (1989). Perceived control over caregiving outcomes: Implications for child abuse. *Developmental Psychology, 25*, 532–539.

Bugental, D.B., & Shennum, W. (1984). "Difficult" children as elicitors and targets of adult communication patterns: An attributional-behavioral transactional analysis. *Monographs of the Society for Research in Child Development, 49* (1, Serial No.205).

Burns, A., Homel, R., & Goodnow, J.J. (1984) Conditions of life and parental values. *Australian Journal of Psychology, 36*, 219–237.

Carugati, F. (1990). From social cognition to social representation in the study of intelligence. In G.M. Duveen & B. Lloyd (Eds), *Social representations and the development of knowledge*, pp.126–143. Cambridge: Cambridge University Press.

Carver, C.S., & Scheier, M.F. (1981). *Attention and self-regulation: A control-theory approach to human behavior*. New York: Springer-Verlag.

Cashmore, J.A., & Goodnow, J.J. (1985). Agreement between generations: A two-process approach. *Child Development, 56*, 493–501.

Cashmore, J.A., & Goodnow, J.J. (1986). Parent-child agreement on attributional beliefs. *International Journal of Behavioral Development, 9*, 1–14.

Caws, J. (1974). Operational, representational, and explanatory models. *American Anthropologist, 76*, 1–11.

Chen, C., & Uttal, D.H. (1988). Cultural values, parents' beliefs, and children's achievement in the United States and China. *Human Development, 31*, 351–358.

Chombart de Lauwe, M.J. (1984). Changes in the representation of the child in the course of social transmission. In R.M. Farr & S. Moscovici (Eds), *Social representations*, pp.185–210. Cambridge: Cambridge University Press.

Clark, M.S. (1984). Implications of relationship type for understanding compatibility. In W. Ickes (Ed.), *Compatible and incompatible relationships*, pp.119–140. New York: Springer-Verlag.

Clarke-Stewart, K.A. (1978). Popular primers for parents. *American Psychologist, 33*, 359–369.

Cohen, G. (1981). Culture and educational achievement. *Harvard Educational Review, 51*, 270–285.

Collins, R. (1981). On the microfoundations of macrosociology. *American Journal of Sociology, 86*, 984–1012.

Collins, W.A. (1983). Social antecedents, cognitive processing, and comprehension of social portrayals on television. In E.T. Higgins, D.N. Ruble, & W.W. Hartup (Eds), *Social cognition and social development*, pp.110–133. Cambridge: Cambridge University Press.

Collins, W.A. (in press). Parent-child relationships in the transition to adolescence: Continuity and change in interaction, affect, and cognition. In R. Montemayor, G. Adams, & T. Gullotta (Eds), *Advances in adolescent development* (Vol.2). Beverley Hills, California: Sage.

Conger, R.D., McCarty, J.A., Yang, R.K., Lahey, B.B., & Kropp, J.P. (1984). Perception of child, child-rearing values, and emotional distress as mediating links between environmental stressors and observed maternal behavior. *Child Development, 55*, 2234–2247.

Crowell, J.A., & Feldman, S.S. (1988). Mothers' internal models of relationships and children's behavioral and developmental status: A study of mother-child interaction. *Child Development, 59*, 1273–1285.

D'Alessio, M. (1977). Bambino generalizzato e bambino individualizzato nella stereotipia d'età. In E. Ponzo (Ed.), *Il bambino semplificato o inesistente*, pp.231–242. Rome: Bulzoni.

D'Alessio, M. (1990). Social representations of childhood: An implicit theory of childhood. In G. Duveen & B. Lloyd (Eds), *Social representations and the development of knowledge*, pp.70–90. Cambridge: Cambridge University Press.

Damon, W. (1977). *The social world of the child*. San Francisco: Jossey-Bass.

D'Andrade, R.G. (1981). The cultural part of cognition. *Cognitive Science, 5*, 179–195.

D'Andrade, R.G. (1987). A folk model of the mind. In D. Holland & N. Quinn (Eds), *Cultural models in language and thought*, pp.112–150. Cambridge: Cambridge University Press.

Deal, J.E., Halverson, C.F., & Wampler, K.F. (1989). Parental agreement on childrearing orientations: Relations to parental, marital, family, and child characteristics. *Child Development, 60*, 1025–1034.

De Grada, E., & Ponzo, E. (1971). *La normalità del bambino come pregiudizio dell'adulto*. Rome: Bulzoni.

Deutsch, F.M., Ruble, D.N., Fleming, A.S., Brooks-Gunn, J., & Stangor, C.S. (in press). Information seeking and marital self-definition during the transition to motherhood. *Journal of Personality and Social Psychology*.

Dix, T.H., & Grusec, J. (1983). Parental influence techniques: An attributional analysis. *Child Development, 54*, 645–652.

Dix, T.H., & Grusec, J. (1985). Parent attribution processes in the socialization of children. In I.E. Sigel (Ed.), *Parental belief systems*, pp.201–233. Hillsdale, N.J.: Lawrence Erlbaum Associates Inc.

Dix, T.H., Ruble, D.N., Grusec, J., & Nixon, S. (1986). Social cognition in parents: Inferential and affective reactions to children of three age levels. *Child Development, 57*, 879–894.

Doise, W., & Mugny, G. (1984). *The social development of the intellect*. Oxford: Pergamon Press.

Dunn, J., & Munn, P. (1985). Becoming a family member: Family conflict and the development of understanding. *Child Development, 56*, 480–492.

Durkheim, E. (1895). Représentations collectives. *Revue de Métaphysique et de Morale, 6*, 273–302.

Duveen, G., & Lloyd, B. (1990a). *Social representations and the development of knowledge*. Cambridge: Cambridge University Press.

Duveen, G., & Lloyd, B. (1990b). Introduction. In G. Duveen & B. Lloyd (Eds). *Social representations and the development of knowledge*, pp.1–10. Cambridge: Cambridge University Press.

Duveen, G., & Lloyd, B. (in press). An ethnographic approach to social representations. In G. Breakwell & D. Cantor (Eds), *Empirical approaches to the study of social representations*. Oxford:Oxford University Press.

Eccles, J.S. (1986). Gender-roles and women's achievement. *Educational Researcher, 15*, 15–19.

Eccles, J.S., Harold-Goldsmith, R., & Miller, C.L. (1989, April). *Parents' stereotypic beliefs about gender differences and adolescence.* Paper presented at meeting of The Society for Research in Child Development, Kansas City.

Edwards, C.P., & Gandini, L. (1988, November). *The developmental expectations of experience: A cross-cultural study of the effect of professional experience on cultural knowledge.* Paper presented at meeting of American Anthropological Association, Phoenix.

Elias, M.J., & Ubriaco, M. (1986). Linking parental beliefs to children's social competence: Toward a cognitive-behavior assessment model. In R.D. Ashmore & D.M. Brodzinsky (Eds), *Thinking about the family: Views of parents and children*, pp.147–180. Hillsdale, N.J.: Lawrence Erlbaum Associates Inc.

Emery, R.E. (1989). Family violence. *American Psychologist, 44*, 322–328.

Emiliani, F., & Molinari, L. (1988). What everybody knows about children: Mothers' ideas on early childhood. *European Journal of Psychology of Education, 3*, 19–31.

Emiliani, F., & Molinari, L. (in press). Mothers' social representations of their children's learning and development. *International Journal of Educational Research.*

Emiliani, F., Zani, B., & Carugati, F. (1981). From staff interaction strategies to the social representations of adults in a day nursery. In W.P. Robinson (Ed.), *Communication in development*, pp.89–107. London: Academic Press.

Emmerich, W. (1969). The parental role: A functional-cognitive approach. *Monographs of the Society for Research in Child Development, 34* (8, Serial No.132).

Engstrom, Y. (1988). Reconstructing work as an object of research. *Quarterly Newsletter of the Laboratory of Comparative Human Cognition, 10*, 21–28.

Entwisle, D.R., & Hayduk, L.A. (1981). Academic expectations and the school attainment of young children. *Sociology of Education, 54*, 34–50.

Evans, M., Barber, B.L., Gadsden, V.C., Paris, S.G., & Park, S.H. (1989, April). *What knowledge do parents have about educational assessment tasks?* Paper presented at meeting of the Society for Research in Child Development, Kansas City.

Ewart, J.C., & Green, M.W. (1957). Conditions associated with the mother's estimate of the ability of her retarded child. *American Journal of Mental Deficiency, 62*, 521–533.

Farr, R.M., & Moscovici, S. (Eds) (1984). *Social representation.* Cambridge: Cambridge University Press.

Fazio, R.H. (1986). How do attitudes guide behavior? In R.M. Sorrentino & E.T. Higgins (Eds), *Handbook of motivation and cognition*, pp.204–243. New York: Guilford.

Feldman, S.A., & Quatman, T. (1988). Factors influencing age expectations for adolescent autonomy: A study of early adolescents and parents. *Journal of Early Adolescence, 8*, 325–343.

Finch, J. (1983). *Married to the job: Wives' incorporation in men's work.* London: Allen & Unwin.

Fischer, J.L. & Fischer, A. (1963). The New Englanders of Orchardtown, U.S.A. In B.B. Whiting (Ed.), *Six cultures: Studies of child rearing* (Vol.5). New York: Wiley.

Fodor, P. (1983). *The modularity of mind.* Boston: M.I.T. Press.

Ford, M.E. (1984). Linking social-cognitive processes with effective social behavior: A living systems approach. In K. Kendall (Ed.), *Advances in cognitive-behavioral research and therapy* (Vol.3), pp.167–211. New York: Academic Press.

Forgas, J.P., Bower, G.H., & Krantz, S.E. (1984). The influence of mood on perceptions of social interactions. *Journal of Experimental Social Psychology, 20,* 497–513.

Foucault, M. (1980). *Power-knowledge: Selected interviews and other writings.* Brighton: Harvester.

Frankel, D.G., & Roer-Bornstein, D. (1982). Traditional and modern contributions to changing infant-rearing ideologies of two ethnic communities. *Monographs of the Society for Research in Child Development, 47* (4, Serial No.196).

Fry, P.S. (1984). Teachers' conceptions of students' intelligence and intelligent functioning: A cross-sectional study of elementary, secondary and tertiary level teachers. *International Journal of Psychology, 19,* 457–474.

Furstenberg, F.F., Jr. (1971). The transmission of mobility orientation in the family. *Social Forces, 49,* 595–603.

Gecas, V. (1979). The influence of social class on socialization. In W. Burr, R. Hill, F.I. Nye, & I.L. Reiss (Eds), *Contemporary theories about the family* (Vol.1), pp.365–404. New York: Free Press.

Gergen, K.J. (1982). *Toward transformation in social knowledge.* New York: Springer.

Gergen, K.J. (1985). The social constructionist movement in modern psychology. *American Psychologist, 40,* 266–275.

Gibson, J.J. (1966). *The senses considered as perceptual systems.* Boston: Houghton-Mifflin.

Gloger-Tippelt, G., & Tippelt, R. (1986). Kindheit und kindliche Entwicklung als soziale Konstruktionen. *Bildung and Erziehung, 2,* 149–164.

Goodnow, J.J. (1976). The nature of intelligent behavior: Questions raised by cross-cultural studies. In L. Resnick (Ed.), *The nature of intelligence,* pp.169–188. Hillsdale, N.J.: Lawrence Erlbaum Associates Inc.

Goodnow, J.J. (1980). Everyday concepts of intelligence and its development. In N. Warren (Ed.), *Studies in cross-cultural psychology,* pp.191–219. London: Academic Press.

Goodnow, J.J. (1984). Parent's ideas about parenting and development: A review of issues and recent work. In M.E. Lamb, A.L. Brown, & B. Rogoff (Eds), *Advances in developmental psychology* (Vol.3), pp.193–242. Hillsdale, N.J.: Lawrence Erlbaum Associates Inc.

Goodnow, J.J. (1985a). Change and variation in parents' ideas about childhood and parenting. In I.E. Sigel (Ed.), *Parental belief systems,* pp.235–270. Hillsdale, N.J.: Lawrence Erlbaum Associates Inc.

Goodnow, J.J. (1985b). Topics, methods, and models: Feminist challenges in social science. In J.J. Goodnow & C. Pateman (Eds), *Women, social science, and public policy,* pp. 1–31. Sydney: Allen & Unwin.

Goodnow, J.J. (1987, April). *The distributive justice of work: Mothers' account of children's household tasks.* Paper presented at meeting of the Society for Research in Child Development, Baltimore.

Goodnow, J.J. (1988a). Parents' ideas, actions and feelings: Models and methods for developmental and social psychology. *Child Development, 59,* 286–320.

Goodnow, J.J. (1988b). Children's household work: Its nature and functions. *Psychological Bulletin, 103,* 5–26.

Goodnow, J.J. (1990a). Using sociology to extend psychological accounts of cognitive development. *Human Development, 33,* 81–107.

Goodnow, J.J. (1990b). The socialization of cognition: What's involved?. In J.W. Stigler, R.A. Shweder, & G. Herdt (Eds), *Cultural psychology*, pp.259–286. Cambridge: Cambridge University Press.

Goodnow, J.J., Bowes, J., Dawes, L., & Taylor A. (1988). *Would you ask someone else to do this job? The effects of generation, gender and task on household work requests.* Unpublished manuscript, Macquarie University.

Goodnow, J.J., Cashmore, J.A., Cotton, S., & Knight, R. (1984). Mothers' developmental timetables in two cultural groups. *International Journal of Psychology, 19,* 193–205.

Goodnow, J.J., & Delaney, S. (1988). *For love or for money: Mothers' ideas about payment for children's work around the house.* Unpublished Manuscript, Macquarie University.

Goodnow, J.J., & Delaney, S. (1989). Children's household work: Differentiating types of work and styles of assignment. *Journal of Applied Developmental Psychology, 10,* 209–226.

Goodnow, J.J., Knight, R., & Cashmore, J. (1985). Adult social cognition: Implications of parents' ideas for approaches to development. In M. Perlmutter (Ed.), *Social cognition: Minnesota symposia on child development* (Vol.18), pp.287–324. Hillsdale, N.J.: Lawrence Erlbaum Associates Inc.

Goodnow, J.J., & Warton, P.M. (in press). The social bases of social cognition: Interactions about work, lessons about relationships. *Merrill-Palmer Quarterly.*

Gravenhorst, L. (1988). A feminist look at family development theory. In D.M. Klein & J. Aldous (Eds), *Social stress and family development*, pp.79–101. New York: Guilford.

Greenberger, E., & Goldberg, W.A. (1989). Work, parenting, and the socialization of children. *Developmental Psychology, 25,* 22–35.

Gretarsson, S.J., & Gelfand, D.M. (1988). Mothers' attributions regarding their children's social behavior and personality characteristics. *Developmental Psychology, 24,* 264–269.

Grotevant, J., & Cooper, C. (1986). Individuation in family relationships. *Human Development, 29,* 82–100.

Grusec, J.E., Dix, T.H., & Mills, R. (1982). The effects of type, severity, and victim of children's transgressions on maternal discipline. *Canadian Journal of Behavioral Science, 14,* 276–289.

Grusec, J.E., & Kuczynski, L. (1980). Direction of effect in socialization: A comparison of the parent's versus the child's behavior as determinants of disciplinary techniques. *Developmental Psychology, 16,* 1–9.

Hagestad, G.O. (1984). The continuous bond: A dynamic, multigenerational perspective on parent-child relations between adults. In M. Perlmutter (Ed.), *Parent-child interaction and parent-child relations in child development, Minnesota Symposia on Child Development* (Vol. 17). 129–158. Hillsdale, N.J.: Lawrence Erlbaum Associates Inc.

Halvorson, C.F., & Waldrup, M.F. (1976) Relations between preschool activity and aspects of intellectual and social behavior at age 7 and a half. *Developmental Psychology, 12,* 107–112.

Hanson D.A. (1988). Schooling, stress, and family development: Rethinking the social role metaphor. In D.M. Klein & J. Aldous (Eds), *Social stress and family development*, pp.44–78. New York: Guilford.

Harkness, S., & Super, C.M. (1983). The cultural construction of child development. *Ethos, 11,* 222–231.

Harkness, S., Super, C.M., & Keefer, C.H. (1986, December). *The directive force of American parents' theories of child behavior and development.* Paper presented at meetings of the American Anthropological Association, Philadelphia.

Hatano, G. (1982). Should parents be teachers too?: A Japanese view. *Dokkyo University Bulletin of Liberal Arts, 17*, 54–72.

Hayes, A., Gunn, P., & Price, D. (1982). Construction of infants' social behavior by mothers and researchers. *Infant Behavior and Development, 5*, 114.

Heath, S.B. (1983). *Ways with words: Language, life and work in communities and classrooms*. Cambridge: Cambridge University Press.

Heath, S.B. (1990). The children of Trackton's children: Spoken and written language in social change. In J.W. Stigler, R.A. Shweder, & G. Herdt (Eds), *Cultural psychology, pp.496–519. Chicago: University of Chicago Press*.

Helfer, R.E., & Kempe, C.H. (1986). *The battered child*. Chicago: University of Chicago Press.

Herzberger, S.D., & Tennen, H. (1986). Coping with abuse: Children's perspectives on their abusive treatment. In R.D. Ashmore & D.M. Brodzinsky (Eds), *Thinking about the family: Views of parents and children*, pp.277–300. Hillsdale, N.J.: Lawrence Erlbaum Associates Inc.

Hess, R.D., Azuma, H., Kashiwagi, K., Dickson, W.P., Nagano, S., Holloway, S., Miyake, K., Price, G.G., Hatano, G., & McDevitt, T. (1986). Family influences on school readiness and achievement in Japan and the United States: An overview of a longitudinal study. In H. Stevenson, J. Azuma, & K. Hakuta (Eds), *Child development and education in Japan*, pp.147–166. New York: Freeman.

Hess, R.D., & Goldblatt, I. (1957). The status of adolescents in American society: A problem in social identity. *Child Development, 28*, 459–468.

Hess, R.D., & Handel, G. (1959). *Family worlds: A psychosocial approach to family life*. Chicago: University of Chicago Press.

Hess, R.D., Kashiwagi, K., Azuma, H., Price, G.G., & Dickson, W.P. (1980). Maternal expectations for mastery of developmental tasks in Japan and the United States. *International Journal of Psychology, 15*, 259–271.

Hess, R.D., & McDevitt, T.M. (1986). Some antecedents of maternal attributions about children's performance in mathematics. In R.D. Ashmore & D.M. Brodzinsky (Eds), *Thinking about the family: Views of parents and children*, pp.95–118. Hillsdale, N.J.: Lawrence Erlbaum Associates Inc.

Hess, R.D., Price, G.G., Dickson, W.P., & Conroy, M. (1984). Different roles for mothers and teachers: Contrasting styles of child care. In S. Kilmer (Ed.), *Advances in early education and day care* (Vol.2). Greenwich CT: Johnson.

Higgins, E.T., & King, G. (1981). Accessibility of social constructs: Inform ation-processing consequences of individual and contextual variability. In N. Cantor & J.F. Kihlstrom (Eds), *Personality, cognition, and social interaction*. Hillsdale, N.J.: Lawrence Erlbaum Associates Inc.

Higgins, E.T., Klein, R., & Strauman, T. (1985). Self-concept discrepancy theory: A psychological model for distinguishing among different aspects of depression and anxiety. *Social Cognition, 3*, 51–76.

Higgins, E.T., Van Cook, E., & Dorfman, D. (1988). Do self-attributes form a cognitive structure? *Social cognition, 6*, 177-207.

Hinde, R.A. (1979). *Towards Understanding Relationships*. London: Academic Press.

Hinde, R.A., & Stevenson-Hinde, J. (1988). *Relationships within families: Mutual influences*. Oxford: Clarendon Press.

Hoffman, L.W. (1988). Cross-cultural differences in childrearing goals. In R.A. LeVine, P.M. Miller, & M.M. West (Eds), *Parental behavior in diverse societies*, pp.99–122. San Francisco: Jossey-Bass.

Hoffman, L.W., & Hoffman, M.L. (1973). The value of children to parents. In J.T. Fawcett (Ed.), *Psychological perspectives on fertility*. New York: Basic Books.

Hoffman, M.L. (1970). Moral development. In P.H. Mussen (Ed.), *Handbook of child psychology* (Vol.2). New York: Wiley.

Hoffman, M.L. (1986). Affect, cognition, and motivation. In R.M. Sorrentino & E.T. Higgins (Eds), *Handbook of motivation and cognition*, pp.244–280. New York: Guilford.

Holden, G.W. (1988). Adults' thinking about a child-rearing problem: Effects of experience, parental status, and gender. *Child Development, 59,* 1623–1632.

Holden, G.W., & Edwards, L.A. (1989). Parental attitudes towards child rearing: Instruments, issues and implications. *Psychological Bulletin, 106,* 29–58.

Holden, G.W., & Klingner, A. (in press). Learning through experience: Differences in how novice vs. expert nurses diagnose why an infant is crying. *Journal of Nursing Education.*

Holden, G.W., & Ritchie, K.L. (1988). Child rearing and the dialectics of parental intelligence. In J. Valsiner (Ed.), *Children's development within social-cultural structured environments*, pp.30–59. Norwood, N.J.: Ablex.

Holland, D., & Valsiner, J. (in press). Cognition, symbols, and Vygotsky's developmental theory. *Ethos.*

Holloway, S., Gorman, K.S., & Fuller, B. (1988). Child-rearing beliefs within diverse social structures: Mothers and day-care providers in Mexico. *International Journal of Psychology, 23,* 1–15.

Holloway, S.D., & Hess, R.D. (1983). Causal explanations for school performance: Contrasts between mothers and children. *Journal of Applied Developmental Psychology, 3,* 319–327.

Holloway, S.D., Hess, R.D., Azuma, H., & Kashiwagi, K. (in press). Causal attributions by Japanese and American mothers and children about performance in mathematics. *International Journal of Psychology.*

Holy, L., & Stuchlik, M. (1981). *The structure of folk models.* A.S.A. Monographs 20. New York: Academic Press.

Hunt, J., & Paraskevopoulos, J. (1980). Children's psychological development as a function of the inaccuracy of their mother's knowledge of their abilities. *Journal of Genetic Psychology, 136,* 285–298.

Isen, M.A., Means, B., Patrick, R., & Nowicki, G. (1982). Some factors influencing decision-making strategy and risk-taking. In M.S. Clark & S.T. Fiske (Eds), *Affect and cognition: The 17th Annual Carnegie Symposium on Cognition*, pp.243–262. Hillsdale, N.J.: Lawrence Erlbaum Associates Inc.

Janssen, A.W.H., Gerris, J.R.M., & Janssens, J.M.A. (1988, July). *Family climate, parental discipline strategies, and the child's development of moral judgment.* Paper presented at meetings of the International Society for the Study of Behavioral Development, Tokyo.

Johnson-Laird, P., & Stedman, M. (1978). The psychology of syllogisms. *Cognitive Psychology, 10,* 64–99.

Jones, E., Farina, A., Hastorf, A.H., Markus, H., Miller, D.T., & Scott, R.A. (1984). *Social stigma.* New York: W.H. Freeman.

Kay, P. (1987). Linguistic competence and folk theories of language. In D. Holland & N.Quinn (Eds), *Cultural models in language and thought*, pp.67–77. Cambridge: Cambridge University Press.

Kaye, K. (1982). *The mental and social life of babies: How parents create persons.* Chicago: University of Chicago Press.

Keller, H., Miranda, D., & Gauda, G. (1984). The naive theory of the infant and some maternal attitudes: A two-country study. *Journal of Cross-Cultural Psychology, 15,* 165–179.

Kelley, H., Berscheid, E., Christensen, A., Harvey, J., Huston, T., Levinger, G., McClintock, E., Peplau, L., & Peterson, D. (Eds). (1983). *Close relationships*. New York: Freeman.

Kendig, H.L. (1986). Intergenerational exchange. In H.L. Kendig (Ed.), *Ageing and families*, pp.85–109. Sydney: Allen & Unwin.

Kessen, W. (1979). The American child and other cultural inventions. *American Psychologist, 15*, 815–820.

Kindermann, T.S., & Skinner, E.A. (1989, April). *Mothers' perceptions of children's progress in developmental tasks: Organizers of contingencies in everyday interactions*. Paper presented at meeting of the Society for Research in Child Development, Kansas City.

Klein, J. (1965). *Samples from English cultures*. (Vol.2: *Child-rearing practices*). London: Routledge & Kegan Paul.

Knight, R. (1986). Parents' satisfaction with progress and beliefs about stability of traits. In C. Pratt, A.F. Garton, W.E. Tunmer, & A.R. Nesdale (Eds), *Research issues in child development*. Sydney: Allen & Unwin.

Knight, R.A., & Goodnow, J.J. (1988). Parents' beliefs about influence over cognitive and social development. *International Journal of Behavioral Development, 11*, 517–527.

Knudson, R.M., Sommers, A.A., & Golding, S.L. (1980). Interpersonal perception and mode of resolution in marital conflict. *Journal of Personality and Social Psychology, 38*, 751–763.

Kochanska, G., Kuczynski, L., & Radke-Yarrow, M. (in press). Correspondence between mothers' self-report and observed child-rearing practices. *Child Development*.

Kochanska, G., & Radke-Yarrow, M. (in press). Normal and depressed mothers' beliefs about their children. *American Journal of Orthopsychiatry*.

Kohn, M.L. (1963). Social class and parent-child relationships: An interpretation. *American Journal of Sociology, 68*, 471–480.

Kohn, M.L. (1977). *Class and conformity: A study in values* (2nd edition). Chicago: University of Chicago Press.

Kohn, M.L., & Schooler, C. (1982). Job conditions and personality: A longitudinal analysis of their reciprocal effects. *American Journal of Sociology, 87*, 1257–1286.

Kojima, H. (1986). Japanese concepts of child development from the mid-17th to mid-19th century. *International Journal of Behavioral Development, 9*, 315–329.

Kojima, H. (1987). *The role of belief-value systems related to child-rearing and education: The case of early modern to modern Japan*. Unpublished manuscript, Nagoya University.

Kuczynski, L., Kochanska, G., Radke-Yarrow, M., & Girnius-Brown, O. (1987). A developmental interpretation of young children's noncompliance. *Developmental Psychology, 23*, 799–806.

Larsen, J.M., & Harris, J.D. (1989, April). *Parent education: Effects on middle class/educationally advantaged families*. Paper presented at meeting of the Society for Research in Child Development, Kansas City.

Leadbeater, B.J. (1988). Relational processes in adolescent and adult dialogues: Assessing the intersubjective context of conversation. *Human Development, 31*, 313–326.

Leonard, R. (1988, August). *Ways of studying early negotiations between children and parents*. Paper presented at 5th Australian Developmental Conference, Sydney.

LeVine, R.A. (1974). Parental goals: A cross-cultural view. *Teachers College Record, 76*(2), 226–239.

LeVine, R.A. (1988). Human parental care: Universal goals, cultural strategies, individual behavior. In R.A. LeVine, P.M. Miller, & M.M. West (Eds), *Parental behavior in diverse societies*, pp.5–12. San Francisco: Jossey-Bass.

LeVine, R.A., & LeVine, S.E. (1988). Parental strategies among the Gusii of Kenya. In R.A. LeVine, P.M. Miller, & M.M. West (Eds), *Parental behavior in diverse societies*, pp.27–36. San Francisco: Jossey-Bass.

Lewinsohn, P.M., Larson, D.W., & Munoz, R.F. (1982). The measurement of expectancies and other cognitions in depressed individuals. *Cognitive Therapy and Research, 6*, 437–446.

Lidz, T. (1963). *The family and human adaptation*. New York: International Universities Press.

Linville, P.W., & Jones, E. (1980). Polarized appraisals of outgroup members. *Journal of Personality and Social Psychology, 38*, 689–703.

Lloyd, B., (1987). Social representations of gender. In J. Bruner & H. Haste (Eds) *Making sense: The child's representation of the world*. London & New York: Methuen.

Lloyd, B., & Duveen, G. (1990). A semiotic analysis of the development of social representations of gender. In G. Duveen & B. Lloyd (Eds), *Social representations and the development of knowledge*, pp.27–46. Cambridge: Cambridge University Press.

Luster, T., Rhoades, K., & Haas, B. (1989). The relation between parental values and parenting behavior: A test of the Kohn hypothesis. *Journal of Marriage and the Family, 51*, 139–147.

Maccoby, E.E. (1984). Socialization and developmental change. *Child Development, 55*, 317–328.

Maccoby, E.E., & Martin, J.P. (1983). Socialization in the context of the family: Parent-child interaction. In P. Mussen (Ed.), *Handbook of child psychology* (Vol.4), pp.1–101). New York: Wiley.

MacKinnon, C.E., & Arbuckle, B.S. (1989, April). *The relation between mother-son attributions and the coerciveness of their interactions*. Paper presented at meeting of the Society for Research in Child Development, Kansas City.

Main, M. (1985, April). *Adult mental organization with respect to attachment: Related to infant strange situation attachment status*. Paper presented at the biennial meetings of the Society for Research in Child Development, Toronto, Canada.

Main, M., Kaplan, K., & Cassidy, J. (1985). Security in infancy, childhood, and adulthood: A move to the level of representation. In I. Bretherton & E. Waters (Eds), Growth points of attachment theory and research. *Monographs of Society for Research in Child Development* (Vol.50, Serial No.209), pp.66–104.

McGillicuddy-DeLisi, A.V. (1982). Parental beliefs about developmental processes. *Human Development, 25*, 192–200.

McGillicuddy-DeLisi, A.V. (1985). The relationship between parental beliefs and children's cognitive level. In I.E. Sigel (Ed.), *Parental belief systems*, pp.7–24. Hillsdale, N.J.: Lawrence Erlbaum Associates Inc.

Mancuso, J.C., & Lehrer, R. (1986). Cognitive processes during reactions to rule violation. In R.D. Ashmore & D.M. Brodzinsky (Eds), *Thinking about the family: Views of parents and children*, pp.67–93. Hillsdale, N.J.: Lawrence Erlbaum Associates Inc.

Meares, R., Penman, R., Milgrom-Friedman, J., & Baker, K. (1982). Some origins of the 'difficult' child: The Brazelton scale and the mother's view of her new-born's character. *British Journal of Medical Psychology, 55*, 77–86.

Miller, D.T., & Turnbull, W. (1986). Expectancies and interpersonal processes. *Annual Review of Psychology, 37*, 233–256.

Miller, S.A. (1986). Parents' beliefs about their children's cognitive abilities. *Developmental Psychology, 22*, 276–284.

Miller, S.A. (1988). Parents' beliefs about their children's cognitive development. *Child Development, 59*, 259–285.

Mills, R.S.L., & Rubin, K.H. (1990). Parental beliefs about social behaviors in early childhood. *Child Development, 61,* 138–151.

Minuchin, P. (1985). Families and individual development: Provocations from the field of family therapy. *Child Development, 56,* 289–302.

Miyamoto, M. (1984). *Parents' and children's beliefs about children's achievement and development.* Paper presented at International Congress of Psychology, Acapulco.

Molinari, L., & Emiliani, F. (1987). Everyday discourses about childhood: Social representations of childhood. Manuscript, University of Bologna.

Molinari, L., & Emiliani, F. (1990). What is an image: The structure of mothers' images of the child and their influence on conversational styles. In G. Duveen & B. Lloyd (Eds), *Social representations and the development of knowledge,* pp.91–106. Cambridge: Cambridge University Press.

Moscovici, S. (1961). *La psychanalyse, son image et son public.* Paris: PUF.

Moscovici, S. (1981). On social representations. In J.P. Forgas (Ed.), *Social cognition: Perspectives on everyday understanding.* London: Academic Press.

Moscovici, S. (1990). Social psychology and developmental psychology: Extending the conversation. In G. Duveen & B. Lloyd (Eds), *Social representations and the development of knowledge,* pp.164–185. Cambridge: Cambridge University Press.

Moscovici, S., & Hewstone, M. (1983). Social representations and social explanations: From the "naive" to the "amateur" scientist. In M. Hewstone (Ed.), *Attribution theory,* pp.89–125. London: Blackwell.

Mugny, G., & Carugati, F. (1985). *L'intelligence au pluriel: Les représentations sociales de l'intelligence et de son développement.* Cousset: Editions Delval. [To be published in English as: *Social representations of intelligence.* European Monographs in Social Psychology. Cambridge: Cambridge University Press.]

Nerlove, S.B., Roberts, J.M., Klein, R.E., Yarborough, C., & Hobicht, J.B. (1974). Natural indicators of cognitive development: An observational study of rural Guatemalan children. *Ethos, 2,* 265–295.

New, R.S. (1988). Parental goals and Italian infant care. In R.A. LeVine, P.M. Miller, & M.M. West (Eds), *Parental behavior in diverse societies,* pp.51–64. San Francisco: Jossey-Bass.

Newberger, C.M. (1980). The cognitive structure of parenthood: Designing a descriptive measure. In R.L. Selman & R. Yando (Eds), *New Directions for Child Development* (Vol.7), pp.45–67). San Francisco: Jossey-Bass.

Newson, J., & Newton, E. (1976). *Seven years old in the home environment.* London: Allen & Unwin.

Newtson, D. (1973). Attribution and the unit of perception of ongoing behavior. *Journal of Personality and Social Psychology, 28,* 28–38.

Niemala, P. (1981). *The housewife's process of identity change in cognition, emotion, and action.* Manuscript, Universtity of Turku, Finland.

Ninio, A. (1979). The naive theory of the infant and other maternal attitudes in two subgroups in Israel. *Child Development, 50,* 976–980.

Oliveri, M.E., & Reiss, D. (1982). Family styles of construing the social environment: A perspective on variation among nonclinical families. In F. Walsh (Ed.), *Normal family functioning,* pp.94–114. New York: Guilford.

Palacios, J. (1986). *Parents' ideas about child development and education.* Manuscript, University of Seville.

Palacios, J. (1988). *Las ideas de los padres sobre la educación de sus hijos.* Seville: Instituto de Desarrollo Regional, University of Seville.

Palacios, J., Gonzalez, M.M., & Moreno, M.C. (1989, July). *Cognitive stimulation in daily life: The role of parents' ideas*. Paper presented at meetings of the International Society for the Study of Behavioral Development, Jyväskalä, Finland.

Parke, R.D. (1978). Parent-infant interaction: Progress, paradigms, and problems. In G.P. Sackett (Ed.), *Observing behavior* (Vol.1), pp.69–94. Baltimore: University Park Press.

Parsons, J.E., Adler, T.F., & Kaczala, C.M. (1982). Socialization of achievement attitudes and beliefs: Parental influences. *Child Development, 53*, 310–321.

Patterson, G. (1982). *Coercive family process*. Eugene Oregon: Castalia.

Pederson, D.R., & Gilby, R.L. (1986). Children's concepts of the family. In R.D. Ashmore & D.M. Brodzinsky (Eds), *Thinking about the family: Views of parents and children*, pp.181–204. Hillsdale, N.J.: Lawrence Erlbaum Associates Inc.

Pharis, M.E., & Manosevitz, M. (1980). Parental models: A means for evaluating different prenatal contexts. In D.B. Sawin, R.C. Hawkins, L.O. Walker, & J.H. Penticuff (Eds), *Exceptional infant* (Vol.4), pp.215–233. New York: Brunner/Mazel.

Pinchbeck, J.M., & Hewitt, M. (1969). *Children in English society* (Vol.1). London: Routledge & Kegan Paul.

Poffenberger, T., & Poffenberger, S.B. (1973). The social psychology of fertility behavior in a village in India. In J. Fawcett (Ed.), *Psychological perspectives on population*. New York: Basic Books.

Poresky, R.H., & Hendrix, C. (1989, April). *Parenting priorities: Stability, change, and impact on young children*. Paper presented at meeting of the Society for Research in Child Development, Kansas City.

Price, G.G., & Hatano, G. (in press). Toward a taxonomy of the roles home environments play in the formation of educationally significant individual differences. In S. Silvern (Ed.), *Literacy through family, community and school interaction*. Greenwich Connecticut: JAI Press.

Quattrone, G.A. (1985). On the congruity between internal states and cognition. *Psychological Bulletin, 98*, 3–40.

Quinn, N. (1987). Convergent evidence for a cultural model of American marriage. In D. Holland & N. Quinn (Eds), *Cultural models in language and thought*, pp.173–194. Cambridge: Cambridge University Press.

Quinn, N., & Holland, D. (1987). Culture and cognition. In D. Holland & N. Quinn (Eds), *Cultural models in language and thought*, pp.3–42. Cambridge: Cambridge University Press.

Radin, N. (1972). Three degrees of maternal involvement in a preschool program: Impact on mothers and children. *Child Development, 43*, 1358–1364.

Reid, B.V., & Valsiner, J. (1986). Consistency, praise, and love: Folk theories of American parents. *Ethos, 14*, 1–25.

Reiss, D., Oliveri, M.E., & Kurd, K. (1983). Family paradigm and adolescent social behavior. In H.D. Grotevant & C.R. Cooper (Eds), *Adolescent development in the family*, pp.77–92. San Francisco: Jossey-Bass.

Richman, A.L., Miller, P.M., & Solomon, M.J. (1988). The socialization of infants in suburban Boston. In R.A. LeVine, P.M. Miller, & M.M. West (Eds), *Parental behavior in diverse societies*, pp.65–74. San Francisco: Jossey-Bass.

Rickard, K.M., Forehand, R., Wells, K.C., Griest, D.L., & McMahon, R.J. (1981). Factors in the referral of children for behavioral treatment: A comparison of mothers of clinic-referred deviant, clinic-referred non-deviant and non-clinic children. *Behavior Research and Therapy, 19*, 201–205.

Roberts, G., Block, J.H., & Block, J. (1984). Continuity and change in parents' child-rearing practices. *Child Development, 55*, 586–597.

Rogoff, B., & Lave, J. (Eds) (1984). *Everyday cognition: Its development in a social context.* Cambridge Mass: Harvard University Press.

Rogoff, B., Sellers, M.J., Pirrolta, S., Fox, N., & White, S.H. (1975). Age of assignment of roles and responsibilies to children. *Human Development, 18*, 353–369.

Rogoff, B., & Wertsch, J.V. (Eds) (1984). *Children's learning in the zone of proximal development.* San Francisco: Jossey-Bass.

Rosaldo, M.Z. (1980). The use and abuse of anthropology: Reflections on feminism and cross-cultural understanding. *Signs, 5*, 389–417.

Rosenkrantz, B.G. (1978). Reflections on 19th century conceptions of childhood. In E.M.R. Lomax, J. Kagan, B.G. Rosenkrantz (Eds), *Science and patterns of child care,* pp.1–18. San Francisco: Freeman.

Rosenthal, D.A. (1984). Inter-generational conflict and culture: A study of immigrant and non-immigrant adolescents and their parents. *Genetic Psychology Monographs, 109*, 53–75.

Rosenthal, D.A., & Bornholt, L. (1988). Expectations about development in Greek and Anglo-Australian families. *Journal of Cross-Cultural Psychology, 19*, 19–34.

Roth, J.A. (1963). *Timetables: Structuring the passage of time in hospital treatment and other careers.* Indianapolis: Bobbs-Merrill.

Rothbart, J. (1981). Memory processes and social beliefs. In D.L. Hamilton (Ed.), *Cognitive processes in stereotyping and intergroup relations,* pp.145–182. Hillsdale, N.J.: Lawrence Erlbaum Associates Inc.

Rubin, K.H., & Mills, R.S.L. (in press). Parents' thoughts about children's socially adaptive and maladaptive behaviors: Stability, change, and individual differences. In I.E. Sigel, A.V. McGillicuddy-DeLisi, & J.J Goodnow (Eds), *Parental belief systems: Consequences for children.* Hillsdale, N.J.: Lawrence Erlbaum Associates Inc.

Rubin, K.H., Mills, R.S.L., & Krasnor, R. (1989). Maternal beliefs and children's social competence. In B.H. Schneider, G. Attili, J. Nadel-Brulfert, & R. Weissberg (Eds), *Social competence in perspective,* pp.313–337. Dortrecht: Kluwer.

Ruble, D.N., Hackel, L.S., Fleming, A.S., & Stagnor, C. (1988). Changes in the marital relationship during the transition to first time motherhood: Effects of violated expectations concerning division of household labor. *Journal of Personality and Social Psychology, 55*, 78–87.

Ruddick, S. (1982). Maternal thinking. In B. Thorne & M. Yalom (Eds), *Rethinking the family,* 76–94. New York: Longmans.

Rumelhart, D., & Norman, D. (1981) Analogical processes in learning. In J. Anderson (Ed.), *Cognitive skills and their acquisition,* pp.335–359. Hillsdale, N.J.: Lawrence Erlbaum Associates Inc.

Russell, G. (1983). *The changing role of fathers?* Brisbane: University of Queensland Press.

Ruth S.E. (1984, August). *The south-west Aboriginal and the law.* Paper presented at the First Australian Family Research Conference. Melbourne, Victoria.

Salzman, P.C. (1981). Culture as enhabilmentis. In L. Holy & M. Stuchlik (Eds), *The structure of folk models,* pp.233–256. London: Academic Press.

Sameroff, A.J., & Chandler, M. (1975). Reproductive risk and the continuum of caretaking casualty. In F.D. Horowitz (Ed.), *Review of child development research* (Vol.4), pp.187–244. Chicago: University of Chicago Press.

Sameroff, A.J., & Feil, L.A. (1985). Parental concepts of development. In I.E. Sigel (Ed.), *Parental belief systems,* pp.83–105. Hillsdale, N.J.: Lawrence Erlbaum Associates Inc.

Sameroff, A.J., & Fiese, B.H. (in press). Transactional regulation and early intervention. In S.J. Meissels & J.P. Shonkhoff (Eds), *Early intervention: A handbook of theory, practice, and analysis*. Cambridge: Cambridge University Press.

Sameroff, A.J., Seifer, R., Barocas, R., Zax, M., & Greenspan, S. (1987). Intelligence quotient scores of 4-year-old children: Social-environmental risk factors. *Pediatrics, 79*, 343–350.

Sarchielli, G. (1984). Work entry: A critical moment in the occupational socialization process. In W. Doise, & A. Palmonari (Eds), *Social interaction in individual development*, pp.261–278. Cambridge: Cambridge University Press.

Schaefer, E.G. (1987). Parental modernity and child academic competence: Toward a theory of individual and societal development. *Early Child Development and Care, 27*, 373–389.

Schank, R. (1982). *Dynamic memory: A theory of reminding and learning in computers and people*. Cambridge: Cambridge University Press.

Schank, R., & Abelson, R. (1977). *Scripts, plans, goals and understanding*. New York: Wiley.

Schütz, A. (1953). Commonsense and scientific interpretations of human action. *Philosophical and Phenomenological Research, 14*, 1–36.

Schütze, Y. (1987). The good mother: The history of the normative model "mother-love". *Sociological Studies of Child Development, 2*, 39–78.

Seginer, B. (1983). Parents' educational expectations and children's academic achievements: A literature review. *Merrill-Palmer Quarterly, 29*, 1–23.

Selman, R. (1980). *The growth of inter-personal understanding: Developmental and clinical analyses*. New York: Academic Press.

Semin, G., & Papadopoulou, K. (1990). The acquisition of reflexive social emotions: The transmission and reproduction of social control through joint action. In G. Duveen & B. Lloyd (Eds), *Social representations and the development of knowledge*, pp.107–125. Cambridge: Cambridge University Press.

Serpell, R. (1974). Estimates of intelligence in a rural community of Eastern Zambia. *Human Development Research Unit Reports, No. 25*, University of Zambia.

Shotter, J. (1985). Social accountability and self specification. In K.J. Gergen & K.E. Davis (Eds), *The social construction of the person*, pp.167–180. New York: Springer-Verlag.

Shulman, S., & Zohar, D. (in press). Family type and three-year-olds' behavioral problems. *American Journal of Family Therapy*.

Shulz, M. (1989, April). *Cognitive complexity, expectations and idealizations during the transition to parenthood*. Paper presented at biennial meeting of the Society for Research in Child Development, Kansas City.

Shweder, R.A. (1982). Beyond self-constructed knowledge: The study of culture and morality. *Merrill-Palmer Quarterly, 28*, 41–69.

Shweder, R.A., Mahapatra, M., & Miller, J.G. (1987). Culture and moral development. In J. Kagan & S. Lamb (Eds), *The emergence of morality in young children*, pp.1–83. Chicago: University of Chicago Press.

Siebenheller, F.A., Gerris, J.R.M., & van Leeuwe, J.F.J. (1988, June). *Towards an interactionist model of child-rearing behaviors*. Paper presented at the Third European Conference on Developmental Psychology, Budapest.

Siegal, M. (1987). Are sons and daughters treated more differently by fathers than by mothers? *Developmental Review, 7*, 183–209.

Siegal, M., & Storey, R.M. (1985). Day care and children's conceptions of moral and social rules. *Child Development, 56*, 1001–1008.

Sigel, I.E. (1985a). A conceptual analysis of beliefs. In I.E. Sigel (Ed.) *Parental belief systems*, pp.347–371. Hillsdale, N.J.: Lawrence Erlbaum Associates Inc.

Sigel, I.E. (1985b). *Parental belief systems*. Hillsdale, N.J.: Lawrence Erlbaum Associates Inc.

Sigel, I.E. (1986). Reflections of the belief-behavior connection: Lessons learned from a research program on parental belief systems and teaching strategies. In R.D. Ashmore & D.M. Brodzinsky (Eds), *Thinking about the family: Views of parents and children*, pp.35–66. Hillsdale, N.J.: Lawrence Erlbaum Associates Inc.

Sigel, I.E., & McGillicuddy-DeLisi, A.V. (1984). Parents as teachers of their children: A distancing model. In A.D. Pellegrini & T.D. Yawkey (Eds), *The development of oral and written language in social contexts*, pp.71–92. Norwood, N.J.: Ablex.

Silverberg, S.B. (1989, April). *Parents as developing adults: The impact of perceived distance in the parent-adolescent relationship*. Paper presented at meetings of the Society for Research in Child Development, Kansas City.

Silverberg, S.B., & Steinberg, L. (1987). Adolescent autonomy, parent-adolescent conflict, and parental well-being. *Journal of Youth and Adolescence, 16*, 293–312.

Skinner, E.A. (1985). Determinants of mother-sensitive and contingently-responsive behavior: The role of childrearing beliefs and socio-economic status. In I.E. Sigel (Ed.), *Parental belief systems*, pp.51–88. Hillsdale, N.J.: Lawrence Erlbaum Associates Inc.

Smetana, J. (1988). Concepts of self and social convention: Adolescents' and parents' reasoning about hypothetical and actual family conflicts. In M. Gunnar & W.A. Collins (Eds), *Minnesota Symposia on child development* (Vol.21), pp.79—122. Hillsdale, N.J.: Lawrence Erlbaum Associates Inc.

Smolicz, J., & Secombe, R. (1977). Cultural interaction in a plural society. *Ethnic Studies, 1*, 1–6.

Snyder, C.R., & Fromkin, H.L. (1980). *Uniqueness: The human pursuit of difference*. New York: Plenum Press.

Snyder, M. (1974). Self-monitoring of expressive behavior. *Journal of Personality and Social Psychology, 30*, 526–537.

Snyder, M., & Swann, W.B., Jr. (1978). Behavioral confirmation in social interaction: From social perception to social reality. *Journal of Experimental Social Psychology, 13*, 148–162.

Soccio, L. (1977). A family in Italy and Australia. In S. Murray-Smith (Ed.), *Melbourne studies of education*, pp. 1-26. Melbourne: Melbourne University Press.

Sroufe, L., Jacobovitz, D., Mangelsdorf, S., DeAngelo, E., & Ward, M. (1985). Generational boundary dissolution between mothers and their preschool children: A relationship systems approach. *Child Development, 56*, 317–325.

Steinberg, L. (in press). Interdependency in the family: Autonomy, conflict, and harmony in the parent-adolescent relationship. In S.S. Feldman & G.R. Elliott (Eds), *At the threshold: The developing adolescent*. Washington D.C.:Carnegie Council on Adolescent Development.

Sternberg, R.J., Conway, B.E., Ketron, J.L., & Bernstein, M. (1981). People's conceptions of intelligence. *Journal of Personality and Social Psychology, 41*, 37–55.

Stevenson, H.W., Stigler, J.W., Lee, S.Y., Lucker, G.W., Kitamura, S., & Hsu, C.C. (1985). Cognitive performance and academic achievement of Japanese, Chinese, and American children. *Child Development, 56*, 718–734.

Stich, S. (1983). *From folk psychology to cognitive science: The case against belief*. Boston: M.I.T. Press.

Stigler, J.W., Lee, S.Y., Lucker, G.W., & Stevenson, H.W. (1982). Curriculum and achievement in mathematics: A study of elementary school children in Japan, Taiwan, and the United States. *Journal of Educational Psychology, 74*, 315–322.

Stolz, L.M. (1967). *Influences on parent behavior*. Stanford, California: Stanford University Press.

Super, C.M., & Harkness, S. (1986). The developmental niche: A conceptualization of the interface of child and culture. *International Journal of Behavioral Development, 9,* 546–569.

Thorne, B. (1987). Re-visioning women and social change: Where are the children? *Gender and Society, 1,* 85–109.

Tinsley, B.J. (1989, April). *A longitudinal study of the relationship among maternal health beliefs, utilization of preventive health services, anc child health*. Paper presented at meetings of the Society for Research in Child Development, Kansas City.

Tinsley, B.J., & Holtgrave, D.R. (1988). *Parental health beliefs, utilization of childhood preventive health services and infant health*. Unpublished manuscript, University of Illinois.

Tinsley, B.J., & Parke, R.D. (1987). Grandparents as interactive and support agents for families with young infants. *International Journal of Ageing and Human Development, 25,* 259–277.

Tizard, B. (1977). *Adoption: A second chance*. London:Open Books.

Toussaint, D.N. (1986). *Beliefs and related factors associated with parental choice of care and educational facilities for their children prior to pre-primary school*. Unpublished Ph.D. thesis, Murdoch University, Western Australia.

Triana, E., & Rodrigo, M.J. (1989, July). *The role played by parental ideas about child development in the elaborations of mental scenarios in text comprehension*. Paper presented at meetings of the International Society for Study of Behavioral Development, Jyväskylä, Finland.

Trickett, P.K., & Susman, E.J. (1988). Parental perceptions of child-rearing practices in physically abusive and nonabusive families. *Developmental Psychology, 24,* 270–276.

Twentyman, C.T., & Plotkin, R. (1982). Unrealistic expectations of parents who maltreat their children. *Journal of Clinical Psychology, 38,* 497–503.

Vedeler, D. (1987). Infant intentionality and the attribution of intentions to infants. *Human Development, 30,* 1–17.

Wagner, D.A., & Spratt, J.E. (1988). Intergenerational literacy: Effects of parental literacy and attitudes on children's reading achievement in Morocco. *Human Development, 31,* 359–369.

Walsh, F. (1981). Conceptualizations of normal family functioning. In F. Walsh (Ed.), *Normal family processes*, pp.3–25. New York: Guilford.

Warton, P.M., & Goodnow, J.J. (in press). The several meanings of responsibility: Children's understanding of "your" job, *Child Development*.

Watson, J., & Russell, G. (1988). *Graphic representations of family structure: Change in structure with therapy*. Unpublished manuscript, Macquarie University.

Wegner, D.M., & Vallacher, R.R. (1977). *Implicit psychology: An introduction to social cognition*. Oxford: Oxford University Press.

Weiner, B. (1985). "Spontaneous" causal search. *Psychological Bulletin, 97,* 74–84.

Weiner, B. (1986). Attribution, emotion, and action. In R.M. Sorrentino & E.T. Higgins (Eds), *Handbook of motivation and cognition*, pp.281–312. New York: Guilford.

Weisner, T.C., & Gallimore, R. (1977). My brother's keeper: Child and sibling caretaking. *Current Anthropology, 18,* 169–190.

Welles-Nystrom, B. (1988). Parenthood and infancy in Sweden. In R.A. LeVine, P.M. Miller, & M.M. West (Eds), *Parental behavior in diverse societies*, pp.75–80. San Francisco: Jossey-Bass.

Wertheim, E.S. (1975). The science and typology of family systems II. Further theoretical and practical considerations. *Family Process, 14,* 285–309.

Wertsch, J.V., Minick, N., & Arns, F.J. (1984). The creation of context in joint problem-solving. In B. Rogoff & J. Lave (Eds), *Everyday cognition: Its development in social context*, pp.151–167. Cambridge Mass.: Harvard University Press.

West, M.M. (1988). Parental values and behavior in the Outer Fiji Islands. In LeVine, R.A., Miller, P.M., & West, M.M. (Eds), *Parental behavior in diverse societies*, pp.13–26. San Francisco: Jossey-Bass.

Whiting, B.B. (1980). Culture and social behavior: A model for the development of social behavior. *Ethos, 8*, 95–116.

Williams, T.M., Joy, L.A., Travis, L., Gotowiec, A., Blum-Steele, M., Aiken, L.S., Painter, S.L., & Davidson, S.M. (in press). Transition to motherhood: A longitudinal study. *Infant Mental Health Journal.*

Wittner, J.G. (1980). Domestic labor as work discipline: The struggle over housework in foster homes. In S.F. Berk (Ed.), *Women and household labor*, pp.229–247. Newbury Park, California: Sage.

Wolfenstein, M. (1955). French parents take their children to the park. In M. Mead & M. Wolfenstein (Eds), *Childhood in contemporary culture*, pp.99–117. Chicago: University of Chicago Press.

Zebrowitz-McArthur, L.A., & Kendall-Tackett, K.A. (1989, April). *Parental reactions to transgressions by baby-faced and mature-faced 4 and 11 year old children.* Paper presented at meetings of the Society for Research in Child Development, Kansas City.

Zelizer, V. (1985). *Pricing the priceless child.* New York: Basic Books.

AUTHOR INDEX

SUBJECT INDEX